BLOOM

Best Arizona Teen Writing of 2014

by
Young Authors of Arizona

DEDICATIONS

To all of the families, friends, teachers, and other voices of inspiration for Arizona's young authors:

Edward Albee; Mitch Albom; Maya Angelou; Jennifer Armentrout; Issac Asimov; Thomas Bergersen; William Blake; Ray Bradbury; Charlotte Brontë; Orson Scott Card; Ally Carter; Julian Casablancas; Theresa Hak Kyung Cha; Brann Dailor; Tom DeLonge; Joan Didion; Bob Dylan; Lawrence Ferlinghetti; Jonathan Safran Foer; F. Scott Fitzgerald; Robert Frost; Ben Gibbard; Andrea Gibson; John Green; Kerstin Hamilton; William Earnest Henley; Nasir Jones; Sarah Kay; Oskar Knoblauch; Dean Koontz; Harper Lee; Madeleine L'Engle; Alan Lightman; Lish McBride; Cormac McCarthy; Heather McHugh; Tim O'Brien; Mary Oliver; Chuck Palahniuk; Justin Pierre; Sylvia Plath; Edgar Allan Poe; Ul de Rico; Maurice R. "Robby" Robinson; Rick Riordan; J.K. Rowling; J.D. Salinger; Jimmy Santiago Baca; George Saunders; Patti Smith; Michael J. Sullivan; Ida Tarbell; Dylan Thomas; Leo Tolstoy; Marshall Trimble; Mark Twain; Jerry Uelsmann; Paula Vogel; H.G. Wells; Oscar Wilde; Jeanette Winterson; Adam Young; Markus Zusak.

CONTENTS

DRAMATIC SCRIPT

SCIENCE FICTION/FANTASY

CONCLUDING SECTION

NOTE TO READERS:
Following the tradition of the Scholastic Art & Writing Awards, this book encourages student writers to express themselves freely, without fear of censorship. These works have not been censored and may contain subject matter that is inappropriate for certain audiences.

ACKNOWLEDGEMENTS

In 1923, Robert "Robbie" Robinson, founder of the Scholastic book publishing company, created the Scholastic Art & Writing Awards because he believed teens should be encouraged to create original and skilled art and writing for earned acclaim without fear of censorship. Over 90 years later, his trust in the young is merited (see page 297 to learn more about the Scholastic Art & Writing Awards).

In May of 2011, Young Authors of Arizona (YAA) co-founders Billy Gerchick and Jay Morganstern flew to New York, where the Alliance for Young Artists and Writers opened its offices, to represent YAA at Carnegie Hall as Arizona's first affiliate in Alliance history. YAA thanks affiliate co-founders Laura Turchi and Kelly O'Rourke for their contributions, as well as the Arizona English Teachers Association (AETA) for its early sponsorship and for AETA leaders like Jim Blasingame, Jean Boreen, and Duane Roen for advancing language arts in this state.

YAA's creation was also influenced by the philosophies of educators at ASU: Drs. Duane Roen, James Paul Gee, and Elenore Long (who is also the proud mom of Hannah Jarvis, one of this book's young authors). Family members are integral to YAA, and the more that supportive parents (like Pearlette Ramos) offer to help, the more we can do for Arizona's young minds.

Well before YAA, State Historian Marshall Trimble has been pickin' his six-string and anthologizing our heritage. Arizona's list of published authors is distinguished, and YAA has enjoyed support from poets like Tomas Stanton and Myrlin Hepworth, novelist Jessica Brody, Alberto Ríos, Tom Leveen, and others. YAA was honored to attend the 8th birthday of the Phoenix Book Company (PBC), whose owners Cori Ashley and Jade Corn have been very generous.

While many inspired the Scholastic affiliate, launching an organization takes commitment, and many deserve thanks, notably these YAA non-profit co-founders: Tracy Weaver brings experience and creativity, while Julie Cain's positivity and brains are paramount. Thanks largely to Jon Jeffery, YAA is also Arizona's Scholastic Art Awards affiliate, which means if you're a grade 7-12 author and/or artist, you can enter the 2015 Scholastic Art & Writing Awards (artandwriting.org) by December 17, 2014.

This first book, *Bloom*, enjoyed a strong editorial board: Gerchick, Cain, Weaver, Morganstern, O'Rourke, Turchi, Chris Marsh, Melissa Williamson, Alyssa Tilley, Heather Nagami, Michelle Hill, Taryn Gutierrez, Chelle Wotowiec, and student editor Haley Lee, who coined this year's book title and whose portfolio begins on page 17. Doing this indeed took "a village," as Haley wrote. Thank you.

Arizona's educators also merit recognition. Volunteers like Debra LaPlante connect judges and librarians, district specialists like Jonna Wallis get the word out, administrators like John Biera and Hadley Ruggles welcome us, and teachers like Stephanie Knight participate each year. Thank you to Arizona's 2014 Scholastic Writing Awards partners and educators, recognized below:

Kathy Abraham; Angela Ackerman; Paty Acosta; Jean Akers; Alliance for Young Artists and Writers; Clinton Anderson; Brian Anderson; Arizona English Teachers Association; Wesley Baron; Zachary Bartlett; Kelly Bathje; Erika Beam; Jim Blasingame; Darcy Boggs; Tyler Briggs; Monica Brown; Angela Buzan; Julie Cain; Andrea Carl; Jan Carteaux; Central Arizona Writing Project (CAWP); Theresa Chavez; Collin Clark; Angela Clark-Oates; Joseph Clements; Randy Cluff; Karen Cockell; Ed Como; Lynn Cuffari; Stacey Cunningham; Lori Dahl; Heather Davenport; Conrad Davis; Carrie Deal; Marcia DeMuro; Nicholle Dockter; Kim Dodds; Eve Donohoe; Sarah Driscoll; Sharon Elisco; Danielle Else; Tracey Flores; LaFrenda Frank; Marie Frantz; Marissa Frazey; Anna Fulford; Billy Gerchick; Jolene Gettig; Darla Grant; Gary Griggs; Cherilyn Guy; Julie Hampton; Alice Hayes; Juli Haynes; Patrick Henry; Lauren Hesse; Lyndsay Holt; Rachel Householder; Meg Howell-Haymaker; Tom Irwin; Hilary Johannes; Angela Johnson; Jack Judson; Daniel Kariuki; Jean Kilker; Deirdre Kirmis; Elizabeth Kittredge; Kimberly Klett; Stephanie Knight; James Kobashi; Rachel Kupryk; Dawn Lambson; Peg Leshinski; Melissa Lopez; Francis Mangin; Christine Marsh; Dixie Lee Maxwell; Mary McBride; Elizabeth McConaghy; Jessica McDonald; Kathleen McGowan; Korin McKelvey; Bryce McKinney-Wain; Tom Mitchell; Lisa Moore; Jay Morganstern; Stan Morganstern; Mosaic; Heather Nagami; Shelley Nicoll; Debbie O'Dowd; Bridgette O'Neill; Ann Orlando; Kelly O'Rourke; Donna Parker; Von Perot; Phoenix Book Company; Tim Ramsey; Robyn Reese; Amanda Riney; rl txt; David Rodriguez; Ashley Rogers; Sean Ross; Anna Royse; Hadley Ruggles; Jennifer Sagoo; Ann Salmon; Erin Seidner; Kevin Sheh; Morgan Smith; Kenneth Sorenson; Rosanne Stapka; Amanda Sweeney; Elif Tanyeri ; Mary Thompson; Lauren Tillman; Laura Turchi; Mariana Van Meter; Jennifer Walker; Jonna Wallis; Lisa Watson; Tracy Weaver; Maren Wenz; David White; Laurie Wiesinger; Susan Williams; Melissa Williamson; Hannah Willis; Robert Witz; Scott Woods; Chelle Wotowiec; Writopia Lab; Young Emerging Artists (YEA).

Our final and most important acknowledgement goes to the over-1,000 authors in grades 7-12 who shared work these first three years. Below are Arizona's 2014 Scholastic Writing Awards Honorable Mention, Silver Key, and Gold Key authors. Congratulations!

Jacob Abukhader; Nick Adams; Oscar Aguirre; Jahnavi Akella; Hira Ali; Arianna Anderson; Dylan Angle; Anissa Aparicio; Lauren Arrowsmith; Anthony Bao; Richard Bao; Katie Barnhart; Maxwell Bartlett; Seth Barton; Hannah Bernier; Lizeth Blanco; Darci Botsch; Cameron Brickley; Nate Brooks; Maryia Bryant; Adwoa Buadu; Raina Burchett; Ashley Burt; Ana Carranza; Brooke Cassaday; Isabel Ceja Ceja; Tori Cejka; Ilija Chabarria; Natali Chausovskaya; Hyeji (Julie) Cho; Jean Chung; Spencer Claus; Christopher Clements; Alex Cohen; Trey Connelly; Natalie Cravens; Navya Dasari; Cameron Divine; Vy Doan; Nicole Dominiak; Megan Dressler; Danna Durney; Mariah Edington; Tal Eitan; Alexandra Elbert; Alexandria Ellis; Grace Elsie; Audrey Ennis; Riley Evanson; Devin Farr; Diane Fine; Kimberly Fiock; Antonio Flores; Nick Forney; BrieAnna Frank; Mackenzie Fritz; Angelica Garcia; Jay Garcia; Justin Garner; Grace Gay; Ryan Gilburne; James Glasscock; Tiffany Gong; Alejandro Gonzalez ; Alejandro Gordillo; Kayvon Gorji; Callie Gregory; Heather Griffin; Kelly Guerra; Anvita Gupta; Elizabeth Hammer; Taylor Hammond; Tyler Hatfield; Anna Hawkins; Samantha Hayes; Angela Hemesath; Madi Hinze; Emily Horton; Anthony Huang; Sara Huddleston; Valerie Huntington; Hannah Jarvis; Connor Jennison; Hyunjeong Jun; Evelyn Karis; Alejandra Katz; Kazhra Kelcho; Lina Khan; Myra Khan; Sue Kim; Grant Knight; Sunskruthi Krishna; Nichole Kyprianou; Kimaya Lecamwasam; Bodo Lee; Haley Lee; Madeline Lee; Grayson Lee-kin; Lan Julia Liang; Daphne Li-chen; Rachel Linehan; Caroline Liu; Stephanie Long; Frida Lopez; Chase Lortie; Katherine Lu; Lauren Ludwig; Christina Luu; Brigitta Mannino; Blake Markovic; Kelly Martindale; Gloria Martinez; Michaela Mason; Nailah Mathews; Stirling McDaniel; Sarah Mckee; Jimmy McKinley; Lillian Melzer; Matt Merritt; Anthony Mirabito; Salah Moharram; Adam Nissen; Jordyn Ochser; Daniel Olson; Olivia Osborn; Yash Pershad; Katie Polcyn; Sydney Portigal; Jonie Pretto; Chloe Raissen; Anita Ramaswamy; Mandri Randeniya; Anirudh Ranganathan; Andrew Rangel; Kolbe Riney; Jullienne Robiso; Sandy Romero; Maxwell Rosenberg; Caroline Ross; Lauren Russell; Emma Rymarcsuk; Gabriel Salmon; Aakanksha Saxena; Maci Segal; Taylor Shewchuk; Aubrey Shuga; Julia Simmons; Krishna Sinha; Archanna Smith; Lydia Spire; Raven Stevens; Henry Uhrik; Diana Urena; Shreya Venkatesh; Bailey Vidler; Madison Waaler; Matt Ward; Samantha White; Shaniah Whitehair; Kade Williams; Kaitlynn Williams; Maison Winkler; Catherine Woner; Alicia Wu; Alicia Wu; Kathleen Wu; Misako Yamazaki; Jaylia Yan; Andrea Yang; Ryan Yiu; Alice Zhao; Justin Zhu; Cassidy Zinke.

Show-and-Tell for Arizona
Editor Introduction by Billy Gerchick

Furry friends; Camp Tontozona; Berenstein Bears; show-and-tell; Basketball Encyclopedia; principal atop a flagpole.
I pride my home state and like an increasing many, set my formative story in Arizona. I recall a toddler's fear, then joy, from feeding furry friends at Williams Deer Farm. Each August, Dad took us to Camp Tontozona to watch ASU football; years later, he welcomed me to attend U of A. I believe shared stories by Arizonans help us learn from, and be closer to, one another. This is one Arizonan's story of learning to invite y'all as Young Authors of Arizona.

I loved school in the era of thermoses. In pre-school, *Berenstein Bears* made us smile, and show-and-tell helped us learn from one another. Writing wasn't so five-paragraph structured, and once a year, if I'd been good, Mom and I played hooky for a Snowbowl ski day. A Suns fan, I got to read the *Basketball Encyclopedia* for a 5th grade book report. Did you know Kevin Johnson averaged 20.4 points and 12.2 assists per game in '88-'89? "Fundamental" could be fun, and my principal, Bob Meko, camped atop our flagpole to promote learning. "Saber és poder" remains the Mendoza Elementary School motto: "Knowledge is power."

7th grade fingerprints; Bono and Flava Flav; another novel set in England.
But things change in middle school. Show-and-tell is gone, adolescents clique into groups, and stolen Kit Kats had Billy's 7th grade fingerprints in the wafers. I was a punk, but school, an accomplice. "Can I read that?" "No." "Can I try writing like that?" "No." "Can we talk in class?" I wonder if your learning story has similar conflicts.

By high school, for me, engagement increased when class ended. Bono (of U2) and Flavor Flav (of Public Enemy) on-stage to get an MLK holiday in Arizona—real. *Another* novel set in England—redundant. Thank Cliff for his Notes, but where were the words that spoke to us? Written, folded, passed-by-friends, avidly read, relevant. If 15-year old S.E. Hinton could write *The Outsiders*, maybe more note-passers would engage if approached as authors. Skill development needs models, but we didn't *study* exemplary peer work.

English 101; War of the Worlds; 9/11; page space.

"What do you want to read?" my English 101 professor asked. "Huh?" "What do you want to write about?" It'd been a while since someone asked. "Baseball." Welcomed to pursue personally relevant content, I turned getting cut, then making my high school baseball team into a polished personal narrative. When Arizona Republic columnist E.J. Montini feuded with then-Diamondbacks owner Jerry Colangelo over the funding of Bank One Ballpark (now Chase Field), I engaged as citizen-reader. And because Dysart Unified's students deserved better, I engaged as citizen-writer, mailing my persuasive paper to their penny-pinching school board. Class mattered again, skills developed, but my story needed its true protagonists.

In the summer of 2001, my best friend convinced me to co-manage a Sabino Canyon Little League team: 13-14 year olds. We loved those punks: Beau with braces, Mo with the fastball, pure joy. But many of these boys hadn't set foot on the University of Arizona campus. "Can I come to class?"

My film & lit. professor agreed to let the team watch *War of the Worlds* (1953 version). Despite rejection from the blond in the third row, my players kept asking questions, some of them about the film. "I like this kind of school," said my right fielder, and perhaps like you, my character found focus as both student and mentor. Exclusion turns learners to punks; inclusion can inspire love of learning. Then, 9/11.

The night of September 11, 2001, I walked, confusedscaredangry, in a wash near River Road. I thought about enlisting, about defending, about harming people depicted on TV. How do we reconcile our fear of the unknown? Then, I thought about feeding deer, about passing notes to friends, about my right fielder's future. We need the enlisted, but we also need show-and-tell, now more than ever in a post-9/11 Arizona.

Do you know that just days after 9/11, at a gas station in Mesa, a man murdered an innocent man because he "looked like a terrorist"? Do you know that, combined, Arizona now has over 1,400 middle schools and high schools and many home schools, each with potential storytellers? Media exposure too-often lets the wrong people define Arizona, and Arizonans, so maybe it's time to create page space for our "punks." They might be authors.

The following words show, in snippets and out-of-context, what 63 Young Authors of Arizona have to tell:

Memories swelling like a gasoline rainbow; the old regime and a fear of apology; your pastpresentfuture; my fusion heritage; prefixes rioting for recombination.

Weird gypsy music for self-pitying goth girls; child at the Diwali party clad in jeans; a little green-bodied, red-stomached hummingbird; our van which was luckily stuck between two coconut trees; my heart that thinks too loudly; the same crumpled blue tee, gray yoga pants, and dusty Converse; that awkward kid; that dreaded five-letter word.

Leaking contradictions that send steam rising off asphalt; fireworks that pinwheel across the sky; a spark; smoke ring love letters; Desolation Row; the ugly Christmas sweater; Heaven's ears; scent of Palo Verde; drawing of a polar bear during recess; three balls to juggle two hands one girl; for who I am and not for who I'm not; blasphemy in the beauty of our fingers intertwined; four-point, thirty-six point, two-thousand, four-hundred point scales; a trophy, a glorified piece of metal; against the rusted fence of the basketball court; hues of lonely blue and shades of bitter belladonna; scowls darting across the room; sardonic interior; the cruel paradox of young men; for La Raza; same way on a zigzagged line; mirror, oh mirror; a rather simple concept; how I feel about myself; chewing bubble gum in the rain; hunched like Atlas and cold like David; eyes like Hera and a voice like Echo; how the other person thinks; just a pat on the back and a few words of kindness; a paper-thin castle made of words; one big chunk of rock floating in space; the stoic stare of glassy eyes; a serpentine wisp of fragile white vapor; haphazardly stitching in hopes of mending; just one last smile; white noise in the
TV; War, Poverty, Death, Sickness, Homelessness, Starvation, Dehydration, Helplessness, Greed, Evil, Obliviousness, Cynicism, Deception, Anger, Hatred, Depression, Suicide, Loneliness; nothing like we expected; the end of the Demon's rebirth; the Bliss of the leaves beneath my feet; unplanted seeds and misplaced house keys; an Arizona sunset; the time you nudged my shoulder with your nose; when sheets of glass rain slandered the asphalt; slowly down from five; no more North or South; all that matters; my twelve years with her; perpetual wave of the naked truth.

Suspension bridge of global culture; hiss of steel ringing;

other side of the Earth; the Guns and Roses tattoo; heartbreak, cancer, and a Catch-22; Frost's heart beat; his wedding ring; paper-thin memories crinkled by time; the last of the Presents.

The annoying red light; the ding of the elevator doors; empty cans of spray paint; a pale patch of dried glue.

The grand opening; phrases and English sayings; a regular high school; a new cultural studies program.

When to speak your mind and when to shut up; that beautiful mixture, half-lion half-eagle; the mental wellness and social conditions of the assailants; "reasonable suspicion" that someone is "an alien."

The chagrin of the zealots who loved the dramatics; the knot that held my entire loincloth; as dirty as that last sentence sounded.

Names, and names, and names of men and women old and young.

12 minutes, 56 seconds; a small breakfast of regulation canned Good Meal; the empty shell of my ghostly body; the ones who live life to the fullest, accept all mistakes made, and truly enjoy life as it is.

If you feel the above words don't merit further reading, I welcome you to close this book. If writing by Arizona teens doesn't belong in your curriculum, ignore this rag and the "punks" that ~~pass notes~~ text in class. If bored by 63 friends passing paperback notes, then stop focusing and express ur boredom. Try an emoticon: :(. Otherwise, enjoy.

This is *Bloom*, the Young Authors of Arizona's *Best Arizona Teen Writing of 2014* anthology, the first of its kind in state history: by young authors, for Arizona, earned publication through the Scholastic Writing Awards. YAA is the only Scholastic affiliate in America making our own "best of" book, and we're looking to make publishing a habit.

As high school and college English teacher, now I'm the one asked "Can I read that?" "Can I write about that?" "Can we talk about that?" Yes, you can.

The YAA non-profit was created to help young authors show-and-tell language and media arts. We welcome you, the reader, the teacher, the parent, the librarian, the partner organization, the partner business, and especially you, the aspiring young author, to help language and media arts bloom in Arizona. Go to YAArizona.org to learn how, and thank you for supporting our first draft.

SENIOR PORTFOLIO

The Way We Burned

Student Introduction by Haley Lee[1]

To the readers: The works in this anthology represent just some of the talent Arizona houses. *Bloom* celebrates the potency of the written word and the students who recognize this power. It is a peek into the minds of some of the state's most creative authors. Perhaps most importantly, it serves as encouragement for students who have not yet discovered the courage to write their first story. The featured writers address difficult subjects bravely and reflect on their own lives with insight. As you read, keep in mind the dedication and heart that went into each piece.

To the Young Authors of Arizona: I remember the day I received a phone call about placing in the Scholastic Art & Writing Awards as an exciting one. In fact, my post-call reaction remains engrained in my mind in frame-by-frame detail: yelling out the news to my parents, e-mailing my mentor (the lovely Ms. Ruggles), rewarding myself with a double scoop of Ben & Jerry's Phish Food. In that moment, the award represented a culmination of my efforts as an author. I had battled many of the common plights to reach that point: self-consciousness about sharing my work, writer's block, a shortage of time. I struggled through it all and viewed the Awards as my chance to put those difficulties behind me.

In a way, I thought a trip to New York and a gold medal would make me immune to the dilemmas that riddled my early writing career. Of course, I was naïve to think that one weekend and a shiny object could dissolve my every obstacle. I came to realize, over time, that my mistake was seeking a cure-all to facets of the writing process I should have embraced in the first place. I recognize now that sharing your prose (or poetry or plays) is the way to refine your voice; that the world is brimming with ideas, you just have to look hard

[1] *All works in this portfolio were created by Haley Lee between ages 14-16. Haley, a*

graduating senior from BASIS Scottsdale in Scottsdale, was selected to write Bloom's student introduction.

enough; that writing is something you must make time for, no matter how busy your schedule. Keep in mind, when you write, that the challenges make the final product even sweeter. Every author's journey is different, but I hope that none of yours end anytime soon.

To the parents, the siblings, the teachers, the mentors: Thank you for all you do. Writing, despite what many say, is not a solitary activity. It truly does take a village, and this book would be bare without your support.

Something Like Hope

On the first day of third grade my teacher
unfolded a world map onto the whiteboard,
Arizona, Alaska, Australia held balanced by two purple
    magnets.
I watched the plastic corners slide like a seesaw
struggling to shoulder one hundred ninety six countries
and the uncut frontier of eight-year-old minds
shaped by tissue paper seasons
and distilled by the science of something like hope.
"Come, come look at your country."
We stood, observed each state colored like Easter eggs
eager to be opened.
Cracked, cradled.
Silence is grace.
This is an exhibition and the ticket is pride.
We are joined at the fingertips by raw heritage
and a promise to please, to be pleased,
but nobody weeps red, white, and blue.
Can't you see that sometimes I am split in two?
The clay walls of my history are crouched on stilts
dissolving in the waters of pure contradiction.
Tender, stitched.
"What are you?" a boy on the playground raises his
    eyebrows,
tilting one question toward my skin and another toward my
    eyes.
He thinks he can tell Truth from Lie;
they always told him to color inside the lines
but this is not a game of show and tell.
The dresser in the empty bedroom is stocked with pictures
from times before I was born.
I sift, shift, shiver.
Memories swelling like a gasoline rainbow lie snared in the
    purgatory
between morning glory and midnight insanity –
there are no absolutes.

The valleys of my spine are artifacts tumbled through time
    and
If you trace my two halves far enough you will find
My violin string fingers trapped in the folds between
my grandmother's garden
and the ship that houses my great uncle's stowaway spirit.
But buried beneath the soil is a heart that will not bend to
    hierarchy.

Anchored, armored.
Come, come look at your country.

2013 Gold Key, American Voices, Gold Medal, Poetry

They Are the Patriots

Soldiers chasing savage beauty tear down the horizon with
    precision.
This is a crusade against compassion, against the old
    regime and a fear of apology,
so raise your weapons.
Boom.
Missiles kiss the skyline and we are done
in a flair of gunpowder and smoked horror.
Children holding hands with skyscrapers
scrape their mothers' blood from the kitchen floor
and every night they wish for the bombs to stop falling so
    they can start living.
Feet muddy,
hearts stained.

They are the patriots.

Land mines triggered by our greed
melt skin from bone,
slitting scars in the Earth deep as the Grand Canyon.
So much for the sanctity of human life.
Our fingers are stained like roses from the wounds of
    another generation
and a bleeding flag keeps a thousand caskets warm.
There are families trapped inside temples set ablaze
that turn to ash with their heads tilted toward the heavens.

They are the believers.

Continents are shaking.
Every time we vote for war can you hear the pulse of the
    innocent?
It is the anthem of the forgotten,
the cry of the victim.
It is the sound of a shovel pounding out midnight funerals
inside a city that weeps for its fallen.
But for every shot fired we are digging our own graves.

Hide behind the pursuit of Justice,
but the terror of a life severed short cannot fit into a seven-
  letter excuse.
Our hate spans oceans and we are using virtue as a reason
  to kill.
Who handed you the right to judge?

2012 Gold Key, American Voices, Gold Medal, Poetry

Expanding

Wings dipped in the iron of the sun slice like butter knives.
Clipped, combed.
You are a cosmonaut, a moon dancer.
Your pastpresentfuture is ripe and blushing,
sweeter than the time the night fluttered on our lips,
	unfurled on our hips.
Locked, looped.
I am sorry
for the broken glass
and the way we were constantly expanding,
but for every breath we spend, the universe takes one more
	step toward chaos.
Fall into me; teach me how to sew the layers of us into
	something new.
Bloom, burst.
Your eyes remind me of velvet mornings when the gray-
	tinged-pink-sprayed-orange
spilled onto our thighs like a prayer.
We are heavenly bodies pickpocketing the cosmos.
Warm-blooded, bold.
I know the way Spring skies will pulse.

2013 Gold Key, American Voices, Gold Medal, Poetry

The Balancing Act

It began with a slice of cantaloupe. True, I managed to fake my way through dinner using a shallow serving spoon and the lip of my rice bowl as necessary crutches. But since clearing the other silverware from the table, my pretense of cutlery coordination had hastily started to deflate. Before I could gather my thoughts, the juicy truth tumbled out in melon form—

I didn't know how to hold chopsticks.

Thump.

The buzz of Chinese chitchat revved and then stalled. It was my first night with my host family on an NSLI-Y scholarship, a program that lists Mandarin proficiency and student ambassadorship as the end goals of a six week stay in Hangzhou. To my horror, visions of hand-eye coordination had trounced those twin specters of fluency and diplomacy by the time my portion of fruit clunked against the wooden floorboards.

Zigzagging under the table and now trailing a sticky rivulet, the orange crescent resembled too closely the arc of a mocking smile. I couldn't help grinning in response, feeling helpless and a little ridiculous crouched on my knees. It was my host father who, after I collected myself and my dignity, spoke. "Do you want us to teach you how to use them?" He pointed to the instruments of my destruction, the chopsticks resting innocently against the broad-brimmed dessert platter.

Presented with this question now, "yes" seems like the obvious reply. At the time, I hesitated before answering. During childhood meals, I vacillated regularly between using chopsticks and a fork. The former promised dexterity and grace, the type of swanlike agility detailed by Amy Tan and wielded by Mulan. But in the end, the precision demanded by chopsticks proved too frustrating for me, and so the pair's pronged American counterpart, commanding in ease and in gleam, won my young heart.

Nobody judged me for choosing between utensils. In fact, at annual New Year's Eve dinners with my Dad's Chinese family, my grandma has more than once slid me a fork after watching oysters come back to life between my trembling chopsticks. My nebulous "Whasian" (half-white, half-Asian) status served as a ready-made excuse for my fumbling. So before my host father broached the subject, I lived for years believing my silverware scrimmages lay in the past. While I cannot claim to know what force compelled me to nod in response to his offer, I do attribute my semi-mastery of chopsticks to his advice that followed:

"Relax your hand. The rest will come with practice."

My fingers slackened. I exhaled, relieved.

As a child, I let the fork triumph at chopsticks' expense. I reasoned seeking refuge in my Mom's American influence would lead to a cleaner daily existence—fewer inquiries about the contents of my lunch box if I toted a ham and Swiss sandwich instead of sweet pork buns; fewer raised eyebrows when I told stories if I dubbed my grandma "Nana" instead of "Ngin Ngin." But as my grip loosened, I began to see that where I had staged a duel, there was no need for a dichotomy in the first place. My hands needed a lesson in pliability, but so did my mind.

Today, lowering my own pair of chopsticks into a bowl of instant ramen, I know that my host father was right: I must pursue the challenge of embracing silverware options and, ultimately, cultures. Being half-Chinese doesn't justify hiding behind half commitments. It took a plunging cantaloupe wedge to dislodge my inertia, but since returning home I have successfully pinned tofu with chopsticks; I have started conversing with my grandma in Mandarin; I have begun to delve into literature on modern China.

Although still a long way from achieving student statesmanship, I am enjoying savoring my fusion heritage. There is room for both a fork and chopsticks on my plate. And sometimes, I've learned, it's more fun to make a mess.

2014 Gold Key, Personal Essay/Memoir

To Critics of the Artist

The first time I set pen to paper
Words played catch and release with
The chambers of my heart.
Like Lucifer casting lines into pools of desire,
Hooks snagged onto right brain matter.
You didn't know it yet
But you lost me then to a lifetime of loving
The way a syllable can call revolutions and revelations
To arms in the same breath.
My lungs expanded—
The empty air is a waiting room for prefixes
Rioting for recombination.
Sentence fragments
Intimate with their own gravity
Petition for a glimpse at reality.
Please.
Better men than me have folded to doubt
Yet I cannot help craving creation.
I have listened too many times to
The exaltation of the electron
at the expense of the easel.
Don't dismiss Degas.
Don't tell the girl who picks the pen
she won't earn a dime
And then bemoan the state
of American innovation.
Debris drives decay;
The poet's fall is collateral damage
On a quest for modern enlightenment.
My brother once instructed me to think practically.
His eyes shined wide,
two blank checks
walking themselves to the bank.
He is the champion of clarity and now charity
But you should look to me
only for vulgarity;
Bowed on my knees, I surrender to art.
Monet painted the river Thames
Almost one hundred times because he said
He liked the light.
All I'm asking for is one chance
To try what feels right.
Please.

2014 Gold Key, Silver Medal, Poetry

PERSONAL ESSAY/MEMOIR

Editor Introduction by Chris Marsh

It is with great pleasure that I am writing the introduction to the personal essay/memoir portion of *Bloom*. There were many excellent essays from all over the state, and choosing these was challenging.

I already know that our state's teenagers are achieving at high levels, and these essays were proof of that. I hope you enjoy these insightful and entertaining works as much as I did.

Navya Dasari tells her story through music, introducing us to the soundtrack of her life. Anvita Gupta swirls together the sands of India and Arizona to acknowledge her great grandmother and ancestors in all lands. Raina Burchett remembers her grandma in the lively flitting of hummingbirds. Mandri Randeniya recounts a survivor's tale of the 2004 tsunami in Sri Lanka. Hannah Jarvis pays tribute to her mother and all of the catastrophic yet beautiful imperfections of humanity. Adwoa Buadu goes to battle with a mirror, and wins. Tal Eitan brings hope to Alzheimer's victims through the universal voice of music. Nailah Mathews discovers infinity in the aftermath of the shared experience of living music. Alice Zhao, inspired by the memory of her grandfather, reminds us to love, and celebrate, and live, and keep hoping, even though our moments above the earth are finite.

This year's personal essays/memoirs stretch into every direction the human heart can go, tousling our memories with our musings to rock our senses of reality. These writers share their insights—the kinds that shape our perceptions of ourselves and our world, leaving us forever changed.

Crescendo

It may be the age of digital music, but there's a certain poetry to liner notes that cannot be denied. The music tells a story, and the liner notes spin it in a new direction: a prologue, maybe, with the story of an album's production, or a dedication, with a message to the people who inspired or helped with the album. My favorites have always been the sort that function as footnotes; I remember lying on the couch with a booklet in my hand, faithfully turning the page when I heard the click of the CD player, letting the musician's notes on each song bleed into the notes themselves. For me, those pages expanded each song's meaning, let me feel closer to the music.

We look for music that speaks to us, so it's always fun for me to imagine my personality distilled into an album— how the "soundtrack to my life" would sound. But my childhood habit asks a different question yet: What might the liner notes say?

If my life were composed of music, perhaps these (fortunately or otherwise) would be mine:

LET'S GO HOME is a sweet ballad about comfort and compassion, which strives to be the musical equivalent of a warm hug (or many) without being sugary enough to cause a toothache. Sorry.

MUSINGS is slow soft rock that lends itself to thought; introspection set to piano music. For days on (or a life in) which your thoughts are so loud and fast only something quiet will balance them out. Also for nights on which you lie under the stars and realize you are the second Plato.

PLAYING WITH FIRE is a punk rock song that celebrates living with passion and thriving on intensity, in a way much more personal and much less obvious. The title is meant to remind you that, contrary to popular opinion, I should have been in The Runaways.

HEARTBEAT is power pop to burn my identity into this world, and make you question yours, all in the most cheerful, open-minded way possible and with a spirit reminiscent of bubblegum.

MISTAKES is a melancholy trip hop song for the days when only gloomy electronica and smooth female vocals can simultaneously indulge your insecurities and make you feel less empty. If you don't have these days, it's weird gypsy music for self-pitying goth girls.

VISION relates the obsession every artist has with her work. A fast beat and rousing chorus, along with an abrupt conclusion, emphasize the relentless pursuit of perfection... and the improbability of achieving it. (It can't be impossible, just can't be.)

CHANGE ME is the ubiquitous angsty alternative rock song about the gap between who you are and who people expect you to be. Loud drums and guitars fulfill the requirement for a song about dysphoria, so shove off.

SOMETHING IN THE HORIZON is a jazzy, bluesy song where hope is tinged with darkness or darkness is tinged with hope and everything is swinging, because I really just want to be Billie Holiday.

STILL SWINGING is a cabaret song for people who don't make sense and aren't about to apologize for it. Embracing your insanity can mean striking the fragile balance between the need for emotional stability and the realization that confusing people can be fun.

by Navya Dasari, age 16
2014 Gold Key
BASIS Scottsdale, Scottsdale

A Chipped Peacock

Shades of blue and green shift through my outstretched
fingers and dance under the light, and out of the jumble of
colors, a peacock arises, his tail chipped from use and a
spike protruding from his back where the earrings are held
to the earlobe. I wonder if long ago he danced to the rhythm
of another girl's footsteps, a girl whose eyes moved in
shades of black, like mine do. Comfortable with her life,
adorned by the money of silver speculators, she probably
had no idea that her family would soon lose everything.
Turning the earrings over in my hand, I feel nothing but a
faint pride that my ancestors were gamblers, that their
wealth was built, and lost, on taking risks in the bygone era
of the British Raj.

The sprawling, dry city of Phoenix hovers in the back of
my mind: the slow sweeping of the sky from blue to orange
to red at dusk, the mountains turned to blood, their rigid
contours defined against the soft light of the setting sun.
This unforgiving vista of desert imparts the people with a
certain rawness, a certain frankness, that makes other
parts of the country appear stifling in comparison. We are
the forty-eighth state to enter the Union, and our newness
is projected in the metallic glint of skyscrapers erected
seemingly overnight. The air used to simmer with the heat
of construction and growth; now, suspended, the half-
finished buildings lie in a state of restless anticipation
before they can begin to boom up towards the sky again.
Only the sunsets go on as before, dyeing the vaults of the
divine with prismatic splendor until the colors seep down,
turning the abandoned hardhats into crowns. But the
memory of the city halts abruptly at the recent depression.
Far off in the countryside, the land still booms with the
melodies of the Navajo. Under our canals lie the ruins of
the Aztec waterways, but we have never been a city to live
in retrospection. In winter, the air is clear not only of dust,
but also of recollections of family members cheated, uncles
killed, desperate veterans buried under the grounds of
family cemeteries.

The stucco walls of my house fondly remember the
growing pains of two babies, but they remain aloof and
untouched by memories of the dead. My backyard is not

broken by freshly broken mounds of dirt on which I can lay flowers and say prayers. And even if it was, what would I remember, standing at those graves? My most vivid memory of my grandmother is from a dim dream I had when I was four. News from my family in India is muted, and even when I talk with my relatives on the phone, their voices are distorted by the distance and their faces are blurs in my mind. My family is a sapling growing in virgin ground, and the roots we are building do not touch the roots of the tree whose seed we grew from. But I don't mind.

Our roots are nevertheless strong because they intertwine around one another. Without childhood friends, my parents turn their attention to me. The only time I feel the lack of family is when Thanksgiving rolls around, and the large mahogany table in our home suddenly feels absurdly large and empty.

At school, my friends sing, *"Land where my fathers died; Land of the pilgrim's pride,"* and I join in with a clear voice, though my heart lies flat at the words. Their fathers died here, not mine. At home, my mother hums *"Come home, O Traveller, your country calls you."* The way the laugh lines around her face twist and the far-off look in her eyes leave no doubt of the country she's remembering and hoping to go back to. But when I hear her sing, a vague sense of loneliness wakes and pushes itself out of my heart. Both my parents and my friends know where they belong, where their mothers and grandmothers belonged, and I feel that I should know as well.

After all, in Hindi, my name means a bridge, one who brings two people or ideas together. As a first generation daughter of immigrants, my name is oddly appropriate; after all, I am supposed to connect the traditions of the old country with the opportunities of the new. But instead of connecting, I am more often teetering over a gaping chasm, feet on one country and hands on the next. I had hoped, as I grew older, that I would stop jolting from side to side on the Indian-American scale, that I would finally find my footing. But I am forever that one child at the Diwali party clad in jeans, among women wearing their best *sarees*, or the kid arrayed in a full-length *lenga choli* at a casual Christmas gathering.

What country calls me? When I was a child, I heard the soft voice of India in the way my parents looked at the flag on Indian Independence day, their lips parted, eyes soft, lost in the light of a childhood they had left behind for a rocky desert steeped with rough people. I thought I heard its cry in the patriotic songs they sang, in the movies of bloody revolutionaries, in the rhythm of Gandhi's march. These impressions are a part of my blood, of my very-conflicted self.

Consequently, I was very excited to visit India at the age of eight, having already decided that any country my parents could love so must be the best in the world. But I found a land of extremes, pulsating to the heartbeats of a billion people living, breathing, working, procreating. With all those heartbeats, would you notice if one stopped? In streets so alive with colors and crowds, do you notice the beggar wheeling himself on rusted wheels, the dark stump of his leg blending in with the shadows? I noticed, because I was less adept at ignoring, more sheltered than my parents were.

Though many years have passed, I still remember a mother coming up to us and asking for money, a son following her with his hands open. Just a few years older than my brother, the little boy had no idea that begging was shameful. A grin overstretched his dirt-covered face as he blabbered in garbled Hindi for some coins. Before I could watch him for more than a second, our burly driver hurled himself at the little boy's mother, arms outstretched to slap her and voice raised, as if he owned her. Cringing, the child grabbed his mother's skirts and began to cry, his dimples and innocence turning to dust.

I knew then that India could never be mine, not in the way it was my parents'. Please don't misunderstand me: I love my culture. I love my religion. I love the way we place candles leading up to our door on Diwali, to welcome the start of the new year. I love the bright colors and popping spice of *chane bhature* and *aaloo paranthas*. I love talking in a different language when I don't want anyone else but my family to understand me. But I couldn't live in the country my parents loved, living their history all over again. Though my mind may not be tinted orange, green, and white, in the colors of the Indian flag, it is certainly not red, white, or blue either. Or, at least, the red is the color of Sedona rock, the white the hue of the glaring sun, and the blue the shade of the Colorado River.

I still laugh at the first-generation Indians who try to totally assimilate themselves into American culture. America isn't really a melting pot or a stew- or, at any rate, it's the first stew I've seen where the carrots distrust the potatoes and the beef is constantly protesting all the other vegetables. To pretend otherwise entails making my name more Anglo-Saxon, swallowing my anger when history textbooks calls our Hindu gods fictional. But still, I hope. I hope that, if not I, then my children will be accepted here, that they will never have to hear the words "go back to where you came from" from a history teacher or a politician.

Go back to where you came from! As if my parents were locusts, rather than self-respecting business owners. No, I couldn't kowtow to the norms of the land my parents had chosen to live in, even though I loved the rugged ridges of the mountains near my home, loved the dripping summers of mesquite trees and chlorinated pool water.

I ponder all this the next time I am in India, mull over my life when loneliness arises in me again, as I realize how little I fit in anywhere. The thoughts rise again to my mind, now, as I roll over the earrings in my hand, feel the chipped tail of the peacock dig into my palm.

"They're for you," my grandmother says, looking at me carefully. "Your father's grandmother kept them for you."

A tingle of warmth goes through my body. Someone thought about me before I was born, before I was conceived in thought or body. My mind drifts back to that strange girl, long ago, with my features, and down the line, through silver speculators and shop owners, until I get to my great grandmother. A small picture of her hangs in the alcove next to my desk, and in it, she grins without teeth. The arms she folds across her chest are dark brown and thick, and I realized long ago that they look exactly like my father's arms. I remember that she raised my grandfather and his brother when her husband died, leaving her a widow, unable to read or write anything but her own name. She sewed to make a little money, cooked and sold relishes to send her boys through school. But throughout her hardship, she never sold these earrings or any other relics of her past. Even at the age of eighty, she was able to smile and stand tall, back unbent by hardship.

Holding the peacocks in my hand, I feel the strength of my great grandmother filling my conflicted veins. As if in a dream, I see that courage passed down to my father and mother in their choice to leave their home and build a new one. They didn't do it so that their children would spend the rest of their lives wondering where they fit in, dilly-dallying between one country and another, unable to choose. I don't belong, I realize, to either the fractured desert of Arizona or the fog filled jungles of Delhi; I belong to values, to strength and determination and the people who exhibit them, no matter where those people are found.

by Anvita Gupta, age 16
2014 Gold Key, American Voices Nominee
BASIS Scottsdale, Scottsdale

Free Bird

I remember my Great Grandma Ruth.

I remember her always cracking jokes and the time my uncle was re-doing her carpet and she rolled my Grandma Wendy's friend Cliff into it. She jumped on top of the roll and sat on it and called everyone over to join her. "Come on everyone, sit on Cliff. CRUSH HIS LUNGS!!!"

I remember making pirogues with her and this is how it went: Mom would make the circles, I'd put a spoon of potato cheese mash, Grandma Wendy would fold, and Ruthie would "inspect them." Then, we'd put the first batch into the large silver pot over the fire of her gas stove and that was Ruthie's time to go outside and chain-smoke. She'd grab a Capri out of the pack, stick it in her mouth, and "click...click," she'd light the cigarette. Then, after she had time to smoke three or four, the pirogues were done, she'd drain them, and she'd "inspect" them. "WENDY! SHANNON! RAINA!!! There are four open mouths out of 30!" "Open mouths" she'd call pirogues that lost their filling in the pot. I remember her voice: so soft, so subtle, but still recognizable.

I remember Easter and the time I got the golden egg, thanks to her. I think she liked me the best of my cousins. I remember going to the zoo with her and Grandma Wendy and Mom. We also went to the Renaissance Fair where she bought me a pretty pink princess hat. She was my best friend.

I remember staying the night at her house and talking to her on the phone. She was always happy to hear me babble about school and second grade kids and she always seemed interested and even fascinated with the words I'd say: "the chill grill," chasing boys on the playground, doing flips on monkey bars. Sometimes we'd talk about birds and she'd asked which bird was my favorite; I was always changing from a quail to a blue jay but hers always stayed the same. "Hummingbirds are my favorite," she'd reply. She was the smartest person I knew and she knew the answer to every question about birds.

Every morning after I stayed the night, we'd throw bird seed into her back yard and fill the feeders. Then we'd feed her koi fish brown flakes and frozen corn and frozen peas and watch the koi swim around. She seemed to know all their names but I think she was trying to mess with me. I finally realized it was funny how she named all of them either "Elvis," "Presley," or "Elvis Presley." She told me that Elvis was a good-looking guy and say funny things like "I hope when I grow up Elvis will ask me to be his hound dog..." Then she'd laugh to herself.

The worst memories I have were her last few months. I remember her bones so brittle and that voice I loved to hear humming as she smoked her morning cigarette with her morning coffee. Like fall leaves, her skin changed from tannish to pale to yellow to orange. I didn't know why this was happening. Why was my best friend Ruthie so ill? So, so hard to look at? No one told me that she wouldn't be okay. No one told me that one of my best friends was going to die. No one told me that she'd get sicker and sicker and suffer more and more. I didn't understand what cancer was.

I remember her last few days when I'd visit her, every day after school. Most of all, I remember that last night.

She was so sick, so orange, so shaky, so frigid and frail. I remember sitting next to her on the couch but didn't understand that this'd be the last night I'd ever see her face or hear her voice. I remember her holding my hand, then smiling at me.

Then, her just crying, ...

tear drop...

by tear drop, more and more rolling down her cheek. She began to sob and I felt her soggy tear land on my shoulder. She hugged me and nestled me into her chest. I could smell her scent: bittersweet, like baby powder and tobacco. I didn't understand why she was sobbing so much. "I love you so much baby," she whispered into my ear. "You will be a beautiful woman with a beautiful soul," she repeated two times.

I remember the next day coming home to see my mom in our two-bedroom apartment. She was sitting in the living room, alone. When I walked in, I could feel the energy of loss. She sat me down on the couch and held my hand tightly. I could see it in her eyes that she was trying to hold back her tears. "Raina, Grandma passed away."

I didn't know what to say. I sat there and stared at her, blankly. My mom began crying a bit but stopped. She smiled and said, "At least she's happy."

I went outside to the front porch and began to water the red roses by the front door. Mom followed. Then, a little green-bodied, red-stomached hummingbird came to see what I was doing. "There, Mommy. There she is!" I said with a big grin on my face, pointing at the hummingbird.

"Grandma."

by Raina Burchett, grade 11
2014 Silver Key
Coronado High School, Scottsdale

Waves

All alone in a barren parking lot waiting for my family to rescue me, a five year old version of myself silently watches a massive dark wall of water rush towards me with the speed of a cheetah hunting its prey. The wall of water got closer and closer while my fear grew exponentially. As the water was about to envelop me, I would wake up trying to scream away the panic and reach for someone's comfort. These dreams became less frequent as the years went on, but even though it's almost nine years later, I still remember the day that my sanctuary became my own personal hell.

Let's rewind my life story to about nine years ago. I was a loud, energetic, dare-devil five year old from the tiny island of Sri Lanka. Being the first born of my family, I got the attention from my parents. I was that child who was always touching things I'm not supposed to, asking questions that were none of my business, and doing things the way I pleased. However, there was another side of me that not a lot of people noticed. I understood things and held onto words that the careless might casually throw away. My memory, even as a child, was occupied with little tidbits and details rather than the actual phrases I was told to remember.

The beginning of my story is a bit hazy, but I remember it being a humid December. Being a Buddhist Sri Lankan, Christmas wasn't too significant. It was the time of year that we got school holidays, and, for two weeks, would travel to various hotels with various family friends. That break started out like all the rest. My father booked about five hotels we were to stay in. The first two hotels are now a fused blur of Santa Clauses, us consuming steaming plate after plate of delicious food and overall, bliss. But the night before *that* day is clear in my head.

We were all sitting around a fire pit with all the adults drinking beer and reminiscing about the olden days. My sister and I were tuckered out after an entire day of swimming in the ocean and the pool. As my eyes were on the verge of complete darkness, I heard, "We should change our reservations to Nila Vali Hotel; it's closer to the ocean, but I guess Blue Oceanic is acceptable, too." With that, I sunk into heavenly dreams of frolicking on the fine sand of the beach.

As the morning laziness subsided, we were all anxious for the next stop on our journey. After we checked out, everyone packed into our clean, brand new, rented white van to travel to our new destination: Blue Oceanic. Blue Oceanic was a plain old lump of coal to people passing by, but only the people who dared to venture inside saw it as a geode. The hotel itself was four stories tall with three buildings and a monster parking lot surrounded by coconut trees. Again, this is one of the times that my memory fails me. I cannot remember anything we did but remember having a great time.

The next morning is forever etched in my mind. We sent the bags downstairs to the front desk in order to make checkout easier. We collected all the small items and met in the hall connecting the two lavish rooms we had gotten on the second floor. My mother desperately wanted to go on a boat ride before we departed, but the rest of us just wanted to get going. We made sure we had all our belongings and started making our way down the steps, then had to turn back because my mother's friend had to use the restroom. Suddenly, there were screams of terror coming from outside. In that split second, the chaos started.

Have you ever had that feeling of sheer terror but the source of it was nowhere to be seen? This was one of those feelings. People ran for their lives, screaming and holding their children close. I have never, to this day, seen so many so scared out of their minds. I knew it was time to be a deer and follow the crowd, but I couldn't move my body an inch, even if my conscience desperately told me to go. My brain had shut down, and so had my body. I just watched helplessly when a familiar hand scooped me up and carried me to the fourth floor, just in time.

The stairs were packed with people struggling for their one chance at safety. Somehow, I managed to end up beside my mother who was hysterically looking for me. My father, whose familiar hands I'd failed to recognize in that moment of panic, comforted my mother knowing that we were all safe. My sister was beside me, asking me questions that she seemed to be picking off my brain. When she realized I had no answers, she turned to my mother. My mother was too busy venting to her friend to notice.

"I thought it was a Tamil Tigers attack," my mother sobbed.

"Didn't you see the waves?" my mother's friend replied. "They were the size of a three story building."

"Look, we're all here, and let's thank Sai Baba and go before it's too late," her husband declared.

The men of the group ventured outside right after the first wave to find our belongings and van. I finally gathered enough courage to glance out the window. Everything was covered in water and the line indicating where the ocean started and the beach ended was nowhere to be seen. I spotted our van which was luckily stuck between two coconut trees that once covered the entire parking lot. All the other vans were floating towards the ocean, offering their owners a death sentence.

My father remembers this part of the story clearly. He and his friend tried to start the grass and mud-covered van once. Nothing happened. They tried a second time. Same outcome. Desperately, they tried a third time... and our van miraculously started! They thanked the gods for our fortune and, afraid the van might stall, motioned for us to quickly come down to the parking lot.

The rest of us speedily exited the fourth floor and made our way downstairs. The lobby was a disaster area. The huge windows that once surrounded the lobby were now miniscule pieces strewn into the brown, grass-filled water that reached up to my chest. The furniture was tossed aside, and the staff had assembled downstairs to come up with a plan of action. Our bags were nowhere in sight, but that was the least of our problems.

We all rushed into our god-given escape, and my father drove because our lives depended on it. Two minutes into the van ride, reality caught up with me: We could very well be dead. That's when the tears came, and they didn't stop for a year. We drove until we reached a small tea shop in the heart of Sri Lanka. When we stopped, the engine of that god-given, once-white van stopped and never started again. Now nine years have passed, and I'm at the same hotel that was once the Blue Oceanic, opening up a red suitcase that was thought to be lost forever. Breaking open this salt-encrusted seal and seeing all our preserved memories shows all the factors that could have changed our lives. What if we had changed our reservation and gone to Nila Vali Hotel? Nila Vali had no survivors. What if we had gone on a boat ride before we left, like my mother wanted? We would have been the first victims. What if my mother's friend had not needed to use the restroom? We would have been those bodies that they still can't find. What if our van hadn't started? We would have been hit with the second and most devastating wave. But, those things didn't happen. I'm thankful to be alive today and will forever be in debt to the gods for keeping me in the world through the 2004 tsunami.

by Mandri Randeniya, age 14
2014 Silver Key
Marcos de Niza High School, Tempe

Still Life, an *Essaie*

An elementary teacher once introduced the essay to me as "a short literary composition on a particular theme or subject, usually in prose and generally analytic, speculative, or interpretive." Dry. Is this all an essay can be, a collection of the vernacular, a cookie-cutter thesis statement sounding off the first argument, five paragraphs lined neatly in a row? What a *flawed* misconception. No, the essay is trying for the perfection that is hiding within the art of beauty, trying despite our flaws.

I take pride in the art of my eyebrows. Generally, though, people never come close enough to see that my right eyebrow is slightly better groomed than my left. On the occasion that they do, they come close enough to see it is these flaws, my heart that thinks too loudly, my mind that feels too deeply, that make me the person I am.

Flawed. I once dated a girl who described herself as so broken, so depressed by the pain within our world. And I saw her as flawed— flawed as a many-faceted diamond is flawed. *Yes, we are all flawed, but if you were a stone you would shine, love, shine.* She learned to make "flawed" beautiful. *Someday, in an essay of your own, you must share with me the secrets to being you.*

Beauty is not easy, but it cannot be worked for. *It comes off of you effortlessly, but you pay dearly for it— "I am not well-adjusted for this world," you say, and that is your price.* Here I am, trying to work for beauty but to no avail; I am not an artist, but a curator. Beauty I can see, and beauty I can protect, but when it comes to creating something both beautiful and significant, I am lost. *Loss is something I'm beginning to grow used to, now, always being at a loss for words, always remembering that loss of you.*

My mother is not strictly religious, but she loves God. Her faith that such a large and unruly power exists, and that it loves her in this loveless world, never ceases to amaze me. Yet, for all this love, by the end of every church service she attends, tears rain a tiptoeing waterfall down her face. Tears of what, I cannot say, and neither can she; they may be of awe, sadness, nostalgia, all or nothing. Whatever they are, they are her price for beauty, for feeling too deeply.

There is a line in Andrea Gibson's poem, *Wasabi,* that sings, "This girl is gonna crush me like a small bug..., but I'm like, go ahead, I'm all yours." On nights where I can't sleep for the rope knotting in my stomach, that line sings over and over in my mind. That's where Gibson and I have something in common; we both love with the entirety of our selves. We know we are going to be broken, but we would rather experience that moment of awe as the lightning flashes directly overhead than hear the thunder from miles away. *Let me throw myself into the storm of you, I am not afraid, not in the traditional sense of the word.* I do live in anticipation of the lightning that surely will strike, the pain of what is sure to come. *I know I will eventually be a bug on the windshield of you.*

Landslides, tornadoes, hurricanes—they are all beautiful to me. The careless way they wield their power, it is captivating, the way they create utter chaos without meaning to. They demonstrate the power nature still holds over us which, despite our genius technology, we cannot escape. Even with our seismographs and careful science, nature manages to destroy everything with what seems an unconscious gesture. *If there was a human embodiment of this chaos-creator, it would be you. You feel with the power of a mudslide, you write with the passion of the sun. You uproot the people who love you in the caress of your monsoon.*

My mother grew up in a household turned nuclear by her sister's case of epilepsy. She describes her and her siblings' ways of handling the stress: her brother became the comic relief of the family, her other sister the "bad child," while my mother strived to look perfect in her parents' eyes. One may think it ironic, then, that she is the one that her parents would consider to be the least perfect. Unlike her siblings, she did not manage to hold her marriage together, to tough out the hard times, to raise the perfect child. To have a "normal" relationship. Her parents see my homosexuality as testament to her failures as a mother which is, in their eyes, the most important role a woman can play. *But is there no beauty in the willfulness of her effort?*

Doesn't it seem that life denies us the things we want very much the most? *My mother and her perfection, you and your quest to never hurt another living soul. I don't know if you realize that you are a tornado, that no matter how gentle and careful you are, things will get destroyed.* What do I want very much the most? To identify something so important seems to almost erase it as a possibility. I want to make something beautiful.

A similar soul is one who sees embarrassments, hidden things, and still says, "I wish I had that. I wish I had friends and parents that would go along with that. I respect you even more for that." Friend, don't worry; together, we will immortalize our embarrassments in the Untitled Essay that makes up our lives. Our essays may be neither beautiful nor powerful but, together, we will ravish in our ugly unimportance.

A French philosopher birthed the essay into this world, only his essay was *essaie,* defined in French as *to try.* Is this not what we do in this short-lived life? Is this not the only thing at which we can actually dream of succeeding?

Life is an essay and it belongs to us, the authors. It is our job to look past our flaws, to build them into the art of perfection, the art of beauty.

It is our job to *essayer;* it is our job to try.

by Hannah Jarvis, age 16
2014 Silver Key
Westwood High School, Mesa

It's a Lovely Day for Fighting, Isn't It?

I like to believe that God made the colors of our skin as package deals. The chocolate package, though generally seen as lacking in tact and abounding in a hell of a lot of sass, does have one trait which I like to lord over everyone else: the ability to dance.

And, I like to say I do it pretty well. It's that sort of inborn quality that people expect and don't expect, the kind of thing where I wake up the Sunday after Winter Formal with makeup still in my eyes and sore legs wondering, *did I do all that for three hours?*

But there's *dance* and there's, well, dance. You know that kind of dance: the awkward, palm-sweating, hand-holding, do-I-really-have-to-move-*exactly*-in-that-position kind of dance. And I'm not ashamed to say I suck pretty darn amazingly when it comes to that.
I do Zumba on Saturday mornings. I see you inferring many things from that statement.

It's not really like I *choose* to, but my parents have this strange notion of "maintaining my health" or something like that and after swimming, gymnastics, that stint with fencing, two arduous years at sports camp, and tennis, my parents started to get more than a little desperate.

And it's not really that bad, I guess. Even if I'm the only teenage girl in the class. And the only one without a license. And the only one under the drinking age... Okay, my parents were *really* desperate.

Anyway, it's about 7 a.m. (which is really late for me) when I wake up. I slip on a blue t-shirt from my closet on top of my pajama pants and yet again unintentionally transform to the Aeropostale cover girl. Then I put on my socks and my Converse (I really should get it through my thick, braided head that maybe I can't really do everything in Converse but I don't have any sneakers.).

After putting on my shoes, I shuffle to the minivan (according to Mom, shuffling one's feet is not ladylike, but I never signed up to be a lady, so who cares?) and wait for my mother to slip into the driver's seat. I decide not to subject her to fifteen minutes of terror by asking to drive (and I'm still kinda sorta really tired). Mom finally arrives, ten minutes to 10 (which means I'll be almost late again), and off we go.

The sun's shining through the late February chill as we drive. While the landscape melts and shifts in front of us, Mom and I discuss the usuals: college, new clothes, her orthodontic problems. I'm able to weave her cacophonous, yet familiar and infectious laughter with the wedding scene I've been mulling for a new story which I'm probably never going to get on paper but modify and romanticize anyway.

Alas, a fifteen-minute drive is a fifteen-minute drive and soon the Honda has scooched into a parking spot near the studio. She's going to leave and come back because she's busy. I remind her I finish at eleven. She gives me a transparent, bracket-decorated smile and tells me to have a good time and to show those women what black girls can do. I turn one of the corners of my full lips into a half smile, telling her I'll try.

Sometimes I wish I didn't have to go there all alone. I'm awfully shy. But I'm a big girl and big girls can't ride on Mommy's arm forever, so I get down from my seat and jog awkwardly across the black pavement.

The dance center isn't a big place. Actually, it's rather small, a tiny alcove in a strip mall sandwiched quite nicely between a karate place and a Thai food restaurant. Despite this, I feel myself slowing, crawling, shrinking into a thick plastic retainer shell that glues my lips shut and sends a course of heat across my cheeks as I push the door open.

I keep my gaze downward, and that's when I notice our regular teacher's vanished into thin air and left a replacement. She's kneeling on the floor, thumbing through a slick iPhone playing the song "Thrift Shop," engrossed in discussion with two women about iCloud only working in certain parts of the house. She looks up and gives me a smile, an I'm-honestly-glad-to-see-you-even-though-we've-never-met-before-and-aren't-you-a-little-young-to-be-in-this-class smile.

I smile back and fill one a Styrofoam cup with cool water.

Several women linger in the studio when we walk in, wiping down blue yoga mats with Lysol wipes, storing them in closets, putting on their shoes. I put my little cup a little ways under a ballet barre on the right side of the room, then walk over near the left-hand corner near the door and the clock. Not that there's a correlation or anything.

Then I turn to the mirror. It's almost identical to many dance studio mirrors: large and almost as big as the wall it's mounted on. I remove the scrunchie from my wrist and pull my loose braids into a makeshift ponytail. On the other side of the mirror, a teenage girl with the same crumpled blue tee, gray yoga pants, and dusty Converse does the same.

I frown a little. Mirror Me looks so *awkward*. So little. So freaking juvenile.

I know it's not really my fault. It's a common thing for adolescent girls to hate mirrors, and themselves, by proxy. Still, some part of me wants to go over and slap Mirror Me upside the head, each whack muttering *Be... more... pretty! Be... more... older! Get... better... grammar! No seriously. You can't talk like this anymore! Grandpa's rolling in his grave!*

The music starts. I silently hope this woman won't kill me.

The second song has started, I've spilled my water, soaked the flood with my jacket, and this woman is trying to kill me.

She's also some sort of mystic genius. Who's so alert at 10:15 on a Saturday morning *anyway*?

Actually, now that I think about it, how are *any* of these people awake? Maybe it's this coffee stuff. I'd drink it, but caffeine gives me the shakes at night and my night literature is pretty fraught with... well... I'd rather not discuss it...

The amazing thing is the way everyone *moves*. Everyone has a certain *strut*: each shake, each curve, head bob, these people... they are *women*.

In comparison, my movements are stiff, robotic, lacking in... well, *anything*. I try not to catch the eye of my reflection but the dark and sweat-filmed smudge keeps shifting in and out of my peripheral vision.

And it's three or four songs later when I wonder why. There is no difference between my reflection and me. Yet, everything is different. My reflection is awkward, clumsy, slightly sticky, but what about *me*? I... well... *like* dancing. I *like* the music, I *like* reveling the self-satisfaction that I can finally maintain a steady and relatively high heart rate on a regular basis for the first time in... well, *ever.*

I look at my teacher. Her bracelets jingle as her hips shake violently from left to right, back and forth, in full circles. And she's *attacking* the mirror.

Poignant, introspective moments don't come to me often, I'm afraid. Usually I spend my energy thinking about food, or guys, or both. But as my feet position themselves and slide on the floor, I steal a quick moment, looking at myself.

I *am* sweaty. And kinda short. And my body is slightly lumpy. But... *I... don't care.* I don't. I really don't. Because it's fun, and the bass is pumping and I'm jumping and... I'm *dancing.* The only thing my reflection and I share is my retainer shell.

But *I...* I am capable of so much more. And I start twirling and smiling and my heart beats faster and faster and it's fun, so fun. And for a moment... I stare at the mirror again.

The girl's movements are still awkward and discordant in comparison to everyone else's. Her eyes lock with mine, silently challenging me to deflate.

Look at yourself.

My smile remains. *Oh, don't worry, I am.*

And with my hands on my hips, I attack the mirror too.

by Adwoa Buadu, age 16
2014 Gold Key
BASIS Tucson North, Tucson

Music Hath Power to
Slay the Savage Beast

Music is often the accompanying feature of "living." It enhances quality of life. Harmonious hums impose themselves on the fleeting shadows of memories, regaining the lost ones and reinforcing the joyous ones, causing a tender, loving rush when such memories are brought to mind. Yet it comes with great grief that some people cannot recall these memories; their minds gaze hopefully at the blank canvas that is their consciousness.

To participate in the effort to help Alzheimer's patients, I initiated a weekly outing to Memory Lane. I fabricate melodious tunes on the tenor saxophone for the residents of Barton House, a home for senior citizens suffering from Alzheimer's. Joining me are my friends and family on different instruments, including the piano and drums. We play popular songs to liven the sleepy atmosphere. Jazz is also in the repertoire. The live music provides the residents a means of stimulation to counter their declining awareness of life.

Entering the home, one is bombarded by the quiet atmosphere. Only the caretaker welcomes us and setting up the band wakens only a few now-intrigued residents. But after the first few notes of Scott Joplin's "The Entertainer," all exhibit some type of groove. Barbara swings her body, Bill taps his finger, the residents experience an awakening.

Music becomes the bridge of time, connecting the past with the present. One of the residents was a ballroom dancer. Now Alzheimer's has erased that memory, yet the music faintly rewrites her past as she dances with the grace of forgotten days. The eager expression on her face, combined with her pure joy of dancing once more, motivates us to play on.

Another resident has a booming voice that only singers have. He cannot recognize his wife, who visits him daily, yet when the patriotic rhythms of Woody Guthrie's "This Land is Your Land" ring from my sax and the snare drum rolls and the piano bounces to the melody, he joins us, sounding each word proudly. He remembers the words to the song. Remembers them. Each one.

These moments are raw proof that music connects lost memories with their owners, who are desperately trying to cling to them. When we leave, the animated atmosphere is gone. This is reality. Yet the momentary expressions of bliss on residents' faces when we play the music are always moving. I'm as exuberant as the residents, if not more so, for I feel accomplished in the sense that we improved the perspective of life for others.

Over the years, we have formed some close-knit bonds with staff members and some of the residents and their families. We've become part of the extended family that is the Barton House. When I see these people, and the suffering they and their families endure, I cannot help but wonder when a cure will be developed. Understanding the complexities of the brain and the causes for such a crippling disease as Alzheimer's has been on the national agenda for years, but now it is on mine. By entering the medical field, I hope to make a contribution to the growing effort to eliminate the power that Alzheimer's has over the lives of its victims.

by Tal Eitan, age 17
2014 Gold Key
Chaparral High School, Scottsdale

Chasing Infinity

I once read this book by a guy called Chbosky. It was about this kid who got abused and was really awkward and wasn't good at making friends. But then out of the blue, he did. He made some friends and this one night after they go to this show, the awkward kid says, "We are infinite." At least I think that's how things went down. It's been a while since I read the book. I never saw the movie.

Anyway, I never really understood what he was saying until this one night when I was coming back from a show with two of my friends. We burst out of the Marquee Theatre with our arms looped around each other. We were breathless and excited and just plain happy to be alive. Fresh out of the pit, our skin was a cocktail of stale sweat and cloying perfume. When we stumbled into the car, I was in the passenger side and the top was down, and I was remembering back to the show.

In the pit, barely three bodies from the barricade itself, there was this moment where I looked up right before the band shot confetti at us. The ceiling was dark because all of the lights were still down, but there was this rush. Everyone screaming along to the words we knew by heart, bodies pulsing and writhing together against each other— united, withstanding the force of storms because we *were* the storm.

We were together. We didn't know each other, but we were brothers. Sisters. Lovers, children, mothers, fathers, friends; and I remember remembering the way I held my breath. Then, there was a flash and confetti was coming down on us. I had laughed, we had laughed, all of us together breathless and still and then we were screaming again. Screaming with our comrades in love and in life, singing back to our heroes, clinging close to our fellow misfits. I had never felt more invincible in my life.

And I remember being in the car with my hands peeking through the sunroof, and my eyes on the stars. I was holding my breath again. There was still confetti in my hair. My friends in the back seat were just as spent as I was. We were all still hiccupping with excitement. Tears had dried at the corners of our eyes from when a lead singer brought out his acoustic guitar and asked us to help him sing. We had cried to the songs that saved our lives and reveled in the wonder at that stupid hiccup interrupting our breath. We were in awe of being alive.

We giggled at moments from the show, blushed about people we fell in love with. We bemoaned broken glasses and jewelry. We sighed about crowd-surfers with wayward feet and praised ourselves for helping the hurt and crying out of the pit. We shook our heads for not getting ourselves out when we overheated or got too hurt. We were shuddering with labored breaths and sweat stained brows, lungs empty and hearts full to bursting.

In that moment, I started thinking about this one time when I read this book by a guy called Chbosky about this awkward kid who couldn't make friends, but then did, and then said, "We are infinite." And I understood what that awkward kid meant.

It was that feeling. That feeling of being completely surrounded and being completely alone. It was being pressed against strangers and laughing and crying with them. It was calling them family. It was what stopped an entire show when a girl passed out. What pulled a kid who didn't have his right arm up onto our shoulders and into our hands and surged him toward the stage. It was that feeling. *That* feeling is infinity.

And that night, I swore to God, to my grandmother's grave, to the stars above my head, to the wind whistling in my ears; I swore to whoever was listening that I was infinite.

That I am infinite.

by Nailah Mathews, age 16
2014 Gold Key
Ironwood High School, Glendale

In the End, You and I

Two years ago, my grandfather asked me to write him a eulogy.

I remember the timid whip of a fan in the corner.

I remember the stick of the table under my palms.

And I remember the way his eyes, serious and solemn, caught mine, as he said in a hush of breath, "Will you write something for me when I'm gone?"

His hands were folded on the table—casual. His legs were crossed as he leaned back in the chair.

We could have been talking about the weather. We could have been talking about lunch. We could have been talking about anything else in the world but that dreaded five-letter word that had suddenly forced itself into our lives—the word that hung over our heads, heavy and choking, its fingers creeping along the back of my neck, breathing into my ear; and what was that knot in my throat, and why couldn't I say anything—a *yes* or a *no* or at least *something*—and only let my mouth open and close again and again like a gaping fish?

I suppose that it was inevitable. After all, according to *Health in the Americas*, the average life expectancy of a human being is 78.3 years. That's about 4,000 weeks, or 700,000 hours, or 2.5 billion seconds—numbers upon numbers, strung together to make a statistic, a hard nugget of scientific theory, empty, cold, and flat. When I say to you these numbers, that this is the estimated expiration date of our human life, our body of flesh and muscles and bone, stamped somewhere in our genetic code, imprinted in our very core—what does that mean to you? Can you hear beyond the sound of their syllables?

But, what if I told you about eyes growing blank, of skin growing cold, of the lungs growing sullen and still, the heart stopped in its once-eternal beats? What if I told you about the sodden grey dirt, of the maw of the ground, of a coffin lowered for a final rest somewhere below the cruel earth, somewhere I can't go, somewhere I can't follow, somewhere where I and you and he and she and all of us in this room and in this world and in this reality will be sent to in our own time?

I saw you grow old.

I saw your fingers shake, your veins grow soft, your skin grow thin. I saw your steps once sure and steady, now stumbling and catching, now sloppy and slow. You used to run with me when I was young—and when you were young. You could chase me around the house, around the street, around the city, around the world—but now you stand still and quiet, and you can't follow me anymore, can you?

You used to paint. You used to paint with oil, the colors staining your fingertips blue and red and green, blushes of the rainbow sinking into your nails. With the stroke of a brush, a blur became an edge became a life—and I see a farm and honey fields and golden trees, a spotted dog barking at an oxen patient, a boy in the distance, satchel over his back, waving a faint hello. With a flick of your wrist, lines became shapes and shapes became art, and I still have that picture we made so long ago, of a lake by our apartment, the tower rising in the distance cloaked by a forest stretching its branches to the sun above, and a boat bobbing in the waves, steam curling from its chimney, and a girl and a man on the deck, leaning over the railing to the water, gazing at a jumping fish, scales smudged blue with ink.

We blew bubbles at the windowsill from detergent, watching them drift through the air and tumble to the ground, our five-second secrets.

We folded airplanes and pretended they were stars, your majesty, your grace, we named them all and watched them fly up above and hoped they never came down.

I remember all of these things, and I wish I could remember more, because those seventeen years of my life with you, I don't remember them all, I wish I could remember them all, so that when you are finally cold and grey and gone, and I'm standing by a headstone, speechless and blank, and rubbing my hand over its pitted surface, I can see you standing just by my side at the corner of my eye, still here, forever young.

Forever young, your skin still smooth, your eyes still bright and winking.

Forever young, faster, stronger, bolder than ever, reckless and rushing toward the future, stretching the elastic of the now, hungry for something new, something more, and how can we be satisfied when the sun is still bright, the night is not yet too dark, when we can still see the full spectrum of colors and taste the full brilliance of our senses, the kisses of grass on our skin, the croon of an owl so far away, the splashes of sugar and salt with every bite, the wisp of lavender brushing against our cheek?

We saw the splendor of life run through our fingers like sands in an hourglass—to think we knew this splendor, we knew it all too well so many years ago, and now it's all going away piece by piece, slipping out of our clutches slow, so slow, that we can't see it going, but then it's gone, not to be found again.

I guess that you and I have to feel it someday, and one day or another, everything will end, we the unconquerable spirits who domesticated our souls, who created the most magnificent structures, who wrote the most magnificent words, who graced this hollow world with our magnificent presence, and who will leave behind our magnificent dust.

What am I supposed to do? What am I supposed to say? What am I supposed to think about our 78.3-year-lives? Where will we head when everything has passed, where will we start and where will we end, and won't it just be so beautifully awful if one day you and I and he and she and all of us look back on those years past and look forward at those years future, and think what is all of this, what was the point?

This thump of this heart, this sweep of these lungs, this ticking of this brain, jerks of nerves in this mind, again and again—this is what keeps us in the now—all of this involuntary and out of our control. Can I hold all of it in my hands, wonder at how charming and horrible it all is, at how fragile and tremulous, a thin rope bending under some great enchanting weight—and can I remember all of those things in my life and your life and his life and her life and all of our lives?

Our mortal, 78.3-year-lives—can I?

Remember the day we fell asleep in our parents' beds, our cheeks pressed against our parents' arms, and how they didn't move, only smiled and placed a careful hand on our heads, and rubbed at our hair, and thought I wish this didn't end, I wish it could always be like this, and how unfair it is, that you will someday grow up and grow old, and look at me from far away?

Remember the day we sat outside with our friend, the mosquitoes snapping at our arms, the sting of the sun on our faces, the scratch of the bench under our legs, and how we looked at each other over our lunches and thought that this was nice, what a wonderful feeling this is, to share the morning with someone whom I didn't know, whom I now know, whom I will forget to know because we will fall apart.

Remember the day when we curled up in our rooms, our fingernails scratching into our skin, our teeth clawing into our lips, our eyes stinging and hurt and hell, and thinking I can't take this, I won't take this, please leave me alone, don't leave me alone, and why can't I be small again, so I didn't have to think about tomorrow, how it "creeps in this petty pace from day to day...and all our yesterdays have lighted fools/the way to dusty death," (Shakespeare, *Macbeth*) how there is nothing more certain and nothing more final than the end of our existence, and how horrible a thought that is—of the inevitability of time.

Remember—this moment and that moment and all these moments, how can we remember all of these things, the ugly and the raw and the pain and the cut of wounds, but the triumph too, and the joy, the celebration of us, as children, young!

One day, you and I and he and she and all of us will be old. Feeble and weak, with all those shades of memories locked up inside but unable to be accessed, with all of those times of laughs and cries and jealousy and rage and obsession and depression and euphoria and greed, and remember that stubborn, awful, beautiful thing we call love—we'll forget that too, thrumming inside of our chests, now sullen, now still, slipped away into the dark of forget.

I wish I could have told you that I miss you, and I love you, and I heard you that time when you thought I didn't, and I care about you, that I know that you think the same way, and we're just two people, you and I, and my arm's by my side, and your arm's by your side, and I want to hold your hand—but now you're gone, and I'm here, alone, so tell me, you, how many feelings did you leave behind, stuck in your trapped lips, that you wanted to tell me, too many, too many—and it's done.

But, for now. For this tiny slice of the now, with you out there, and me right here, and all of us together for once—

can I say that we're still young? We're still young, we're still stupid, we're still lonely, we're still jealous, we're all of those bitter human things that swell inside of us, but with those seconds, with those hours, with those days and months and years we have left, drop your walls, drop your layers, let's look at each other face-to-face, I'm alive, and you're alive, so what could be wrong with that?

Our internal clocks are ticking down, yours and mine and his and hers and all of ours, clocks that we can't see, that we won't ever see, that we don't want to see, that exist anyway.

Let's make the best of what's left—that's all we can hope to do, and for a second, just a second, mind you, because yesterday has been sealed off, and tomorrow is as inscrutable and foreign as always, let's reach out our hands and touch that thing that we call being human and being young and being alive, can you see it, can you see this now, look carefully, this thrumming, beating, wonderful, charming, horrible, dreadful, tasteless, rude thing, we're standing at a field, honey and golden, it's rye I think, we're standing in a field of rye, and there's nobody to catch us at the edge of the cliff, no catcher this time, and we can run off right now, we can run off and feel that breath of air as we fall down into the abyss, down to the end of time, hoping to change for the better or for the worse, real, we're real—and eternal and cut short—and maybe, just maybe, can you believe this, in our 78.3-year-lives—

There is still hope for us yet.

Works Consulted

Health Organization, 14 May 2013. Web. 3 October 2013.

Shakespeare, William. *Macbeth*. New York: Washington Square Press, 1992. Print.

"United States of America." *Health in the Americas*. Health in the Americas – Pan American.

by Alice Zhao, age 17
2014 Gold Key, American Voices Nominee
Phoenix Country Day School, Paradise Valley

POETRY

Editor Introduction by Tracy Weaver, Laura Turchi, Heather Nagami, and Kelly O'Rourke

William Wordsworth postulated that "poetry is the spontaneous overflow of powerful feelings: it takes its origin from emotion recollected in tranquility," and later, Ralph Waldo Emerson posited "what lies behind you and what lies in front of you, pales in comparison to what lies inside of you." The young poets in this section have far exceeded what Emerson dictated. They *have* taken what lies within them and blossomed into their own.

Some are seasoned poets, some new, but they all create an urgency that their words and messages are for the ages, are for the masses, and are for generations of poets to come. Wisdom lies not only in their ideas about life, but also in how they carefully chose and placed their stanzas, lines, words, and nuances.

All poems demonstrate an incredible control of language while expressing strong emotions, evoking a special depth. The musicality of the lines vacillates and impresses the ear to reveal the skill of careful and hard-working writers who notice the greatness in subtleties.

Watching our young writers move from the world of childhood into the world of adolescence, or from adolescence into adulthood, is one of the immense joys of teaching. These young poets show a multitude of journeys into self-acceptance, imperfections and all; they ponder the mysteries of the universe, reminding us how important it is to allow our young people to think and write in their own way. Theirs are stories of love and loss expressed in images well beyond their years.

We are indebted for being allowed to work with these young, brilliant minds who have much to say about the human condition. As Thomas C. Foster expounds, there is only one story to be told, and that *is* the human condition—how we interact, conflict, love, respond and grow. This growth is eloquently illustrated in each piece. Please let each poem resonate within your soul, for you will be truly blessed by reading and learning from these young authors.

Passion

My palms sweat
jarring promises, fingertips hot.
There are no gentle corners.

There is an electric urgency
that stretches from my throat
to my heart.
I live heavily,
crackling.
I used to grind together
bright flowers, fragrant leaves
but they only left brown stains

on burning pavement.
I am leaking contradictions
that send steam rising off asphalt.
Don't tell me to hide the cracks
where weeds grow.
I have nurtured my insanity,

let it crawl through my veins.
Let it pump my heart full of passion
that sings in my blood
now. This is not healthy,
but I'd be lying if I said
I didn't love the way I think.
I know how to let my nature tug
until it pulls me to the brink.

by Navya Dasari, age 16
2014 Gold Key, Silver Medal
BASIS Scottsdale, Scottsdale

Trust

We have sacrificed the siesta
but the sun still drags us into
its worship: the soft, buzzing, drowsiness
of afternoon languor, the cadence of beating
warmth and steady light.

Our lightning fear has been eclipsed
by our obsession with the electric,
but we are still disturbed by the first
crack of thunder tearing across the sky.

The power of the sea,
the crash of water and salt against sand,
still tugs at our souls with the first sound,
first song, the rush of our mother's blood
in the womb, the beating of her heart.

I could never understand a Creation based on
order, order, order—
I know only the world spiraling out of control,
the beautiful breakdown
into the apocalyptic.

Disintegration, not freedom.
Not like fireworks that pinwheel across the sky
on nights you allow yourself to believe
in magic.

The tragedy is this:
That we are creatures of chaos unable to exist without
    walls.

Still,
I want you to break them down.
Let me believe I am powerful enough not to care.
Take me to nature, let our souls
mix a little. We might find ourselves
when we find each other,

and that chance is enough.

by Navya Dasari, age 16
2014 Silver Key
BASIS Scottsdale, Scottsdale

The Start

And it begins.
Your blood starts to pump
You feel yourself being thrown
Your palms so sweaty
It's no longer your dream even though you feel asleep
It's now a solemn truth
It's like you're on a trip to meet God
But there's no one home.

Empty an endless endeavor
Then your humanity kicks in like a punch to the gut
The sky now a black empire,
Wind knocked out of you
Then the beauty settles around you
Open on our onset
Like a crow, subtle yet deadly.

You're speechless
Breathless
Thoughtless
But as you feel like everything you know
is slipping from your memory
There's a rumble like a landslide.

A spark ignites.

Then the stars reveal themselves
        a beacon yelling in the endless dark
Clear as night
So beautiful
And then there's Earth
A structure so detailed but so simple
Screaming out blue
A world of life in a place of death
Your blood now running.

You see the sun coming up on the horizon
The earth now a silhouette with a sea of rays holding it
You laugh,
She's smiling
So you're not afraid when the fire finally catches you
You close your eyes.

And it begins.

by Jacob Abukhader, age 15
2014 Silver Key
Mountain View High School, Mesa

Cupid's Bow

Cupid placed his bow upon her mouth
and left it there for safekeeping.
She guards it with a quirk of her lip;
infatuation tucked into the corner
where she holds her cigarettes.
Sweet nothings perch
on the swell of her smirk.
She tips ash forget-me-nots,
blows smoke ring love letters
around frantic first times,
bittersweet goodbyes and
better things to come.
She blows a kiss: an arrow flies.

by Nailah Mathews, age 16
2014 Gold Key
Ironwood High School, Glendale

Safe in Ruin

We stopped running
When we found the city,
Concrete, cold,
Windows broken, cuts of glass
Catching sunlight, tossing it
Into millimeter pupils
Dilating in ecstasy—it has been years
Since we have seen the sun.

We stretched our skeletons
Open, filthy palms, fingertips—
Bullets into the heavens.
We unhooked our jaws and howled
In joy memoriam celebration,
Echoing down Desolation Row

Where skyscrapers were long ago
Banished to the ground
Like Babel for their ambition.
Cars littered in the streets,
Rust cradling them like lovers, mothers
Where vermillion and rose
Made their footholds,
Taking back what men had claimed.

We carved ourselves a home
In an old high rise
Abandoned, dusty, grey
Tattooed the walls with
The days that lingered on
Deep dug in the pits of our bellies
Dyed each other's hair
The colors of the saturated sky
Pastel fluorescent neon
Hummed 'hallelujah' out of key
Out of tune out of time
But still alive
We are safe in ruin.

by Nailah Mathews, age 16
2014 Gold Key
Ironwood High School, Glendale

The Hipster Manifesto

Wake up & have a bowl of Nutella with your Cap'n Crunch.
Dishevel your hair so it doesn't look like you care too much.
Wear jeans you haven't washed since the beginning of time.
Add the ugly Christmas sweater even though it's July.
    Affix the thick rims
    And hold your holy woven bracelets
    Close to your heart; put those on, too.
    Slip on your dirty shoes;
    Turn up your Dave Matthews,
And remember the mantra that you hold closest to you:

Nothing is any good if other people like it.

by Megan Dressler, age 17
2014 Silver Key
Mojave High School, Bullhead City

Ones and Sixes

Lay me out on the table;
Probe my mind, know my secrets
'Cause I'm not very simple.
Here's my life, hear my regrets.
If you've given me one chance
I've taken six,
And I've screwed up every single one
'Cause lessons don't stick.

Three cheers for Heaven's ears:
I'm glad they never learned to hear
About how I never listen
And you still trust me.
It's a wonder how the universe
Hasn't intervened.

I will tell you a story;
Based on my past, I'd say I'm lying
'Cause I'm really quite boring.
Though I laugh, know I'm dying.
Although you say you'd take me
Any way I come,
My pride keeps me lying
'Cause I've got too much.

Three cheers for Heaven's ears:
I'm glad they never learned to hear
About how you are the victim
Of all my crimes,
And you never seem to see
That all I do is lie.

by Megan Dressler, age 17
2014 Silver Key
Mojave High School, Bullhead City

Scent of the Desert

Modules of water
falling from the sky
plummeting to Earth
and landing
with a sigh
you know
they're coming
when the sky
clouds up,
when the
heavens darken
and the sunshine's
all dried up
and when they
begin to fall
here in the desert
the scent
of Palo Verde
runs through
the air
with such a force
that this
individual scent
has come to represent
those few moments
every couple
of months
when the
heavens open
and the sky
begins to pour.

by Emma Rymarcsuk, age 13
2014 Silver Key
Desert Canyon Middle School, Scottsdale

If My Mind Was a Book

If you were to turn my mind into a book
you would discover
dog-eared pages full of bright-eyed hopes for the journey
I'm embarking on,
and the sloppy notes
on what I should
bring along with me.

You would read about the time
I kicked my teacher's door because
I wanted to make sure she knew how angry
I was about not being able to stay inside and finish my
        drawing of a polar bear during recess.

You would chuckle about how every night
at the age of six I would pray to God
to make me a horse
because that was my idea of a perfect career.

You would learn of the raging jealousy
I sometimes feel when the boys look at other girls,
and the quick-to-follow shame
as the red rushes to my face
because good Christian girls
don't dare to think of such things.

You would see my sharp-taloned worries
and red-eyed fears
lurking around the words,
sinking their teeth into my shoulders,
reminding me how they can never truly be slain.

You would feel the pain
I felt when someone I slowly fell in love with
quickly fell in love with someone else,
and the utter embarrassment when
I fooled myself into thinking maybe
I've finally found someone who will smile
at my sayings and laugh at my jokes.

You would rub your fingers across old pictures,
drawings of what made me happy
and what dared to make me cry.
You would find the lyrics to an old Diana Ross song,
and faded photos of friends who have come and gone.

You would find a letter to my future child,
and a note to my favorite author that I never mustered the
     courage to mail.

You would feel the warmth of a campfire where I finally
become brave and share my story to faces
I finally learned to trust beings who somehow changed my
     life in just over eight weeks.

You would read a chapter on my yearning for a happiness
     that I must discover for myself as I make my map of
     where I want to go. Little slips of paper would fall from
     the pages. They would have scriptures that give me
     peace when the world I so carefully built decides to
     cave in sometimes.

You would find conversations with God
about anything and everything,
begging him to reveal to me the purpose of my existence.
An old red ribbon would mark the pages where you paused
     your reading,
one which I used to tie my hair back
so it wouldn't get in the way of my drawings.

You would find pages of unfinished homework
that I gave up on because I decided
I would never use it in my lifetime.

You would find famous quotes from J.K. Rowling bouncing
     around in between the paragraphs of unfinished stories
     and skeletal outlines, motivating me to finish what I
     once started.

Of course, my book would also have many blank pages;
pages waiting to be filled one at a time with memories
and experiences all waiting to happen as I go along my
journey, photos taken because the moment was perfect
and I felt an indescribable happiness inside of me.

If you were to turn my mind into a book, the cover would be
worn and folded in the corners, and the spine would be
falling apart from too many pages forced into it.

You would find thoughts and confessions I've yet to confess.

You would discover the wonders of my mind, and how I
work.

If my mind were a book, it would forever remain
unfinished.

by Madeline Lee, age 18
2014 Gold Key, Silver Medal
Mountain View High School, Mesa

The Juggler

Three balls to juggle
Two hands
One girl

Finals
Knotted stomach
Last minute scramble
Rambling, draining study sessions
Hope, desperation, fear, anxiety, stress
Chunky, broad review packets
Exhausting, sleepless nights
Sweaty palms
Tears

Relationships
Departed friends forgotten
Current friends lost along the wayside
Brief contact, hazy and fleeting memories
Splitting time with separated parents
Lifeguard for drowning friends
Striving for equality
Unavoidably flaky
Helpless

Duties
Clean room
Acquire a job
Attend all church meetings
Apply for a plethora of scholarships
Submit multiple college applications
Fixate on future
Earn money
Prepare

One girl
Two hands
Three balls to juggle

One always on the ground.

by Heather Griffin, age 17
2014 Silver Key
Dobson High School, Mesa

I Wish to Be Famous

I wish to be famous for being the one who is like a book of
   secrets but never tells a single one.
To be famous for who I am and not for who I'm not.
One who knows past quotes and can make her own.
The one to explain the wisdom behind them, even if I know
   it is something I need to work on.
I wish to be remembered as the loyal dirt that everyone can
   step on for support.
To be the one who can see everyone else's view even if I
   don't admit it.
I wish to be a famous photograph worn down by stories,
   tales and memories.
To be a constellation, never just a star alone.

by Samantha Hayes, age 13
2014 Silver Key
Tesseract School, Paradise Valley

Blasphemy

You look at me,
salt-stung eyes full of lies
you cannot bear to hear.

The rippling emotion of our love
has never had enough power
to break the barrier of their words
and your sapphire veins bleed into
more bodies of water than even the
most skilled scientist could ever discover.

Your body hovers above mine like
a moon lacking enough gravity
to bring in the tide and I wonder if
you can see the words written in
my mind like unsent love letters
sealed with the eternal promise of
a kiss that could never be properly executed,
even though we could have been—
because people didn't agree with our love,
still don't agree with our love,
and days like this, sometimes
you wonder if everyone ever will.

They see blasphemy in the beauty of our
fingers intertwined and speak hatred against
the connection we never thought we could find.

They put oceans between our instincts,
built dams around our feelings,
tore us down to nothing,
and called it religious necessity.

They have taken our love and
put it under a microscope,
held a gun against our heads
and a knife across our throats.

We never called our love conventional,
but how the hell is this "unnatural?"

They are standing with armies against
our weaponless bodies and claiming to be
offended because I asked to hold my lover's hand.

They deny us our rights, holding the book
of God in their hands, forgetting that not
everyone follows the scripture that not
even they can understand.

This God they speak of is not the God
I would like to know, and even if He was,
I wouldn't be afraid to show the world
of my love—just like they do with His.

I do not wish them a fraction of the curses
they have laid upon me and yet,
I have never asked them to put down
the book they read.

Choosing my battles carefully
should be more of a metaphor
than it is a reality and I'm beginning
to question the possibilities—

No, I will not let them win.
I will not bow down to a God I don't believe in,
I will not sacrifice something *beautiful*
for the sake of your agreement—

I will not allow *them* to pretend they are *Him.*

by Madi Hinze, age 17
2014 Gold Key
Desert Mountain High School, Scottsdale

What Is Good Enough?

There is a constant stream of questions
you are subjected to, being a senior.

Like, "What's your GPA? Are you applying to any
Ivy Leagues? Have you written your college essay?
Have you thought about staying in-state?
Have you gotten accepted yet?"

Or, my personal favorite: "I know how much
you hate it, but if you majored in math, do you
know how much money you could make?"

And it's funny, you know, how people begin to care
more about your class rank than they do
your ability to string 26 letters into something beautiful
or how your family obsesses over four-point, thirty-six
point, two-thousand, four-hundred point scales as they're
pulling your grades apart like flower petals—
Good enough, not good enough, yes, no, yes, no, no, no—
until you are left with nothing to provide,
nothing to say, because your grades speak for you now.

You wonder why no one ever told you that
the infamous plague senioritis is actually
contracted through the effect of the
words of the people you love most.

Your own family is wrapping their expectations
around your neck—so tightly, so tightly,
that you can barely breathe, let alone think.

At this point, you are gasping for air by the time you say,
"Well, I did get accepted—to Portland State."
But you already know the petals have determined your fate
and you're moving your lips along with them
as they say, "not good enough."

Just like they have said about your aspiration
of studying English, because apparently,
following your dreams has gone to bullshit
and apparently, teaching the next generation is not
worthy enough of my time, when they're the only reason
I am able to use this mind of mine—

This mind that you are polluting, corrupting, breaking
        down
into nothing, just because I am not the kind of person
who wants to live a life I am inclined to dislike.

And it's sad, you know,
how the only letter of rejection I have received
so far has my home as the return address.

by Madi Hinze, age 17
2014 Silver Key
Desert Mountain High School, Scottsdale

Metal

Human history has always been a conquest of metal:
The Bronze Age, the Iron Age, the Steel Age,
All culminating in the final conquest of juvenility—
Who has a trophy, a glorified piece of metal
Against who does not.

The applause of meaningless people rings and echoes
Like some hideous, cyclonic thunder—
Again, again, and once more:
Constant repercussion off of gymnasium walls.

As kids, we were all told that everyone is a winner,
But that's not true.
Some walk away, their arms buckling
Under the weight of their own grandeur and awards.
Others aren't so lucky;
They walk away, tears pouring down their disappointed
    faces.

They offer a round of applause for the runner-up and third,
But no one ever remembers the fourth-place,
The fifthsixthseventheighth.
Disillusioned to find that they aren't good enough.

The only thing colder than the shiny surface
Of the award won by few
Is the cold shoulder given to the hoi polloi,
The people who never had, don't have, and won't have
Metal.

by Alex Cohen, age 15
2014 Gold Key
BASIS Scottsdale, Scottsdale

Schoolyard

In elementary school
We stood—just pushing five feet tall—
Against the rusted fence of the basketball court,
And teams were picked.

Come, you can all join in—
Except for you, the bookworm,
Who would rather have his face buried in dusty pages
Than the dust of a soccer field.

And you, the fat one:
You run slower than the honey you eat.

In fact, nobody different can play:
The blind, the deaf, the crippled, the Jew,
The ugly, the poor, the mature, and you.

In high school, we sat in our first-floor bedrooms—
Not posh or popular, but plaintive and poor.
We saw, through our tears,
Iridescent lights cascading out of open windows.

Explicit party music abused our eardrums
As girls we used to color with stumbled home drunk.
We ostensibly believed we were better, but that wasn't true:
We were only jealous, and we were never invited.
Not once.

It was as if life were some purgatory that put us through
    trials
So as to expunge our sins from a past life unknown,
As if life were cries to a deaf God.

Maybe time didn't pass at all:
Maybe life is the same people and the same year.
Maybe the sands of time felt the heat of two atom bombs
And melted into an immutable glass.

Either way, whether it be that life is punishment,
Or that Father Time's hourglass creeps like molasses, filled
    with glass—
The fingers wrapped tightly around the bottles
Are the same fingers that wrapped around the rusted coils
    of fence.

Still, we stand, five feet tall.

by Alex Cohen, age 15
2014 Gold Key
BASIS Scottsdale, Scottsdale

Impasto

Impasto: The process or technique of laying on paint or pigment thickly so that it stands out from a surface.

Inspiration,
You stated.
That was what you needed.
We danced upon keys of every kind,
thrashing, waltzing,
you even had me belly dance.
Inspiration.
You dowsed with wines of every shade,
shared your shadowy visions with me.
Inspiration.
You indulged in decadence,
injecting me with pain and selfish pleasure.

Alas, a revelation! A masterpiece yields, engulfing your
soul, your mind and self-control:

You paint tender blossoms with your fingers
In hues of lonely blue
And shades of bitter belladonna,
Vivid with scarlet rivers that pulse
Beneath the petals.
You capture
Confusion with such care,
In whorls of blood and brine—
These pirouetting whirlpools
That drown all sense and thought.
I cannot understand your artful machinations,
For I am not an artist.
I am a simple canvas.

by Christina Luu, age 17
2013 Gold Key Poetry, 2014 Silver Key Portfolio
Coronado High School, Scottsdale

Mother Was Wrong

Mother,
What shall I do, when the words you have taught me
have left me without a clue?
When "don't hit," "stand up straight," and "don't cry"
apply to big-girl life?
The monsters that haunt me lay no longer under my bed.
They're real and alive; they're in my head.
The menacing taunts of girls
with heads larger than their lives
devour my soul, inhabit my thoughts.
Scowls darting across the room.
My mind racing towards impending doom.
"Be the bigger person."
How can I,
when I am my own enemy?
The internal conflict lingers in my mind.
I let them get to me; that is their prize.
But, Mommy, when I'm being called *whore*,
there's simply no way to ignore
the agonizing spirit in my soul.
The urge to bite and scratch until I feel whole
prods at me all night while I scream without control.

by Tiffany Gong, age 18
2014 Silver Key
Dobson High School, Mesa

The Monster Within

Monsters, predators, demons lie in wait within.
Scratching to get out, but need not claw to get in.
Contemptuous mind overtaken by lust,
"I want to see pain. See it, I must."
Awaken, you beast, you vile creature.
Prey upon the weak, destroy, until you feel better.
The vile lies you speak to maintain your stature,
you false prophet, you Jezebel.
All eyes upon the monster, yet they do not know.
The monster hides, lies in wait for the show.
Sardonic interior, why must you feed on despair?
Why must you feel so superior when you compare?
Calamitous figment with your corrupt crimes,
I have tried killing you a thousand times.
You sleep buried deep within my innards.
May you never come out; I dared let you in.
Discard the remnants of my former self.
Burn it, remember it, place it upon a shelf.
I have relinquished myself to the monster,
the disease has engulfed my heart.

by Tiffany Gong, age 18
2014 Silver Key
Dobson High School, Mesa

To The Young Men
An Ode to Honor Jimmy Santiago Baca, The New Godfather of Poetry

An angel overwhelmingly with sorrow,
An artist trying to get an education,
Because his mom wanted him to have
A better life than she had.
But the cruel paradox is young men are
Condemned to live without any of
Those humane principles that
Expand across the entire continent.

These young men had to fight off a
Dreamless hope
That all Latinos bring power from
Insight of oppression
They lived in daily with an
Impurity of heart and body.
These young men trying to survive
The streets where gangbangers
Fly face-up in their grill
And creativity starts to die.
Where homelessness and poverty are
Ignored in society.
Amazing powerful organizations above
Don't give nothin' to no one.
But Jimmy gives great respect
To the young men
Because they love the magical
Aspects of poetry
Jimmy had gangbangers in their
Seats,
Across from bars on the walls,
Writing poetry
And hoping for much more than this
Condemned life.

by Antonio Flores, age 16
2014 Silver Key
Mountain View High School, Mesa

Sí Se Puede

We are cursed at birth

because our skin can speak.

It says that we steal,

that we work for a meal,

that we break every law

and can't keep a deal.

How do you feel

to prove the racist bigot right?
Have you forgotten

that we did not get here
    without a fight!

You are ungrateful and
    ignorant.
You are a fool.
You are belligerent.
Can you hear the echo
    ya basta!?
End the stereotype.

Do it for La Raza.

Let us tie our skin's
    tongue in a knot,
Let us recall
    the struggles our
    ancestors fought.
Let us be the vision
    our forebears sought.

Can you hear the echo de El Grito de Dolores?
Throw away your stupid gangster colores!

My vision is burned
    by the things you do.
Flashing your guns,
all badass with your crew.

You demean us all,
    and we are not few.
They are afraid,
    but for the wrong reasons.

Let us rise up

Elevate

Levitate

Let us prove them wrong.

by Oscar Aguirre, age 18
2014 Silver Key
Maryvale High School, Phoenix

Linked

Chains can bind
And blind the mind
Yet chains are all linked
In some place, some time.

For one person's doubts
In another they bout
In the same way
On a zigzagged line.

Everyone's pain is connected.
Every trouble erected
Can be found in another.
If you seek you shall find.

So no matter what you may think
You're never alone, for not even a blink
No matter how unusual your worry
There's another, with whom you are aligned.

by Katie Barnhart, age 12
2014 Silver Key
Desert Canyon Middle School, Scottsdale

Reflection

Mirror, good mirror,
Show me my face
For today my sorrow is more than at bay.
Ignorance is bliss, this is the way,
Mirror, good mirror,
Show me my face.

Mirror, cruel mirror,
Don't show me my face.
Not now, not today, I am too afraid
Of my eyes looking back, hanging on by a thread.
Mirror, cruel mirror,
Don't show me my face.

Mirror, oh mirror,
What I feel, I don't know.
Nothing around me truly feels real
Life is a blur, how to know how I feel?
Mirror, oh mirror,
Back to life, I don't want to go.

Mirror, oh mirror,
I need you no more.
I know who I am, I don't need to see
The reflection's corrections, never perfection.
I don't need criticism. I see myself clear,
So, good bye, we traveled, and now we depart.
My new life of heart's mind I must start.

by Katie Barnhart, age 12
2014 Silver Key
Desert Canyon Middle School, Scottsdale

We Are All Equal

October 11th, 1864,
This is a day that changed many lives.
This is a day that Maryland abolished slavery.
This is a day that should be known,
and remembered.
It took centuries for people to understand
a rather simple concept.
A concept that we are all equal.

Built big like a hippo or as small as a mouse.
Naturally tall like a giant or as short as a midget.
Weighed fat or skinny?
Hair blonde as day or black as night.
Skin color flashing white or hidden black.
That doesn't matter,
It shouldn't matter because we are all equal.

And we can't stop.
And we won't stop until this idea is
as plain as day in all our hearts and minds.
No more eccedentesiast faces and
being judgmental without knowing a person.
Treat everyone with respect and dignity.
Make everyone feel equivalent and especially
important.

by Lauren Ludwig, age 15
2014 Silver Key
Mountain View High School, Mesa

What We Have the Power to Do

Why are we so proud?
We are all the same.

If only beauty was measured
By kindness,
And not by what is
on the outside.
Being made fun of as a
child in elementary school
Makes me think—
Every day
What I need to do
So they will stop teasing me.
But then I realize,
All those names,
Don't really mean anything.
All that really matters,
Is how I feel about
myself.

No one can make me feel of less worth
Than I really am.
I am the only one
Strong enough to tear myself down.
I am the only one
who has the power.

We all have the Power within.

by Taylor Hammond, age 15
2014 Silver Key
Mountain View High School, Mesa

Birth of Courage

There was a boy at the bus stop today.
He was hunched like Atlas and cold like David,
Glaring at the earth like it stole his name.
He pulled his hair like angry weeds,
Breathed long and hard with iron lungs,
And paid no mind to the man beside him.

The world is his oyster but he is the grain of sand
Stuck between rough outlines and motherly love.
His fears the shadows stealing change from his pockets
And double knotting his heartstrings.
He waits for the sun to melt his wings
Or the pressure to make him invincible.

There will be a man at the bus stop tomorrow,
Standing tall like Zeus with eyes like Androcles,
Staring at me as if I knew his name.
He will fold his hands like water lilies,
Inhale the breeze as it saunters by,
And pay no mind to the boy beside him.

by Jordyn Ochser, age 17
2014 Silver Key
Chaparral High School, Scottsdale

Birth of Grief

There was a girl at the bus stop today
With eyes like Hera and a voice like Echo,
Staring at the sky like it stole her heart.
She twirled her hair like woven garlands,
Swayed with the wheat in the wind,
And paid no mind to the woman beside her.

Her head in the clouds but no shoes on her feet,
She waits for the moment when the air stands still
And plucks her spirit like an overgrown weed.
She chases the future and buries the past,
Begging the sun to circle round one more time
To fend off the eager shadows playing at her heels.

There will be a woman at the bus stop tomorrow
With hands like Arachne and a mind like Cassandra,
Watching the clouds like they know her pain.
She will hold her purse tight like it holds her last penny,
Lean into the wind like a stubborn old tree,
And pay no mind to the girl beside her.

by Jordyn Ochser, age 17
2014 Silver Key
Chaparral High School, Scottsdale

Ordinary Courage of a Normal Teenager

I think that those people
Who reel in their emotions
Before things get hot and
Think about how it might hurt
Before they talk and
Wonder how the other person thinks
Before making assumptions
Ought to be recognized for and given a medal for
Their ordinary everyday courage that
Keeps the world spinning.

by Lydia Spire, age 13
2014 Silver Key
Tesseract School, Paradise Valley

Ordinary Courage of a Father

I think that those fathers who
Are unrecognized
And buried in the tides of the earth
Ought to be given the spotlight sometime.

To the fathers who give
Without a thought to receiving.
To the fathers who serve
Without a thought to thanking.
To the fathers who let go
Without a thought to homecoming.
To the fathers that respect,
Without a thought to their own dignity,
To them, perhaps not a flashy medal,
Or a trophy of gold,
Or an official certificate.
Perhaps just a pat on the back and a few words
Of kindness
For all they have done.

by Lydia Spire, age 13
2014 Silver Key
Tesseract School, Paradise Valley

Lament—An Elegy for the Fairy Tale

In a paper-thin castle made of words,
I lived my childhood as a princess.
Expecting,
My life struggles to disappear with a warm and golden
    flourish:
Every painful finger-prick sleep would end
With the perfect kiss of fortune.
Both the shoes and men I lost at midnight
Would appear expectantly on my doorstep.
If I felt distant, trapped, and alone
Then I could just let my hair down.
Everything,
Fell into picture-perfect place,
Illustrated by the author of my mind.

Until I grew too tall for my home,
Thrust into the world of giants
By a turning, twisting, beanstalk.
I learned what it meant to be human.
Even the greatest kingdoms fall,
Priceless dreams end up smashed pumpkins,
Families slaughter golden-egg laying geese for
    Thanksgiving dinner,
Hoodie-clad Prince Charmings ride in and out
    in their beat-up Chevy trucks.
Life knows just how to end every Happily Ever After.

by Anna Hawkins, age 17
2014 Silver Key
Mountain View High School, Mesa

Would You Believe Me?

What if I told you
That the world is just one big chunk of rock
Floating in space
And we are just the sad little creatures
Looking up and saying,
"That is a ball of fire,
And if you wish on it,
Your wildest dreams will come true."
And we walk around in our little minds
And think,
"That is the sky,
and that is a bird,
and I am myself."
But all we really are
Is a big mass of flesh,
    Made up of
        Protons and
            Neutrons and
                Electrons
Whose consciousness happened to be
    Snapped into focus
By a little spark of fire.

by Hannah Bernier, age 13
2014 Gold Key
Desert Canyon Middle School, Scottsdale

Teddy

The stoic stare of glassy eyes still since
The child's content. If only you would breathe—
In growing hearts slowly losing cadence.
For tiny hands a gentle soul beneath;
Reluctant minds, we in-betweens desire
To revive these flat lines that blind our eyes.
Of tea, of ribbons, memories admire
In mirrors now reflecting frozen lies.
My glance, now brief, my love eternally
For marbles two that never ceased your gaze—
Imagination leaves hyperbole;
It leads me to believe for all my days
Our love is cherished, unified at least.
Naivety conceals facetious beasts.

by Hyunjeong Jun, age 15
2014 Silver Key
BASIS Tucson North, Tucson

Eastbound

My pale bare feet dance across the icy metal strip.
A grey sky questions me. November chills caress my skin.
A distant scent of smoke rises from the suburbs.

Dreams were dreamt to someday arrive at a destination.
Left behind are blackened tracks and ashen pebbles.
I longed to pursue that train, to shatter the arbitrary
    chains
That desired to bind my clawing remains.

To shake the mockers and scoffers,
To remember what it was that I held dear to my heart.
To search for the child that I abandoned—
A long time past.

Yet the very essence of my being is as tired as my body,
The flame of my courage has turned as cold as my soul,
My guilty hands are as crimson as the child's neck, and
There will be no use collecting pieces of a broken vase.

Raindrops pierce my skin with every pitter patter.
Dark clouds give my dry eyes the tears that left me then.

The hem of my fluttering white dress kisses the smooth
    metal body of the train.
Dangerously close.
Heat rising from the once Arctic rails that I walked upon.
Breathing in, I stand inches from that powerful monster.
The blurring of handles, boxcars, and wheels fill my vision.

A serpentine wisp of fragile white vapor escapes my lips
As I exhale into the northern sky.

Shut my eyes and topple backward.
Spite my screaming scalp. Head. Mind. Thoughts.
Locks of hair are ripped out in the vacuum
Of the merciless locomotive fuming ahead.

A blue sky invites me
To its envious embrace.
The angered waves of the cyan sea slap against my cheeks.
I drift away into memories of a young tree and its luscious
    fruits.
In my greed, I could not choose one.

A delicate and firm hand pulls me forward by the arm.
The child glimmering with radiant sunlight guides me.
A ticket stamped in golden letters.
Eastbound.

> *by Hyunjeong Jun, age 15*
> *2014 Silver Key*
> *BASIS Tucson North, Tucson*

Chewing Bubble Gum in the Rain

Chewing bubble gum in the rain.
My feet are bare on the normally vibrant green grass,
    overcast today with a shade of gray reflected from the
    angry clouds above.
I can feel the pliable mud ooze lazily between my toes.
Each stalk of grass, wet with cool, therapeutic moisture,
    tickles the top and sides of my feet.
Chewing bubble gum in the rain.
Drops of rain attack my clothes which provide a momentary
    barrier between the liquid and my skin.
But my arms have no such protection as they are thrust out
    in welcome to the voyaging droplets of condensation.
The raindrops collide with my arms in a frenzy. Some are
    absorbed into my dry, thirsty skin, while others roll
    slowly off and fall, defeated to Earth.

Chewing bubble gum in the rain.
While the rest of me stands with nearly divine serenity, my
    mouth moves with purpose.
I roll the sticky wad of sugar around in my mouth until it
    forms the shape desired.
I form it onto my tongue, and blow.
 A balloon of perfect pink gum cascades from my pursed
    lips, contrasting wildly with the murky background of
    dark grays and greens.
Rain assaults the bubble, berating it until the thin, stretchy
    surface breaks and it falls like a windless parachute
    over my lips.
I bring it back into my mouth, as I have so many times
    before.
As I did many years ago, standing in the same spot with
    littler feet, shorter arms, bigger hopes, and smaller
    fears.
But no matter how old I get and how much has changed,
    some things will always stay simple, and stay the
    same.
Like chewing bubble gum in the rain.

by Alex Elbert, age 17
2014 Gold Key
Chaparral High School, Scottsdale

Patchwork

Tearing cloth,
Cutting string,
Patching worries,
Pushing batting back,
Haphazardly stitching
In hopes of mending.

Each time a loss,
Each time a scrap torn away,
Poor little tatters—badges of pain
Frayed edges forever the same,
Once unspun, never whole again.

Cloth quilted by Love,
A seamstress to loss
Will try to sew the heart right,
No matter what the cost.

Yet
    No buttons, no tailors
        Can refasten these threads
            For memories will continue to pull
           On loose ends

by Archanna Smith, age 17
2014 Silver Key
Home-schooled, Chino Valley

Last Smile

Once I could've smiled.
Remember the summer
We spent in "Cancooon?"
The water was warm,
And Daddy held my hands
So I wouldn't get washed away.

You told me to dry myself off,
And wrapped a towel around
My new book
So I could carry it
And it wouldn't get wet.
I smiled then.

Sometimes in the shower
As I feel the drops
Fall hard on my scalp,
I'll remember when we
Played tag in the rain
Until I got a cold.

I'd sneeze and sniffle
But, you'd feed me that soup
And I'd feel better.
Then, you'd brush your long, blond hair
Into a satisfied ponytail.
I was still smiling.

Last week
I went to a ball game.
And the dirt and the grass
Their scent filled my nose
So I remembered
How you would cheer

You would say "now!"
And I knew when to swing.
Home run! Home run!
I ran fast
I wasn't looking ahead
Because I saw you smiling.

But then you stopped.
I think it was because of that
One scary phone call.
When your eyes turned sad.
And you pulled out your hair
Like you weren't my mommy anymore.

And you ignored me
When I asked you
What was wrong.
You just stared at our
Dirty, linoleum floors
Now, I'm sorry I made you say it.

I thought you said Daddy
Would be okay.
Naïve as I was
I knew that wasn't true
Because my right eye twitches
When I lie, too.

At school
My friends would ask me
Why my mommy doesn't smile
And I would tell them
When a mommy loses half of her heart,
It splits and breaks and frowns.

I wasn't trying to annoy you
When I made a funny face
Or danced around.
I just wanted to make you laugh
And you just didn't say a word.
I could take a hint.

I think you forgot I was there.
No,
You just pretended I wasn't.
You thought you could hide
The empty bottles,
But I knew.

You'd disappear behind the house
And come into my room with stumbling feet

When you thought I was sleeping.
You would say goodnight,
But your words didn't sound like words.
Just sounds that tried so hard but were too sour.

That's when I stopped smiling.

They say Mommies
Are supposed to be
Role models and teachers.
That's what you were,
Once upon a time.
So long ago, I can barely remember.

I know you're
In so much—
So much pain.
I know you think
Those bottles will
Make you forget.

And Mommy, they will.
But, you're forgetting everything.
Your life
Daddy
Me
Yourself

My smiles are fake.
I want to see you smile.
But I can't make you do it.
Not if I sing
Not if I crack a funny joke.
Not if I play your favorite song.

Please
Please
Put those bottles down.
They won't bring Daddy back.
And I just want to see your smile.
Just one last smile.

by Angelica Garcia, age 15
2014 Gold Key
Flagstaff High School, Flagstaff

Suspension of Disbelief

The world does not know me.
Their ignorance causes them
To mistake me
For the white noise in the TV.

You have been fooled.
Shall we tolerate,
And lose our identity?
Shall we love
And forsake our judgment?

My existence has been shattered.
"Nothing can be known"
There is no knowledge.
Where I have been extracted.

You cannot think
Lest you be damned
By those who wish to
Take me away,
And indoctrinate you with falsities.

Yet are most cowards?
Because they desire to
Be liked, loved, appraised
With need to fit in.

I am the inverse of corrupt lie.
But I am under-heard—
Neglected like a used tissue.
I have been called irrelevant
And *relative.*

There is a contagious phobia—
The fear of hurt and sacrifice
Are you afraid?
Are you afraid of me?

by Angelica Garcia, age 15
2014 Gold Key
Flagstaff High School, Flagstaff

Sour Milk

This world is full of sour milk.
It stinks, doesn't it?

I'm not talking about the milk that
"Smells a little funny,"
I'm not talking about the milk that
Is *maybe* a day past the expiration date.

No, that's not what I'm talking about.

I'm talking about the sour milk
That sat in the fridge years too long.
I'm talking about the sour milk that started out okay,
But eventually it got really, really, really awful.

I'm talking about the sour milk
That is full of disgusting, horrifying chunks,
The sour milk that leaves its stench behind for weeks,
Even if it was brought in the room for only a minute.

I'm talking about
War, Poverty, Death, Sickness, Homelessness,
Starvation, Dehydration, Helplessness, Greed,
Evil, Obliviousness, Cynicism, Deception, Anger,
Hatred, Depression, Suicide, Loneliness,

I'm talking about the darkness
Of the world.

I'm talking about those people,
Who have the power.

I'm talking about those batrachophagous people,
Who walk everywhere with their head in the air,
Who talk all the time with their pretentious attitudes,
Walk around every day like it was their day,
A holiday just for them,

Those people who have the power,
Who have the ability,
To make a change in this world for the better,
Yet they don't, for their own personal benefit.
That is the sour milk I'm talking about:
The worst possible sour milk.

The sour milk that everyone hates,
But always sticks around.
The sour milk that leaves behind
Stains, and mold, and bacteria, and diseases.
Everywhere it goes.

They all say that we live in the
"Land of the free, and the home of the brave,"
But truly, I tell you that no matter how many times we sing
    those lyrics
No one,
NO ONE,
Will ever be free of the sour milk.

The greed and corruption and darkness of the world
Affects everyone.
Definitely not equally,
Light years from it, in fact,
But it affects everyone in some way.

And our leaders of the
The World Council of Sour Milk,
They can try everything
To make the stench go away,

But as long as the
Greed and hatred and selfishness
Is still there,
Nothing will free us of that foul stench.
NOTHING.

We are the world,
We are the only ones that can
Change it, whether that be for the
Better or for the worse.
So let's make that change.
Let's be that change.
Let's change the world for the better.
Let's feed the hungry,
Help out the poor,
Let's stop the fury,
And end the war.

Let's fix these problems.

The solutions are within reach,
But it's up to us,
The inhabitants of this world,
To rid ourselves of this wretched sour milk.

by Devin Farr, age 15
2014 Gold Key, American Voices Nominee
Mountain View High School, Mesa

Diamonds

We are all born innocent,
Without any words or sight,
Merely breathing,
And crying,
And sleeping.

We are all born innocent,
Without any perception of the world,
Completely oblivious to the immense amount of
Pain, suffering, greed, deception, hate, and corruption in
    the world.

We are all born innocent,
Unknowing of the world around us,
Unexpecting of what is coming,
And unprepared for the life ahead.

As we are growing up,
Years are passing by,
We begin to realize that
Life is nothing like we expected of it.

As we are growing up,
Years are passing by,
We begin to realize that life
Is something that even an education
Won't fully prepare us for.

Life is hard.
It's difficult.
It's surprising,
But not every surprise is a
Surprise *Party*,
is it?

One needs to pay close attention
To even the smallest grain of sand
To fully understand all of the
Sand on the beach.

And if one is down and depressed,
No matter how thick the trees in the jungle become,
They must find the courage to keep searching for the light,
Even in all of that darkness.

The world often seems
Like a magnet for evil and destruction.
Life often seems
Like a magnet for evil and destruction.

But I assure you,
If you dig deep enough,
Your shovel will hit those shiny diamonds.

So dig deep.
Dig, and dig, and dig, and dig, and dig.

It won't be easy to get to that happiness.
After digging for so long,
Your body will ache.
There will be a ton of suffering,
And hardship,
And pain.

But, trust in the fact that one day,
You will thrust your shovel into the earth,
Only to hear the *Clang!*
Of the happiness you have discovered.

by Devin Farr, age 15
2014 Gold Key, American Voices Nominee
Mountain View High School, Mesa

The Devil's Bane

A cold day dawned, a mounting fear
To reality its time was near
Legends proclaim in aging print
Texts gleam with malign glint
Myths that whisper of deathless fate
Increase their cries at frightening rate
For soon He comes, soon He treads
The stain of His darkness, now it spreads
An immortal Demon, rivaled by none
Yet defied His power by more than one
Blackened eyes scarred by time
Surge upward as they begin the climb
His wordless terror is known to all
His killing breath shall soon befall

And with a boom, a thunderous quake
The bowels of the Earth begin to shake
Trenches spewing an ashen tide
Rip the land into new divide
Rolling shadows creep up the walls
Writhing masses answer the calls
Sounded by their Master, bellowed in the deep
The minions of Hell awaken from sleep
Hope falls silent with impending doom
Already encased in a morbid tomb
The shadows rise, their vapor so thick
They cover the ground, haste so quick
Born from the black, the teeming horde
Rose the Behemoth of Evil, Defiler of the Lord

He lifts his head, massive in size
And roars at the world to welcome His rise
With a stomp of his foot, a slam of His fist
The life of the land should cease to exist
Engulfed by creatures so wicked and foul
That abuse the rocks in continuous growl
And the Demon, He grins
A wash of demise leaks from His sins
With none to defy Him, strike down His reign
He orders the Earth be violently slain

An endless army pours from the Pit
Enough to crush any foe to submit
Consumed in lust was the fearless Beast
Blind, He became, to The Power unleashed

Far up in the Heavens, past the sky
A shudder disturbs the Watchful Eye
Tremors that stir an ancient rival
Spark the need for His revival
A flick from His wrist, a tap from His toe
The wrath of Creation shall confront any foe
His touch sires peace and symbolizes life
Under his care there would be no strife
A pact was made long, long ago
That the Demon would rot under Earth far below
And when this truce be utterly broken
The time for words said become past spoken
The force of the angels rains righteously down
Behold, the might of the Lord's fair crown

As the stench of the Devil reeks through the hills
Their beauty and grace suddenly stills
The animals shriek in terrible pain
Their life already beginning to drain
Face to face with utter despair
They lift their heads in one last prayer
Pleading for Him to climb down His throne
Knowing they will perish if left all alone
Suddenly, a peace, a calming breeze
Drifts through the air and floats by the trees
As if in answer, as if in consent
The breeze demands immediate repent
The Demon screams His defiant denial
And the Lord, He stands, to lead His Trial

A magnificent light, descending from the east
Flared, then brightened as all movement ceased
Emerging from the clouds, bathed in glory
Came the Devil's ruin, His final quarry
Rushing beside Him on wings of white feather
Flew the keepers of the Kingdom, soaring together
They dressed as one, in the fairest armor

And ranged from queen to the tenant farmer
In a mass of blinding, dazzling fury
The creatures fell, bound by justice's jury
Those that withstood were left with no choice
But return to the Pit, obey that Voice
The creatures of the Depths remained so cruel
Leaving their Master to fight the ultimate duel

Opening His arms, The Lord shed His cloak
Revealing His heart, never to be broke
He summoned His sword, artfully made
And beckoned His shield to match with the blade
With a brilliant display of marvelous power
He graced the hills with love in that hour
The Demon growled, foul and grim
Wisps of shadow curling from each limb
They swirled and shifted, molding into form
Conjuring a flurry of stygian storm
He reached within the raging whirl
And withdrew a whip He began to unfurl
Filling His fist with a wicked mace
The Demon advanced, closing the space

With a snarl and a swipe, the Demon swung
And to defense the Lord nimbly sprung
He parried each slice, each ruthless blow
Till the Demon's movement began to slow
The Lord, ever watching, saw His chance
He launched His attack, a deadly dance
Slowly but surely, the Demon gave ground
Fighting His way to the place He was found
The Lord pressed on, His strokes a blur
An attack the Devil could hardly deter
They reached the ledge, the entrance to Hell
Where the sins of the masses dismally dwell
With one final stab, the blade that was blessed
Found Evil's origin, deep in Its chest

An explosion that thundered all across Earth
Signaled the end of the Demon's rebirth
To his knees the Defiler fell
The Lord sent Him tumbling to the depths of His Cell

Then He held up His hands for all to see
And in His loudest voice, did He decree:
"Though you may walk through the darkest canyon
I will be by your side, I will be your companion
Let evil hold no place within you
And into my Kingdom you shall pass through
Let it be known, on this fateful day
The Demon is banished, locked far away
His bonds are sealed in holy chain
And I. Am. The Devil's Bane."

by Anthony Mirabito, age 15
2014 Silver Key
School, Gilbert Classical Academy

Faith (Bridge)

Whenever we drive into the city, we cross over a bridge
A plain overpass, but the dammed water beneath is
    anything but
a grassy plain

Whenever we cross over this bridge, I can see you standing
    there,
feet precariously balanced on the edge,
face bent down toward the water and your
hands facing up, like they believe in a god.

Why would you ever tell me that?
Why would you ever tell your little daughter that many
    times
you imagined throwing yourself off that bridge,
into the icy churning below?
I would never tell you that
I know the names of all the prescriptions our bathroom
    cabinet cradles
in its eerily-cheerful light,
that I've dreamed of becoming a barista,
making myself a prescription cocktail just to see how long
it would take my body to become as disorganized as my
neverstopthinkingneverbequietnosleepneverstopping mind
    is.

Because I have faith, faith that I'll never
let myself get that bad.

Why did you tell me that?
Still, four years later, I can only imagine your death
on that bridge.
I still blame myself sometimes.
Would you be as you are now if I had never left?
If I had never forgone the Bliss of the leaves beneath my
    feet,
never forgone my breathing home, my best friend,
for the chance of having a healthy ending to my
earthworm-eaten childhood?

Sometimes, I hurt too. Seeing you in pain
for so many years punched holes in my ever-faithful
heart.
I dream for the day I can let go, move on, start my own life
we're taking steps in that direction already
but I suppose we'll always be connected by the pretty blue
    blood that lies in our wrists
and begs to be cut open.

Faith was the cord that pulled me back from the
edge, never a faith in a god, but the faith in my own
resilience
It was almighty, never faltered until she blew in,
name like a hurricane and winds that blew my faith
out to sea.

Now I can see why people hold on so firmly to their god
there is nothing so disappointing as a Loss of faith,
nothing else that turns every surface, every step
into an icy churning.
into the edge of a bridge.

by Hannah Jarvis, age 16
2014 Gold Key
Westwood High School, Mesa

a (blind) science

Benjamin, don't Rush.
not everything's as straightforward
as your blade.
you don't know what's best for me.

i could follow you, glittery messiah,
but eventually i will grow tall.
your blanket statements won't keep me
covered all night long.
your silhouette will grow so vague,
and all i will have is a tradition of keeping
quiet and opening up my legs.

pinch your cheeks
because the autumn
leaves
fall fast and it
leaves
your tree barren.
fire burns
but doesn't last
with no grounds to stand upon.
ideas forgotten; theories disproven—
the world is not so easy to figure out.
we pale
in comparison.

everything fades
when you don't write with ink.
so let's flirt with speculation and correlations
because anything can be right
when it's up for interpretation.
we'll rearrange the map
until we make something pretty enough
to cover up the perplexed
expression on your face.
it's a social experiment—
ignore all dissent.
we'll find the cure to this plight
of unplanted seeds and misplaced house keys.

maybe then we'll never see
that we're the root of this disease.

Jack, Son,
you didn't want to be
conquered,
and so you let the red flags
that you put at the mast of your battleships
run down your wrist;
but you were wrong.
you are wrong.
it was us that didn't belong.
but we can't stop fighting,
the discord is the only purpose we have—
to be.

Tears will continue to Trail
along our cheeks
as we pretend to know our places
in the platoons marching home.
and we'll pretend to know where home is
as we grope through the gunfire smoke.

we could blame it all on
an apple and a snake;
an imperfect man and woman;
a knowledge of good and evil, a mistake—
but it sounds trite, even to me.
our anthem has been reduced to mumbling,
as if the lyrics were items on a grocery list
that we were trying not to forget.

across the way someone is laughing,
he must know just how lost we are.

by Katherine Lu, age 16
2014 Silver Key
BASIS Peoria, Peoria

Missing in Action

Dust collects on pine book shelves, carven with intricacy
        and care.
It's been a long while since you left
the vague remnants of a hug still on my chest.
Since, the dust has gathered, awaiting your arrival
droves and droves still settle upon the hard wood.
I alone know why you departed
"My country needs me," you said,
donning your camouflage uniform.

Our bed creaks with the extra weight
as you lie down next to me
smelling of caramel and mint tea.
Your breathing,
heavy, fast,
slows to a steady rhythm.
I remember your heart next to mine,
the warmth and utter completeness.

Eyes wide, I turn to study your face once more,
memorizing the subtle upturn of your lips
red, like an Arizona sunset, pursed, as if in thought.
And the hair you wrestle with at any given time
a curly brown mess, with strands that cover your right eye
which matches your hair in color, as does its counterpart.

I can't see them now, resting on our bed
nor can I enjoy your laugh,
a pealing giggle that rises in pitch, depending
whether or not the joke's a pun.
You rise now, at half-past two
A bright yellow cab idles by the curb.

The hug I was speaking of comes
on our front lawn, shining with dew.
Our lips meet for a final time,
the ring in my pocket burns with an intensity to match
        the Sun.
But I cannot bring myself to act on the moment.

If the time comes
and the dust is cleared from the shelves
it might happen.
If that same lovely smile remains.
So many "ifs" and
so little chance of my love returning.

Red lips never return to our home,
and yes, I still consider it ours.
I am never graced with a whiff of mint tea again.
Even now, the ring remains on the carven pine bookshelves
where the dust has grown thicker
and thicker.

by Dylan Angle, age 13
2014 Gold Key, Silver Medal
Desert Canyon Middle School, Scottsdale

Hidden Tiny Things

I.   I am made of stories;
when I tell them to you, they may not make sense
(but trust me, they fit as well as gears.)
"Listen," you told me, "I know why none of your stories
have a climax.
None of the songs you listen to have one, either."
And I'd wished I'd smiled and told you, "Neither does life."
This I have found to be true, except in the mostly hopeless
      cases;
for when it does, the entire thing savors of longing and
      tapers off and
that is not the way I wished to be living.
The French call a climax *'la petite mort'*—the little death—
the little death of all things good and holy in a book and
this makes sense because life is made of little deaths.
Little microscopic endings exist (in the time you nudged my
      shoulder with your nose,
the drop in my throat when I stood to kiss you goodbye for
      good, and
the time I was below absolute zero on your backseat) and
life is not short, sweetie; life is long—it is the memories
      that end in the blink of an eye.

II.   Know that, since I have met you,
there are soft fluttering things inside my ribs, and
when you look at me from the side,
a faint glow emanates from beneath the skin,
reminiscent of the dust particles from my place of origin.

III. You hate France, but even you will admit their
      expressions are
the most reasonable expression of my mind.
So when I say that I am fascinated by an appendectomy,
you can at least remember that my favorite expression is
tu me manques:
"I am missing to you." As if I were an organ,
blood, air to keep you breathing,
and you can pull me closer instead of wrinkling your nose,
like you do at so many of my gossamer tales.

IV. You once told me that the funniest things are the
      startlingly specific.
If you want, you could kiss me five times,
rub my belly in a clockwise motion and tie my hair in a knot
around your ring finger.
I don't mind.
If the startlingly specific is what makes you laugh, then
the startlingly specific is in the map-work palm of my hand.

V. My words like to jump from the attic of my throat
to the pavement.
"You are chatty when you're tired," you said, smiling.

I laughed and said that the words needed to jump to the
      ground
      and gravity pulls them out faster
when I'm hanging upside down (if only from the rush of
      blood to the head). You did not understand, but you
      smiled anyways.
You always smile anyways.

V. I am a liar.
When you find that out,
you will be crushed by the weight of it.
but I don't know how to function any other way
(because the stories that I'm made of
are not always enough for the long haul).

VI. We speak with our knuckles.
I bump your shoulders, your palms, your face, your belly,
and the words scatter throughout your bones
like the rubble from the end of the world.

VII. "You are the poet," you said,
"I have never needed to untangle the meaning of ocean and
      the feel of a summer's day."
But you are a poet because you know that,
if only our words were made of glass,
how much more careful we would be when we spoke.
And you know that, despite what the physics teachers say,
the universe is not made of atoms;
the universe is made of tiny stories.

IX. When I was younger, I had a jewelry box with a
ballerina on top that spun with each wind-up turn.
It wasn't until I found that box last summer
(in the attic, covered with tiny molecules of dust)
that I realized that the dancer wore a tiny locket,
with a tiny image of another ballerina inside,
a white swan, hope (something to keep deep inside for all
    that is to come).

X.   Once, when we were drunk, you were
washing dishes and you accidentally threw a plate at the
    wall.
It left a crack in the tile the size of a fist, but
come next summer,
the vines covering our front porch were
tangling through the cracks like webs of light from the
    outside.

XI. Sometime in chemistry class, I realized that
the world is not the only thing
to be made of tiny stories.
And I am not the only thing
to be made of dust.

    by Kolbe Riney, age 16
    2014 Gold Key
    Catalina Foothills High School, Tucson

Sleeping Boy

On a night when sheets of glass rain slandered the asphalt
    streets,
and police sirens howled as they faded through the blinking
    eyes of the restless city,
a young boy fell asleep underneath a flickering streetlamp
    light.

You were utterly lost when you found him,
stumbling over the cracks in the crooked sidewalk.
You were trying to find your way home after a long day in
    an unfamiliar place.

The sleeping boy was waiting for you underneath a soft
    golden halo of light, while
crystal shards of glass fell quietly like snowflakes before
    crashing like cymbals into the cement ground.
Your ignorance pushed you past the boy, but your
    passionate heart gently led you back.

This was the desolate part of the city, and you were
    wandering
in a maze of streets that seemed to always catch up to you
    despite your attempts to escape them.
You feared the glass rain and its loud noise that shouted
    murder in your ear.

You wanted to ignore the sleeping boy because you could
    hear home calling your name, but
once you noticed that the boy's body was coiled unnaturally
    like a snake,
you knew you had no other choice but to take your pause
    and approach.

You touched the sleeping boy and searched his chest for his
    heartbeat, but
nothing.
He had the expression of tossing dreams in his childish
    head, but his sickly skin reminded you of a corpse laid
    to rest.

Your ear aches to hear the sleeping boy's name because
the boy was too young to simply slip away in the dark
without anyone to at least hold his hand.
The sleeping boy was all alone until you came, and you
should've reached him quicker, because now it's too
late.

On that night when sheets of glass rain slandered the
asphalt streets,
and police sirens howled as they faded through the blinking
eyes of the restless city,
a young boy fell asleep underneath a flickering streetlamp
light.

by Gloria Martinez, age 14
2014 Gold Key
BASIS Oro Valley, Oro Valley

The Mahogany Dealer

The sun-kissed devil, they call her
with crimson lips that blow me away.
She wears the white hat stained with blood, never fading,
    never dying.

When her sharp heels click by like knives,
smiles weaken and strip themselves bare.
The dumb man's words flourish without thought, saying
    goodbye before realizing.

The mahogany dealer cripples my heart,
accepting the name second daughter to the devil.
The dealer, the monster, enraptured with what crimes it
      has done, seeking and craving and thirsting for the dry
    sugar taste of adrenaline.

A few hours ago, in this very bar, she captured me
with just one tip of her spiked smile and
asked me to play her game.
I listened helplessly as my lips voiced *yes*.

A dead man, that's what I was
ever since that cursed devil laid eyes on me. She calls the
    game pension for her job, but
it's more likely fuel for her addiction.

The dealer adores and allures elegant vinaceous wine,
but I wouldn't take a sip when she offered some to me.
She tells me blood beads taste sour, and
glass tears are sweet.

When the devil speaks, I think of a sunflower
bathed in fire from a burning sun as it
slips into an ocean of salt crystals.
Count slowly down from five.

Pity the man with a weak human heart.
Five.

There's no escape, no transfer.
Four.

The monster deals with blood currency.
Three.

I've lost the deal by playing her game.
Two.

My currency is gone, fake rose petals pacing in my veins.
One.

These are the thoughts of a dying man.

by Gloria Martinez, age 14
2014 Gold Key
BASIS Oro Valley, Oro Valley

Farewell to the South

Goodbye my new home.
My motherland, my people call me to return.
I no longer have business here in the South.

Goodbye my new brother.
You treated me like your blood.
Thank you for teaching me how to trust beyond myself.

Goodbye my new mother.
I had nothing and no one, yet you found me.
You taught me how to love without condition.

Goodbye little boy who gave me sausage sticks,
Goodbye pretty girl who helped me sweep,
Goodbye Happy the jindo dog,
Goodbye hibiscus plant, dangling laundry, pots of kimchi,
mechanical fan, rickety bike, black-and-white newspaper,
Things and people and places woven into my every hour.

I will miss you all.

I'm sorry for the deception, the lies, the betrayal.
It was my sole duty.
I'm sorry for the eavesdropping, the pretending, the spying.
It was for the greater good.

You don't have to forgive me or pity me.
Just stay healthy, don't worry, don't cry.
I'll be fine, so carry on with your lives.
But please remember:

I once existed.

I once sang with you, helped you cook,
ate your sausage sticks, swept your yard, played catch with
     you,
watered you, hung you, ate you, felt you, rode you, read you.

I was here.

I really must leave now—orders from Above.
I trudge away from home,
The blood red sun casting my shadow on the dirt path.
Maybe one day I will return.
Maybe I can stay here forever.

But the weight of the pistol tapping my thigh at every step
Reminds me of my duty, my sacrifice.
So I continue my irrevocable departure
For the Reunification.

See you again when there's no more North or South.
See you again when we become One.
See you again in Heaven.

by Hyeji (Julie) Cho, age 16
2014 Silver Key
BASIS Scottsdale, Scottsdale

Unholy Trinity

Curled up like a fetus, but
Isolated
    from the womb.
People ask with concerned masks;
People who have never worried about
Meals of only air and water,
Still attached to the umbilical cord.

But it has been
    severed;
No longer connected to family,
No longer connected to money.
Now sleepless nights must be sold to exchange
The only thing left
For the only thing that matters:
Money.

Money,
       money,
             money
All around.
Engulfing the child who is
Bowing down
    to someone else's God,
Laying down
    at the altar to survive.

People say
    "money can't buy happiness,"
But when love is sacrificed for
    a cold meal,
When the sleep only brings
    demons back to life,
Maybe money does make miracles.

Because happily-ever-afters don't exist.
And God doesn't listen.
Happiness can't buy money.
Neither can hope.
Then, why even try?
All that's left is
All that matters is
All people live for is

Money,
   Money,
      Money.

by Hyeji (Julie) Cho, age 16
2014 Silver Key
BASIS Scottsdale, Scottsdale

A Mother's Love

My mother was a special person.
She had a light that radiated around her,
Touched everyone she met with her warm smile and
compassionate heart.
She had bright red hair cascading down her pale shoulders,
Eyes bluer than the sea in the morning,
A teal hue.
Her name, Lynette.
Although not very tall or big,
her heart outweighed her body.
Her past was brim, filled with
words of resentment and rancor,
She said her kids were the light of her life.
She was the light of ours.
My twelve years with her were joyous.
But too short.

One day, not to feeling well, vomiting, unable to move:
To the doctor she went and got the diagnosis.
Cancer.
Told the news, my walls closed in,
I could not breathe.
My beloved mother could not die.
She assured me with gentle voice,
"It'll be alright. I will survive."

Admitted into the hospital almost immediately.
Even with ailing illness,
she remained in good hope and spirit.
Even happy for my twelfth birthday,
when I know she was hurting.
The day, vividly sits in my memory.
I got the call from my father at the hospital
to come and see her—

I had a false sense of being, something was not right.
As I got to the hospital, my senses were right.
As I opened the door to the ICU, I realized she was dying.

The once beautiful face of my mother was snow white
Her blue eyes fading to a cloudy gray
Her bright auburn hair, diminishing and growing gaunt
over thin shoulders.

I knew this would be the time to say what I needed to say
Before she passed.
I told her I loved her,
That I would see her someday.
I will miss her.

She told me to continue my karate,
the goal to a black belt inching closer.
A day I'd hope she would see.

Three years have passed so gradually,
Hurting
Tearing up at any memory of her.
It is hard.
It's not getting any easier...

And it will never get easier.

by Callie Gregory, age 15
2014 Silver Key
Mountain View High School, Mesa

The Nature of Humanity

Although I temporarily escape the oppressing pain and
                    sorrow, reality somehow ensnares me.
I attempt to reject the absoluteness, but I continue
                    to find no solace within myself.
I am instantly drowned by a relentless, perpetual
                    wave of the naked truth:
The world is corrupt, prospering the wicked,
                    incarcerating innocence.
Plastic people surround and expound
            through artificial masks.
Concealing the hypocrisy and vileness within.
There are no authentic individuals here.
The innocent are martyred by evil.
The unique are ridiculed.
The guileless suffer.
Evil always…
Wins.
But,
There are
Glimpses of Hope
Within the infinity of sinister.
Through all of their sin and wickedness,
A façade might veil Pain, Fear, Loss, and Suffering.
I, then, realize that even if there is Iniquity within us all,
Humanity is but a speck of ephemeral dust floating in the
                                        Universe,
Too insignificant to make an impact; acted upon by
                    uncontrollable forces.
    Yet, there are those unexpected kindnesses
        and heroic acts of altruistic courage
That obscure Iniquity, if only for a moment,
and I acknowledge that Hope
is an everlasting…
Possibility.

by Chase Lortie, age 16
2014 Gold Key
Red Mountain High School, Mesa

FLASH FICTION

Editor Introduction by Jay Morganstern

The key to good communication is... brevity.

Flash Fiction captures a single idea conceived in a manner of form such as a snapshot, a single moment in time. The effort for the ferocity and precision of thought contained in this category earns these young writers the credit they deserve as published authors. Our pen-smiths have wrought forth spontaneous and original, classic literature steeped in detailed brevity.

The taste of words will linger in the reader's ears and be heard within one's heart and felt within one's breath.

Brevity loans itself to language that lures the senses, providing an exquisite look at Megan Dresser's "One Thousand and One Pieces" that make up the true identity of a person. Technique has been honed into as fine an edge as the sword of Anthony Mirabito's "The Inquisitor." Audrey Ennis' "The Preference of Darkness" evokes deep emotional responses with an incredibly provocative look at growing up, understanding inspiration, and hoping for the best. Sydney Portigal's "Too Rockstar for Starbucks" shows the measure of lives and self-identities in color of clothing. In Lina Khan's "Woebegone," we watch the power of intent in a self-imposed unraveling. Megan Dressler's "King of Gods" challenges mortality with the creation of art. Pieces, instances, and fragments of life bind the reader and the subject; holding hands through a flash of Gloria Martinez's "Abandoned Memories." Where writing begins and will never end is always inspiration and hope for more! Vy Doan tells the "Rain" to go away, and yet it always comes again, whether or not we have another day. Finally, Kimaya Lecamwasam's "The Presents and the Gone" whispers to remind us to draw life and death in circles instead of clear, straight lines.

One Thousand and One Pieces

My sister told me: "Minnie, you wanna get anywhere in this world, you keep your braids tight and your jeans tighter."

So I wore my hair in dreadlocks, and I preferred skirts over pants.

My cousin in Atlanta told me: "Minnie, don't ever trust whitey."

So I dated a marshmallow-cream Jewish boy.

My aunt in Kenya told me: "Minerva, always stay true to your roots and yourself. If something doesn't feel right in your heart, you cannot give in to it."

This was the only advice I got from my family that ever made any sense. My body was a modified map of the world, a map of *my* world, of all my pieces and parts. My skin was a mix of my mama's and my dad's, a combination of her strong Kenyan dark brown and his pasty French. My eyes came from my grandmammy, dark amber from the Nile, Egypt through and through. My freckles were from Ireland, and my cheekbones, straight from the Cherokee Nation. I had a Persian jaw line, along with long arms and long legs that hailed from Haiti. I had a melting pot within my soul; I was the product of cultural harmony and blind love. Each body part came from its own unique place, and each place was born from its own unique history, and each history deserved to be celebrated in its own unique way.

I celebrated Ireland by drinking Jameson on my rough nights and kept Egypt with me eternally with an ankh tattoo on my left shoulder. Beaded necklaces graced my neck to remind me of the Cherokee who came before me. Haiti was represented by the hand-made Kanaval masks hanging on my wall, and I kept France in my heart by speaking the language. My Persian culture lived and breathed in the copy of *One Thousand and One Nights* I kept from my childhood and in my adoration for Scheherazade's wit. I kept Kenya, the largest part of my identity, close by visiting the country yearly to spend a month or two with my favorite aunt who gave me the best advice, with the woman who always told me African tales and recited proverbs and sang ancient songs while she cooked or cleaned. She was one of the few people in my family who never judged me for accepting my "white side," and the only one who supported it. No one understood my spiritual connection to my heritage except for my aunt; even my boyfriend Max questioned my in-depth interest in his Jewish culture.

I liked to think that I was a cable, holding up the suspension bridge of global culture. With awareness, all the pieces were in place, and the road ran smooth, but if one cable snapped, that could mean the downfall of peace and harmony for everyone. I didn't want to be that cable; I didn't want to be the catalyst for hate.

Don't get me wrong, I loved my family to death, but their advice didn't feel right in my heart.

My aunt from Kenya always told me to stay true to myself. That if something felt wrong, I could not give in to it. I had firm roots all around the world, no one place was more important to me than another. No place except the one in my chest where my heart resided happily, skipping beats when I watched Max light his menorah or when I saw my aunt after a year away from Kenya. No place except my world, the world of all my pieces and parts.

by Megan Dressler, age 17
2014 Silver Key
Mojave High School, Bullhead City

The Inquisitor

I settled against the wall in the corner of the tavern, my lightweight, sheepskin boots crisscrossed out on the table. The cowl of my cloak was pulled low, almost over my eyes, concealing my face in shadow. My gaze drifted across the room, flitting from person to person. A large man, belly bulging out from his waist, bellowed with laughter, slamming his tankard onto the table. He and three portly friends were engaged in some kind of foolish card game.

A fountain of ale sprayed across the table, spewing from the laughing man's mouth. Two of his companions erupted in mirth, obnoxiously slapping their dejected-looking friend on the back. I dipped my head in a wry smile; he had just been cheated out of his weekly pence.

My eyes resumed their third sweep of the room, this time watching two pretty girls argue in the opposite corner. One of them was waving her hands in the air, clearly agitated, while the other unsuccessfully attempted to calm her down. The man I came here to find had not arrived.

Rain hammered the roof of the tavern, and lightning cleaved the sky, accompanied by the threatening rumble of distant thunder. Inside, the weather was warm and comfortable. A candle on each table lit the small space and the smell of wood smoke wafted from the fireplace. Behind the bar, the only barmaid cleaned dishes in a giant, soapy bucket, while the owner filled another round of frothy drinks for the men playing cards.

I withdrew a silver pocket watch from my cloak and popped it open. My superiors had informed me, on reliable intelligence, that the man I am hunting comes to this tavern every night to order whiskey at exactly the eleventh toll. The hour had almost struck. With a flick of my wrist, the watch disappeared, and my left hand lowered to grip the worn leather hilt of my sword.

Minutes later, heavy footsteps plodding down the road signaled a new arrival. The door flew open, and a gust of cold, stormy air followed the soaking customer into the tavern. He shrugged off his dripping coat and handed it to the barmaid, who accepted its moisture without complaint.

She led him to a table in the back of the tavern and pulled the chair out, giving him a grimy grin as he took his seat.

The visitor's movements were slow but deliberate, and he reclined back in his chair as if he hadn't a care in the world. When the barmaid came with his glass of whiskey, he snatched the drink with a grunt of thanks and took one, long draft. As he set the cup down, his own gaze wandered across the people in the bar, stopping far too long on the pretty girls and not paying any attention to me.

I brought my legs down from the table and rose smoothly. The man did not suspect a thing. He had reached the bottom of his first glass, and the other tavern occupants were well into their third. Not making any attempt at subtlety, I grabbed the neck of the man's tunic and hurled him onto the floor. His cup slid off the table and shattered on the polished wood, announcing the atmosphere's abrupt change into turmoil. My sword seemed to slide itself from its scabbard, the hiss of steel ringing throughout the room. The firelight reflected itself in the blade and cast my face into an even deeper, now indiscernible shadow. I leveled the sword point at the man's chest, years of experience steadying my hand.

The customers exchanged various reactions of shock and terror. "Get out! Now!" I commanded, the blunt authority in my voice assuring none would dare challenge me. Fearing for their lives, the patrons scrambled to the door, knocking over more furniture, and they ran into the night, screaming for the guards. I turned my attention back to the man, who was visibly trembling, his eyes frantically searching for an escape route.

I shifted the sword from his chest to press against his shoulder, feeling him shrink away from the cool metal. I used the blade to lift the cloth from his skin, revealing an inky tattoo. It was a crocodile, its jaws clamped around the frail body of a dove. This was the man.

Under the obscurity of my cowl, a demon masked by darkness, I whispered to him. "Shall we begin?"

by Anthony Mirabito, age 15
2014 Silver Key
Gilbert Classical Academy, Gilbert

The Preference of Darkness

Young children run through fields of daisies and poppies and daffodils, laughing as the sun shines down from directly above them, caressing them, nurturing them, loving them. Flowers tickling her ankles, a small girl prances through the sunny meadow. The sun's liquid rays dance across her cheek, and the comforting warmth evokes a flush that matches the brilliant colors permanently staining the sky: pink, orange, yellow, red. Her blue eyes stare up towards the sun, clashing with the gilded rays. She smiles and jumps—up and down, up and down—curly blonde hair bouncing up and down behind her. Golden strands stroke her back as they fall and rise repeatedly. The sun is the one thing in her life that has always been and will always be. For this half of the world is forever steeped in sunlight.

Earth is held in one small spot in space. Earth does not rotate on its axis. Earth does not orbit the sun. Earth stands still, half of it exposed to light and half of it enveloped by darkness. The world is divided. Light. Dark.

On the half of the world where the sun never sets, children forever play in fields washed in golden rays, forever laugh with warmth stroking their tongues, forever breathe in summer air that vitalizes their lungs. There is no coldness, no darkness, no sadness. Light nourishes the innocence of these young children, allowing it to blossom and flourish like the flowers of the fields they run through.

But where are their parents? A soul over the age of twelve years is nowhere in sight on the half of the world where the sun never sets.

They dwell on the other side of the Earth, untouched by sunlight, by warmth, by happiness. This is where every person of this divided world is destined to come. They come here willingly. They remain here willingly. They die here willingly. With the human heart having been forged in darkness, all people are drawn to this place, even when they are raised in sunlight, in warmth, in happiness.

The bright side of the world is the one of perfection, but humanity is far from perfect. On the side of the sun, adults do not fit in. On the side of darkness, they are welcome. In darkness, a starving man, his stomach ravaged by pain of hunger, can steal a loaf of bread from the marketplace without being exposed by light. In darkness, a woman can count money she took from her neighbor, the reassuring coldness of coins against her palms, without being caught. Night is where humans can be humans—people can be people—without the pressure of the sun to keep them in line, to keep them innocent, to keep them battling against their inherent nature. To keep them battling against the need to deceive, to fight, to kill.

The children are the only ones whom the adults pity. Why should the young ones be forced to grow up in darkness, in corruption? The soft bundle of warmth in a mother's arms must be innocent, must be saved from blackness, must be worthy of living in sun-rich meadows on the other side of the world. Shiploads of children, just old enough to fend for themselves, are sent across the sea to the light with ample supply of food and water, all in desperate attempt to spare them from the eternal dark.

New parents, warm hands linked in the cold, hear the lapping of ocean waves against the wooden hull of the ship that is about to take their son to the sun. They hope that he will never return, that he will always be the innocent baby they once cradled in their arms, living in a world where there is no crime, no deceit, no imperfection.

But they know that he *will* return. After all, he is human, and he has their blood running through his veins, and he will crave darkness as they once did, and he will come sailing across the whole world to obtain the blackness he craves. The father grips the mother's hand tighter. They know that he will return, and they are happy about this fact, but too afraid, too guilty, to show it.

While the mother and father hold hands on the dark shore, sending their son away, a group of children gather on the coast of the light side of the world, about to return to darkness on the ship that once brought them into light. The small girl with the blonde ringlets and the blue eyes is hesitant. She wants to board the ship, but she loves the sun, the flowers, and the fields that have nurtured her in place of a mother.

Suddenly, a rumbling sound shakes the earth. The girl stumbles. A shadow engulfs her. Glancing up, she sees a cloud overtake the sun. The sky is dark, welcoming her, beckoning her. Rain. Cold drops flow over her skin, through her hair, down her back, sending a thrill of tiny bumps across her limbs. As the blue of her eyes harmonizes with the gray of the cloud, her heart leaps. Rain. Cloud. Darkness. Beauty. Mesmerized and relieved, she follows her friends onto the ship, heading to darkness.

by Audrey Ennis, age 15
2014 Gold Key
BASIS Scottsdale, Scottsdale

Too Rockstar for Starbucks

They walk in, their black clothes seemingly out of place at a Starbucks. As they come closer, their tattoos grow larger. The Guns N' Roses tattoo is on the man with the exotic musician name. Aldus paradoxically orders a strawberry Frappuccino that doesn't match with his black clothing. He walks outside and sits in a chair and lights his 10th cigarette of the morning, contemplating what to wear to tonight's party.

His girlfriend is more complicated. Her parents named her Daisy and she resented them for it up until the day she was 18 and changed her name to Chloe. She felt as if "Daisy" was the antithesis of who she was as a person; although, she didn't quite *know* who she was and wanted to be. The day she changed her name is the day she left home. It wasn't like she had much to go back to.

Her dad would come around once in a while, usually to take money from her mother or to look for a place to crash for the night. Her mother, although she meant well, didn't have enough hours a day between shifts at the hospital to spend time with her. Alone to raise herself, Chloe left without looking back.

During her junior year at college she met Aldus, who was exactly what she (thought) she needed. He was perfectly shallow and simple in his desire to become a musician/artist. Chloe found him to be an endearing, refreshing change from her over-complicated life.

Chloe takes her sunglasses off and orders a black coffee. She takes her drink outside to accompany Aldus. She plucks the cigarette from his fingertips and takes a long drag. She, too, was contemplating, but not about what party they were going to, but if they even had to go to a party. All they did was socialize and "party," and she was getting tired of it. They sit at the table, drinking their drinks, together but apart.

On the outside, they seem oblivious to the world's opinions; on the inside, more self-conscious. Aldus got his tattoos one drunken night with his friends. He hated them for a while; they made him look "silly." Aldus took himself *very* seriously. But ever since his mother bought him his first black Dior sweater, he realized that the black totally complimented his tattoos, in particular, his Guns N' Roses tattoo. So, from that point on, he only wore black to keep up his "image." Chloe wore black for a different reason. The black clothes at the Goodwills she shopped at tended to be in better condition than the other clothes. She didn't have an "image" to keep up.

"Hey Chlo?" Aldus finally spoke, coughing as he finished his cigarette.

"Mhmm." Chloe was still lost in thought, and Aldus's voice caught her off guard.

"What are you wearing tonight? I need to plan out my outfit according to yours."

"Oh, Aldus. I don't know. I just don't know..."

Aldus went silent, knowing that Chloe's reply held more meaning than her outfit choice. As he sat trying to figure out what to say, Chloe stubbed out her cigarette and started to get up. She knew how uncomfortable her reply had made Aldus and was unsure wasn't sure if it upset her that they never talked about anything of substance. She smiled a solemn smile at him.

"Let's go home. I think Law and Order SVU is on."

Aldus smiled, overjoyed that they were talking about something easy again.

"Wanna play a drinking game? We take a shot every time Stabler hits the criminal. It'll get us in the mood to party tonight!"

"Sure... Sounds fun."

Chloe answered without listening, for she was pondering whether she should spend the money to buy clothes in *any* color other than black.

by Sydney Portigal, age17
2014 Silver Key
Phoenix Country Day School, Paradise Valley

Woebegone

Her parents were in love. They loved each other almost as ardently as they loved her. Her mom was a homemaker, and her father worked for a non-profit that paid him well. Her brother was studying to be a doctor, all the while managing a budding professional baseball career. Every year, he would get her a new charm for the bracelet he bought for her when she was ten, and he never missed a birthday. Her best friend called her every night at eleven, and the two would talk until the sun came up about everything and nothing. She was popular. She was valued and valuable. She was beautiful. She was five-foot-seven with long tan legs, straight blonde hair, and bright blue, chatoyant eyes. Her boyfriend was a preacher's son, and he took her to church every Sunday. They were going to get married.

She was a candy striper down at the children's hospital and a volunteer at the retirement home. Her name was at the top of the honor roll, and she was a beauty queen. She laughed at the right times and cried when appropriate. She was never left hungry. She was the smell of rain after two seasons of drought. She was adventure. She was a muse. She was home. She was nirvana. She was youth. She was a dream. She was truth. She was a paper doll. She was warmth.

She was the top of Everest. She was expectation. She was the calm before the storm. She was a cluster of stars, and they called her a constellation. She was a meteor shower. She was a house of cards.

She was never in want of anything except chaos.

Her dalliance with virtue was over, and she wanted to feel something go wrong after years of life going right. She wanted illness, she wanted sadness, she wanted disappointment.

More often than not, she would imagine scandalous ways of falling from grace—she wanted addiction and rehab and relapse. Heroin appealed to her, and she pictured her teeth rotting away from meth and her olive complexion turning sallow from coke. She dreamed dreams of seedy bars and faceless men. She begged for disease, heartbreak, cancer, and a Catch-22. She wanted to be stuck between Scylla and Charybdis. Her dulcet voice was the lull of a siren to a man at the end of his rope. She was an earthquake, a tsunami. She was a car accident and a drunk driver. She was living in a test tube. She was a cocktail, at the will of the hand of a bartender with a medical license and a lab coat. She was all white knuckles and chapped lips, crossed fingers and broken promises. She was the pulsing ache in her mother's chest. She was terminal.

You're crazy, they told her.

I'm fine, she assured.

She was the noose scratching at her own neck. She was full of blame, but she filled the holes in her life with termites and forged more holes and more problems where there weren't any before. She broke things after they were fixed. She painted demons on her angel face. Locked away in the labyrinthine confines of her own mind lay a version of herself driven to the brink, withering away, blowing away at the slightest breeze.

Perfection isn't all it's cracked up to be, she contended.

You're crazy, they told her.

I'm fine, she replied, *but I don't want to be.*

She was a winter of discontent.

by Lina Khan age 16
2014 Silver Key
Phoenix Country Day School, Paradise Valley

King of Gods

I call myself Noel Jupiter, not because I consider myself a god but because I want nothing more than to feel... alive. To feel as if I am something ethereal, moving through space with the planets, or even as a moon to a planet, even if I am only one of sixty-three. Nothing puts me closer to achieving my celestial aspirations than painting. I wasn't blessed with a golden tongue or any measurable sense of self-esteem, but I see deeper into things than others do. Putting it into words? That's a matter of translating sight into speech. I'm nothing special, linguistically. Because, though I was born with Frost's heart beating faltering in my chest, I was given Dali's hands. Now, I'm trapped, a realist in a world of my worst nightmares, surrealism caving in around me.

I make the best of my affliction. Visualizing, getting paint on the canvas, it comes easily. I've got stacks feet high of decay and death on my canvases, and they never stop coming. Because the accomplishment I get when I finish tearing my heart to shreds and creating art with the remains is unmatched by... anything. Angels sing my name, my skin buzzes with ecstasy; I've contributed to the earth something more than my carbon dioxide exhalations. It's like... when I place my last stroke, my heart shines through my chest and suddenly... Noel.

Suddenly Noel *is* Jupiter.

Suddenly he is alive.

Suddenly his heart beats as if it is sure of its steps.

Suddenly Noel leaves his shell of a loft.

Suddenly he is among us.

Suddenly we love him.

But suddenly is fleeting, and Noel cannot stay this way forever.

And I sink back into my skin from on high, realizing that planetary hopes require more than one gallon of fuel. Realizing that I live and die by the stroke of a brush, and that if I want to stay afloat in a world that was not built to accommodate paper skin and baby-boy emotions like mine, I have to keep creating. Maybe one day, the feeling of being alive, of being something more than a sad excuse for a man will stick, and I'll create something that lasts in my soul forever. But, for the meantime, Frost's heart beats faltering in my chest.

Faltering, faltering, fading, fading, shallow, and suddenly....

Suddenly it looks like his tightrope-walking hopes are falling from their precarious perch.

And no one remembered to put up the safety net.

by Megan Dressler, age 17
2014 Silver Key
Mojave High School, Bullhead City

Abandoned Memories

There's a tiny crack in the glass pane of my bedroom window that's as thin as a strand of spider silk. It grows with each passing day as the winter wind blows her freezing breath along the pane, forcing the crack to spread like branches of a barren winter tree. The crack has turned my window into a beautiful and dangerous mosaic, and even though I know I should probably have it fixed, I can't bear the thought of destroying such beauty.

When the first rays of dawn reach my window, the crack causes fractured waves of light to scatter throughout the small confines of my dull room. One of these waves rests upon my cheek and slowly moves into the corner of my eye, inducing a yawn from my mouth as I slowly wake up.

Dragging myself out of bed, I allow my feet to carry me down the dim hallway and into the dining room where I prepare some breakfast for myself. Then I pull out a chair and sit down at the kitchen table.

My heart freezes in my throat as my eyes land on a golden wedding ring that rests within a halo of morning sunlight. The halo of light is entirely unintentional, but even so it feels like it's meant to soften the pain I feel. It doesn't. Not in the slightest.

My dad never takes off his wedding ring, and yet here it is, sitting upon the table as if it had been waiting for me this whole time. When I was younger, my dad used to tell me that his wedding ring was a reminder of all the good memories he had, such as his wedding day and the birth of me and my sister. Because of that, he cherished his wedding ring. But now he has abandoned all of his memories and walked away from me, Lena, and Mom. The message he left with his wedding ring is so loud, and maybe that's why it hurts so much. It's clear-cut, not shrouded in subtlety.

Without realizing it, my hand has slowly crept towards the ring, fingers outstretched in an attempt to grasp at it. But I'm not leaning forward enough, and my fingers touch nothing but air. However just being this close to the ring makes it feel like I have something to hold on to.

I think about leaning forward and closing my hand around the wedding ring, possibly hiding it from Mom and

Lena, but I instantly feel guilty as the thought crosses my mind. Mom and Lena deserve to know that Dad made a conscious decision to leave, and it would be wrong of me to hide this from them.

However, the muscles in my body still ache to selfishly hold on to the ring, so that I have a piece of my dad to cherish, but my heart quietly asks me if I have any right. Lena is much younger than me, and her mind is still so fresh. Maybe she deserves the ring, if only to remind her that some memories are worth cherishing. But then again, maybe Mom needs the ring more than either of us. After all, the bond between a husband and a wife is much stronger than between a child and a parent, and maybe Mom needs to remember why she decided to trust her heart to a stranger. I can't measure myself to my mom or my younger sister, so I don't even try. I give away the ring without ever truly having it in the first place.

I hear a sound come from somewhere down the hall, and it causes my fingers to unconsciously flash forwards and snatch the ring from the table. I draw it close to my chest and directly over my heart as I listen to the rapid thump of an ensnared muscle pounding against metal.

Mom shuffles into the dining room with a blanket wrapped around her body, even though her hair has been recently washed, and her clothes are neat and pressed, suggesting that she has already showered. Her eyes and cheeks are flushed and wet with tears, and the sight makes my heart ache as I realize that she already knows. She has probably known ever since she first woke up and started getting ready for work.

Mom and I stare at each other for the longest time, neither of us quite sure what to do. Her eyes drift over to the clenched fist that rests over my heart, and I slowly remove it from my chest, unwrapping my fingers from the ring as if it were an uncertain rose bud opening for the first time.

I offer the wedding ring to Mom, but, to my surprise, she doesn't take it. Instead, she walks over to me and presses her lips to my forehead, lingering there for a few moments before pulling away. She gives me just the smallest of smiles before unwrapping the blanket from her shoulders and tossing it onto the couch. She rubs her hands over her arms and through her curls of hair before shaking her head and heading into the kitchen.

She leaves me alone to stare down at the ring in my hand, and I wonder what I could possibly do with it. I close my fingers back around the ring and slowly stand up from the table, my limbs feeling like they are entrapped in stone. My body leads me down the hallway and into my room where I quietly close the door.

I stare across the room at my broken window and then wretch my arm back, hurling the ring directly at the cracked mosaic. The ring hits the crack at just the right point so that the entire glass pane shatters, crystals of glass and tears raining down to the floor. For once, I admit to myself that being broken isn't beautiful.

by Gloria Martinez, age 15
2014 Gold Key
BASIS Oro Valley, Oro Valley

Rain

[*Rain, rain*]

Nostalgia is a strange thing. Seeping into those pauses of the day when no one is looking. A retrospective notion lost to paper-thin memories, crinkled by time. The bittersweet taste that lingers on tongues seeking for the right words, the right feelings, the right *time.*

Nostalgia is the ice-cold distinction of raindrops and the fine, hazy mist that creeps into morning air. A word saturated in sentimentality and imprinted with bold typeface onto greeting cards. A whisper from childhood, a yearning for things lost to time.

[*Go away*]

Tongues thick and laden with monosyllabic words. Asphalt-tinged air seeping through a clammy morning market. Peddlers crying—"Hot noodles!", "Fresh chickens!"

You led me through the winding market. Your hand swallowed mine until my fingers melted into your flesh. I struggled to keep up on two splintery legs. I was ten, you were twelve—both of us drunk on youthful temerity. You said you had something to show me, something extraordinary; we should go on an adventure.

Our feet danced upon dirt patted down by daily shuffling. *Clomp. Whoosh.* You shielded my eyes as knives made contact with the once living—now soon to be on the dinner table. You want to get away. I wanted to linger, stay close to the pretty hairclips with blots of dried hot glue. You tug me along, despite my high-pitched pleas.

Where are we going? I asked.

Some place where the living can't ever go to, you whispered.

I numbly let you pull my hand, no longer feeling the energy to resist.

You led me to the edge of civilization. We stood upon dense forestry, at first in awe of the noiselessness around us—we had connected with Nature on platonic grounds. You dared me to abandon my shoes so as to further this Earthly connection. How could I resist a venture beyond what I knew?

You pulled my hand again, this time with more force than what I had been used to. You said we had to hurry before the roots started to pull us under, before the sky cracked open. My breath exhaled salty unsaid syllables. I was too afraid to feel the ground beneath me, too afraid to wipe the dirt particles off my cheeks, lest I should lose souvenirs of our adventure.

Muggy sunlight flickered in and out from dappled trees. I wanted to swallow the sunlit air, fall under a scorching spell of happiness, and lose myself under dizzying heights. I wanted you to take me back to the erasable black land, where we could both play God. I wanted you to draw me ships on topological waves, roses half-shaded in bloom, figures smudged because of your left-handedness. I wanted you to introduce me to your chalk people—the woman in the pink skirt, the man with the blue tie.

But you never did.

[*Come again*]

Running behind you, I see that you've grown out your once-short hair; now it is an ebony cascade. Your sweat-stained shirt clung onto odd little places—the arc of your shoulder blade, the uneven knobs along your spine. Your once-crooked knees have started to stand straighter, unbending themselves, eased by the cadence of running. I wished you would turn around sometimes, just to let me examine your face. I want to see if you've stopped painting that mask of superficiality—the neon pinks, the powder whites, the drooping blacks. But you haven't.

Lost in your thoughts, you swerved from tree trunk to tree trunk. You don't notice that an evil sheen of sweat has loosened our clasped hands. You don't notice that my fingers are slowly unraveling from yours. You don't notice that you have left me with nothing but air and sunlight.

I sit upon rough-hewn grounds, waiting for you to realize the missing piece of our adventure. The sandals I hold no longer have much use for my dirt-encrusted feet. I wait in this empty-handed forest. *Seconds. Minutes. Seconds. Minutes. Minutes.*

You didn't come back for me.

I shuffled through the shrubbery, keeping my ears alert

for any cries of the rooster. Above the foliage, I saw fat curls of smoke fading into dusk. The fragrance of incense and moist air tickled my nose, urging me to travel forward until I reached you. Thunder pulsed through the sky as a fine mist settled to the ground.

[*Another day*]

I believe I will always regret that moment I saw you standing there. I should have known before I saw the glistening ivory, the speckled black stone. I should have known before I saw you reaching for that engraved lettering—"Beloved"—and the flowers, long dead, under days of heat. I should have known before I saw the tears race down your cheeks. I should have known before I saw you unraveling.

by Vy Doan, age 17
2014 Gold Key
Chaparral High School, Scottsdale

The Presents and the Gone

A dusty white car went bump, bump, bump down a red dirt road. The air was thick and soggy; the humidity was stifling. It rumbled through a sea of coconut trees, palm fronds, rice fields. Closer, closer, closer to the house that sat at the heart of the dense greenery, the house that was crumbling, shaking, sinking. They wait there: men, women, children, ever so patiently. They have waited for a long time. They have missed living company. In this world, in this time, in this place, the past bleeds in to the future; those who have moved on are never truly gone. But they live out their afterlives unseen and unheard; they are the Gone and their descendants are the Presents. They linger in the shadows, and watch time pass them by. Watch their families grow old and move on. Watch the world forget them...

The van arrives and creaks to a halt. The inhabitants of the house fly down the arching steps, laughing, shouting, cheering. *"You're here! You're here! Let's celebrate!"*

"My goodness, this place. It's so... dead," a little boy says when he descends from the steaming van. "It looks so lonely." How does he not see the girl running around merely a foot in front of him? How does he not see the legions of men, of women, of children scrambling to the front of the house to welcome the Presents home?

"We've kept the house nice for your visit."

"Look at this place, it's a mess." And it was. The white latticework was chipping and falling off the house's green-painted exterior. The doors were missing. The walls were steeped in sadness. The last of the Presents jumps down from the van, and they begin the trek up the crumbling steps to the house.

An echo of a laugh, long lost to the Presents, bounces up and around the walls like a babbling brook. Shadowy children play hide-and-seek amongst sheet-draped furniture and boarded-up crates. Men sit cross-legged on the floor, discussing long-gone politicians, ancient village affairs, new family faces. Spectral women bustle around the kitchen, squawking and gossiping. The Gone fill the house with life.

"I've never seen this place so empty." The Presents amble listlessly around the house, floating through seemingly empty corridors and rooms, sighing with regrets. How could they have let this precious place fall in to such ruin? They think they have let their ancestors down.

In this world, the Gone are cursed. A grandfather sees his grandchildren for the first time; sees his son after twenty years. He places a strong hand on his son's shoulder, and envelops his grandchildren in a warm embrace. But, the grandfather's joy is tempered; they do not see him. They do not feel him. The grandfather feels. Are the Gone truly gone?

In this world, the Presents are cursed. They do not see their past standing right in front of them. They do not see the Gone waving desperately to grab their attention. They do not hear them whisper encouraging words into their ears when they are afraid and alone and forlorn. The Presents live with the memories of those that have moved on. They are fixed to the past like flies stuck to molasses. They sink into the regrets of things left unsaid. The Presents may live on, but do they truly live?

by Kimaya Lecamwasam, age 15
2014 Gold Key, Silver Medal
BASIS Scottsdale, Scottsdale

SHORT STORY

Editor Introduction by Chelle Wotowiec

There is something to be said about the subtle creation of zealous plot and depiction of emotion in a piece comprised of less than three thousand words. Doing so requires a knowledge and command of our language and its rules that is not always found in the classroom. This is the knowledge found through experience, through reading, and through practice. While some may say the short story is of a dying breed, I ask you to take a close look at the short stories comprised in this collection.

I ask the reader to dissect Cassidy Zinke's "The Young Dreamer," tinker with the definition of love while you contemplate with Brigitta Mannino on whether or not you should have taken the stairs, teeter along the edge of sanity and infinity with Christopher Clements, and try to feel what the narrator feels in Nicole Dominiak's "Gifts, Ghosts, and God," this year's state of Arizona American Voices Medal-winning composition. When finished, ask yourself what you have found. You will certainly find the authors have breathed pain, desperation, humility, and love into their works.

Above all, though, you will find the very real depiction of what it means to be human in these short stories.

The Young Dreamer

A young girl sat in a car seat.

It was way past her bedtime, and her mind was a little fuzzy with exhaustion. She shook herself from drifting off once again and peaked out the window. They were passing by a neighborhood the girl didn't recognize as her own.
Not home yet.

Street lights played across the car with dancing shadows illuminating the calm girl's face. She didn't like the lights. It reminded her of standing on stage with a whole audience gawking at her. She didn't like the whispers of the audience to each other, even though they were actually adoring how cute she looked in her fluffy pink tutu. The whispers would make her brain spin because she couldn't concentrate on all of the voices at once. The whispers seemed to grow louder and louder and spin around her head tauntingly. She tried to run away from them, but something cold had wrapped around her chest and was pulling her down. She kicked and struggled until the world spun and she found herself on the car seat with the seat belt tied around her right arm.
Again she shook herself and again she looked out the window. They were passing by a corn field with tall bulky stalks of corn.
Not home yet.

She continued to watch the stalks of corn. They were all lined up into neat rows that seemed to move while sitting in the car. The long rows turned into huge legs running aside the car. She could hear the steady *boom boom boom* as the giant's feet ran. The legs had a beat of their own. They never missed a step or sped up or slowed down. The booming grew louder, and the girl tensed up in fear. Her wide eyes darted back in forth, for fear of the giant's face. *BOOM, BOOM, BOOM!* She squeezed her eyes shut, as a flash of yellow and a *vrooooooooooom* sped past her and dissolved eventually into the distance. The girl opened her eyes to find a fancy two-seater car racing down the road in front of her. The car's windows were down, and they were blasting a song with a blaring bass drum. The girl uncoiled herself from her seat and sat up, shaking her clenched muscles loose.

She snuck a glance out the window and saw enormous telephone poles lined up at the side of the road.

Not home yet.

She watched in awe as the lines of string crisscrossed and hung attached to each pole. She could see the electrical wire morph into a tightrope string. A lady wearing a tutu and swinging a pink umbrella leaped and swirled on the tightrope. She kept in pace with the moving car with soft fluid motions. Though, the girl didn't see nor feel the car anymore. The car had dissolved into her imagination. Instead, she could hear the loud carnival music blaring on speakers. The smell of kettle corn filled the air so strongly, the girl could taste the warm kernels on her tongue. Flashing multicolored spotlights spun and swayed all over the circus stadium like they couldn't find a place to rest. But then, they did. The lights all spun one more time and landed on the girl in the pretend crowd. The crowd was cheering her name in glee. She looked up and saw the tightrope lady holding out her hand and beckoning with it so she could pull her up onto the tightrope. The girl smiled in delight and was about to grab the nice lady's hand when a loud roar filled the stadium. The girl cowered back into her seat and looked around for the source of the noise.

An enormous lion had entered the ring, and a lion tamer was trying to contain it. The lion tamer held a cheap wooden chair in his right hand and a whip in his left. He threatened the lion by waving the whip around, but the lion took an enormous leap far above the lion tamer and landed in front of the shaking girl in the crowd. There was screams of terror in the crowd, and the tightrope lady in desperation stretched out her hand again. The lion eyed the girl like a tasty snack; he crouched and then charged towards the girl. The tightrope lady beckoned again. The frozen girl managed to free herself from her trance of fear and reached for the hand—only her hand slammed into an invisible barrier. She tried again and again. The tightrope lady's face was full of panic, as was the girl's. The lion took one last leap to land on the girl, and she squeezed her eyes shut.

When she opened them, she found herself sitting on a car seat, breathing rapidly, with a wild heartbeat, sweating all over. Her hand was scrunched in an awkward position against the window like she had been banging at it. The girl, shaking still, looked out the window. They were passing by groups of stores and restaurants.

Not home yet.

The stores all glowed cheerfully, flashing their neon signs. The girl could see the people laughing and eating in a restaurant. She wondered how they could be so awake at such a late time. "Well, they are grown-ups," she reminded herself wearily. "Grown-ups have a later bedtime. I can't wait 'til I have a later bedtime, too." She checked the clock again and smiled with the known fact that she was awake past her bedtime. It made her feel older and more privileged.

She felt the car slow to a stop. She peeked out the window and saw the annoying red light glaring down on her. She loathed the red light. It reminded her of an adult's eyes when she got in trouble. The light was screaming, "Stop! Wipe your feet on the rug first!" It made her angry, so she urged the light to change to that joyful green that would send them on their way. "Turn green, turn green, turn green, turn green!" she chanted silently. Finally, the light turned green. But they were still. . .

Not home yet.

There was one more red light episode, along with one more enticement of turning green until the little girl grew sick of the red lights. She was impatient with this random stopping. She thought of only one solution.

To fly.

She closed her eyes and felt the tires and engines moving and chugging along. She recalled her dad saying something about their uncle's car that had broken down because of a malfunction in the heart of the engine. The girl imagined a big pink heart in the center of the car, glowing with beauty.

"We're gonna fly," she told the heart.

The heart grew brighter, as if responding in agreement.

"Okay, I'll help you," she replied reassuringly.

She saw the tires spinning as usual on the ground. With everything she had in her little body, the girl poured her hope and faith into the tire to fly.

She felt the first tire rise, then the second, and the third and fourth together. She pushed the car higher and higher into the night sky. When they finally reached the height the girl desired, she looked out the window again. Then and only then, did she like the lights. She liked the streetlights that would flash each car with a bright white light. She liked the stalks of corn lined up in rows that no longer looked like legs, but the stitches of your mother's quilt that you would snuggle with in the winter. She liked the telephone poles that rose high and proudly in the air, as if trying to reach her.

The girl remembered the bonus word for her spelling test then. Something like "purpsektive." She remembered asking her mom what it had meant. "It's the way you look at things," she had said. The girl had nodded her head then, pretending to understand.

But, now she did, and she could feel her head nod now.

"You can choose to look at things whatever way you want, but everyone always sees it differently," Her mom had said.

"This must be my better purpsektive," the girl thought to herself. "I like it."

She continued to admire the millions of multicolored lights, imagining each of them as people. Each person had a different color no matter what, because they each saw everything differently. Some people see the light brighter, or duller or a mix of colors. "I wonder which color light I am," the girl thought. "That one, of course."

She saw her house with its bright Christmas multicolored lights.

Home.

Oh, how much she loved the word.
She could hear it now.
"Home..."
She wasn't imagining it this time.
"Jessica, we're home."
Jessica was too tired to even open her eyes.

So, her dad carried his princess into her bed, so the 6-year-old's imagination can take her to worlds that no grown-up will ever understand nor experience again.

by Cassidy Zinke, age 13
2014 Gold Key
ASU Preparatory Middle School, Mesa

I Should Have Taken the Stairs

Oh man... It's been an hour already, seems more like an eternity being stuck next to him in this elevator. *Where* is the operator?

My eyes quickly sneak a glance at the person stuck in here with me. I despise him; though I can't help but notice the gorgeous way his dark hair falls across his forehead. He's grown it out since the last time I saw him. It darkens his features, giving him a severe look. What am I saying? Snap out of it, Jules! Remember what he did to you. Remember who he is. His arrogance, his stubbornness, and he has the nerve to squeeze into *my* elevator just before the doors close—now look where we are.

Wow, it's getting hot in here, or maybe it only feels that way because his 6'2" frame is crammed in dangerously close to my side. We haven't said anything since the elevator jolted to a halt. Well, I certainly won't be the first to speak, not after what he pulled.

He keeps glancing at his watch. as if he can will the time to speed up. A few more minutes tick by, and suddenly the silence is shattered by the screeching of metal as the elevator begins to plummet. A scream escapes my lips, and suddenly, strong arms surround me, sheltering me from the inevitable impact. As fast as the fall began, it abruptly stops. Images of Disneyland's California Adventure ride *Hollywood Tower of Terror* flash through my mind, sending chills up my spine. We could die up here.

Realizing his arms are still around me, I stiffen as our eyes meet, brown on crystal blue. We awkwardly break apart.

As if this is some queue to begin speaking, he finally says, "Well, are you going to say something, or are we just going to continue to stand here acting like nothing ever happened between us?"

"I have nothing to say to you. I'll just patiently wait until the operator calls and gets us off this godforsaken square deathtrap." He looks at me with those eyes that used to comfort me when no one else could. Though, this time, there's something more there, a certain sadness gleams behind them before disappearing into his stern look. I throw away these thoughts immediately, *knock it off*

Jules; he doesn't feel anything toward you.

Noticing I still haven't responded, he continues on anyway.

"So that's it, then. You know, this is so like you! Always avoiding the situation and pretending like it's someone else's problem. When in reality, it's your stubborn attitude that puts you in that bad place."

"Don't you dare blame this on me, Jared," I retort. "You're the one who left, remember—you don't get to judge me. Urgh, of all the people to be stuck in tight quarters with, it had to be with you!"

"And you think I'm particularly pleased with the standing arrangements?" he replies, coming up into my face. "You should be glad this happened, because now you have the perfect opportunity to tell me what a jerk I've been. Well you don't have to say anything, because I already know, and it's been killing me every minute since I left you. Every moment I've spent away from you has left me feeling deprived of oxygen. There isn't a single day that goes by that I don't regret leaving you."

I still haven't said anything. It's as if his words have frozen me in place, and my mouth has refused to open. Still, he has more to say.

"I guess I was just too afraid to let myself feel, because feelings make you vulnerable, because someone like me just doesn't deserve to have someone like you. That's why I never let you in. That's why I said and did those things. I hurt and pushed away the one person I ever truly cared about."

Stunned by his sudden revelation, I shake myself out of this daze, my body unfreezing at last. I'm about to reply with some snide remark, but I hold my tongue when I see the look in his eyes. The scary part is that they seem sincere.

Minutes turn into hours as we both keep our distance from each other, or as much as we can in this 5' x 5' square. He breaks the silence yet again. "Please say something Jules." He's looking at me now. "Juliet?"

"I... I don't know what you expect me to say... Suddenly you've had a change of heart, and we can just ride off into the sunset together? How can I ever trust you again?" Tears are prickling at my eyes now, but I hold them back; I will *not* let him see me cry.

Pain fills his eyes this time as he says, "You have to know that leaving you was the hardest thing I've ever done, and the biggest mistake I ever could have made. I understand that it will take time to earn your forgiveness and trust, but you're going to have to talk to me if we want to get out of here. It's been almost two-and-a-half hours; clearly, no one is coming to save us anytime soon. It's up to us to help ourselves. So for now, let's put aside our differences and work together."

Understanding the situation, I nod my consent and relent. As soon as we get out of this nightmare, I never have to see him again. Though I can't deny there is a small part of me that wishes that weren't true.

"Okay, I think if I give you a boost up, you can knock out that top panel in the ceiling of the elevator and climb out. I'd say we fell about four floors; there should be an emergency hall that connects to the inner workings of the building. You can reach it and call for help."

I don't understand how he could possibly know this, but then, I remember he always was full of odd facts, and never let on at how intelligent he was. I reluctantly agree to his plan, and honestly I don't see any other way of getting out of here. The operator isn't responding, and there are no sounds coming from outside to indicate that work is being done to rescue us.

"Are you ready?" I look down at Jared's hands, already cupped with his palms open, and nod, stepping into them. Gaining the height needed to reach the ceiling, I begin pounding a panel over and over, but it doesn't budge.

"It's no use, Jared, I don't know what these panels are made out of, but it's definitely damage-preventable."

"Don't give up just yet, come on," he urges me on. I pound for what feels like hours; finally, he sets me down, both of us panting. I look up at our progress, and my heart sinks, the most damage I've managed to make is a crack in the panel and a dent in the ceiling. Not to mention, both my fists and my shoulders are now on fire. I'm not sure how much longer I can keep at this. And I certainly don't know where Jared has gotten the strength to hold up my weight this long. At this rate, our energy will give out long before the ceiling panel will.

"Any more bright ideas?" Sarcasm leaks through my voice, exhaustion making me irritable.

"Well, at least I did something. I didn't see you coming up with a plan."

"Well, we know how well your plans with me have worked out in the past," I mumble under my breath. He hears me, though, and before he can respond, the floor drops out from under us again. The fall is fast, this time coming to a stop much quicker than it had before, leaving me breathless and dizzy. Jared puts a hand out to steady me, but I flinch away.

His hand recoils, and I hear him take a deep breath. "I'm trying to make amends here, Jules. Why won't you just accept that I'm sorry?"

"You think that one heroic act that gets us out of an elevator will fix everything? It's going to take a lot more than that to even begin to make this okay," I say, getting into his face.

My initial anger toward him has grown into outrage. That, combined with the fact that we have been trapped for hours in this stifling air, moves me to take it out on him. I shove him in the chest. "You arrogant," I shove him again, causing his back to ram against the wall, "lying, no good—"

His lips are suddenly crushed against mine, kissing me with all the fervor that has built between us. The air rushes out of me, and I let him consume me with all the hunger of a starved man. Somewhere in the back of my mind, I hear the ding of the elevator doors sliding open, but for the first time in the past five hours, I'm in no rush to get off.

by Brigitta Mannino, age 17
2014 Silver Key
Basha High School, Chandler

No Life Worth Living

It is midnight, and I feel like doing something irrational.

Like, something completely out of my mind. Maybe I'll go graffiti the school gym, or set fire to a hot dog stand and roll it down Parker Avenue, but whatever it is, I can sure as hell tell you it will be crazy and stupid, and maybe, just maybe, it will get me to sleep.

I wake up in the gym. Empty cans of spray paint lying next to me, a roaring headache and—how did I get here?

I wake up in the theater. I'm suspended from the catwalk by a strip of linen tied around my ankle. I'm dangling around the stage like a worm on a fishhook.

No, wait—this is all wrong. I wake up in my house. I get dressed, go to school, skip French, skip band, just hanging out in the theater. Underneath the stage there's a whole system of classrooms nobody uses anymore, except for storage. The yellow paint in the attic is so old it's peeling off, and the only illumination in the room is an old light bulb. Piles upon piles of boxes, boxes marked 'markers' and 'old yearbooks.' These aren't why I'm here. I'm here for the boxes marked, 'miscellaneous.' These contain journals and worn out novellas, student-produced writings all the way from the Sixties.

It's reading time. I read these journals; I live by them. The people who write them always vary, but more or less, they're usually like me. Kids with nothing else better to do. I am a playwright. I'm working on a play, "Oh, Brother of Mine," a story about a pilot who crash lands in the Australian outback. All you need to know is that I wrote it, and it's a hit. Critics are already raving. Which critics, you ask? Mostly professors and school faculty. My plays always turn out great. I have received numerous offers from prestigious universities, and I've accepted one—Yale. All that's left to do is direct this play. And I'm off to a promising start, with the set for the first scene made and my actors in place, and my cameramen working on some minor, technical difficulty, when I see her—Marie Bennett. She's the star of my play. I can't believe I never noticed her before. She has beautiful auburn hair and dark green eyes. But it's the way she moves that's really enchanting—almost like a river, with such grace you would expect her to be a dancer, but she's not. Instead, she is acting in my play.

We begin the rehearsal.

I finish the rehearsal. Where did the time go? Who knows? All I can say for certain is that I'm lying on the ground in a pool of saliva in one of the classrooms under the stage. When I leave and go to look outside, it hits me. The day, all gone—slipped through my fingers like sand.

This is narcolepsy.

Well, not really. I can't be sure. I've been plagued by rampant sleep disorders ever since my parents divorced. I read an article about narcolepsy one day, and I realized I fit the bill.

Dream-like hallucinations.

Loss of short-term memory.

And now, I can't function correctly. I don't want to go home, either. I pretty much live here. This theater is the only thing keeping me here. Without it, I'd have abandoned this town years ago. I need to get this play finished. The only problem is, now I'm having trouble telling the difference between dreams and reality. The main cause to my narcolepsy, I believe, is reading the journals. Specifically, my own.

That's right. I've discovered my own journal, buried under mounds of yellow paper, coated in layers of dust and bound in red leather. It isn't possible, I tell myself, I'm just a kid, and this journal is dated nineteen sixty-five. Whoever wrote this should be about forty by now. But there's no mistake in the writing. This journal is my own. In its depths, I discuss the issues with my parents and my school.

I talk about my alcohol abuse.

I talk about my principal's death.

And I talk about my narcolepsy. It seems to be my most frequented topic. In my journal I find list after list of things about me, little summaries of my life so far, in sharp red ink. It looks like I was trying to remember something.

I have two divorced parents.

I have a brother who died in the war.

I am depressed.

I have deep psychological issues.

And I—

Yes, I know. The last one is always cut off. It really kills me, too. I feel like that last bullet is the one that will free me from my nightmare. Anyways, reading my own writing is sending me on some trip. It's this that keeps me from sleeping, and that makes me sleep at times when all I want to do is just stay awake. Deep down, I'm aware I won't last another week sleeping at school and skipping classes. If I even am, I can't remember anymore. It isn't important. What's important is staying focused and working on my play, and—

I wake up on the road. A trail of fire curving down the asphalt road indicates the crime I've perpetrated. Well, I think, I've gone and done it this time. This time, I've set fire to and rolled down Barry's Hot Dog Stand down Parker Avenue. A second or two later and I hear the resounding crash that means it hit home.

Just like I wrote in my journal.

Funny, isn't it?

How everything I read in that godforsaken book turns to truth? And now I'm starting to question whether or not this is even happening. But it has to, because pinching myself never works, and it always did before. In my hand I find a can of black spray-paint. Time for some graffiti. Even in this dream-like state, I can correctly orient myself towards Downside School. I hop the fence and enter through an open window. When I get inside, I turn to a blank wall somewhere in the bowels of the administration building and write, in shining black paint—

Is this the real life?

I used to be a real Queen fan. I say 'used to,' because nowadays, nothing I do is similar to my old self.

Is this just fantasy?

This isn't a tragedy. This is real life.

Caught in a landslide, no escape from reality.

The paint drips down from letter to letter, creating a strangely satisfying effect.

Open your eyes, look up to the skies and see.

I write the last letter and all turns to dark. Oblivion.

I wake up in my private room in the theater. Mr. Baker gave me my own room after my fifth production at Downside.

Everything is becoming disjointed; memories from years past are becoming harder and harder to recall. Whoever I once was, he's dead now. He's not important. In my bag I find my book. I skip to the entry made thirty-two years ago today:

March 3rd, 1965

Today was an amazing day. For the first time, I feel like I've slept. And it's all thanks to Marie Bennett, the star of my show. I feel like I really connected with her on a deeper level. We talked all hour in theater, since a leaky roof needed mending, and rehearsal got delayed. She's really amazing. I can only hope she feels the same way as I do.

Reading this, I know too well that it is true. I check my watch. It reads, "7:34 a.m." I know that if I miss today, due to some horrible relapse into my narcolepsy, I'll be finished. I need to talk to her. Standing up, I search the room for a marker.

Finally, I find a bright red one. I heard my brother talking about this before. He used to have narcolepsy, as well. His method for combating it was to draw a dot in his palm, so he would know whether or not he was asleep. When he saw the dot on his hand, he knew he was awake. Somehow, this didn't stop him from getting a bullet straight through the chest. With this in mind, I do the same thing. This way, hopefully, I will stay awake long enough to speak with Marie. I also grab my journal and toss it in the closet. I'm not going to risk reading it today.

Time passes quicker than usual. Before I know it, it's theater. Just as my journal entry reads, today's rehearsal is set back due to a leaky roof. Most of the cast and crew are talking or playing cards. Normally, I'd sit with my friends, but when I see Marie sitting alone, I can't pass up the opportunity. At first, she is surprised. She doesn't see me very often, and when she does, I'm either asleep or focusing on the play. As we talk, more of her life unveils right before me.

She was born in Maine.

She doesn't know her father.

And she loves acting.

She's also very rich, and her stepfather owns a handsome villa right outside of town. Would I visit her sometime, maybe? I don't know, I tell her. It's too early to say. When the flow of conversation turns to my own life, I find it hard to talk about. I don't allow her to find out anything interesting about me. I do not know if this is a mistake or not. When the period ends and it's time for lunch, I find myself more sleepy than ever. It's the best I can do to work my way to my room and collapse near the closet. I inch towards it pitiably and manage to grab my journal, the journal that shouldn't exist, from a mound of clothing. I turn to tomorrow's entry and try to read, but I decide I'll have time for it later, and I promptly pass out.

I wake up at Marie's villa. I've been sleeping out on the soft, grassy ground, and all of a sudden, I fear for her. What have I done, from the time I slept in theater till now? I try to recall what the entry read but can't. I approach a room I know must be Marie's and, acting on impulse, rap on her window softly.

She answers. We talk. I explain everything.

She's quite distant at first. The idea that someone could be plagued by a disorder as laughable as narcolepsy seems impossible. But the more I explain it to her, the more she realizes my symptoms directly correlate to the disease.

I tell her I don't have much longer.

She answers, why? Why can't I just tell a trusted adult and go to the hospital?

"I wish I could," I say. "The problem is, I don't trust any adults. And," I laugh, "I'd probably fall asleep in the middle of the conversation. Soon," I explain, "my rampant absences from school will reach the breaking point. The administrators will be notified, as well as my deranged parents."

"This isn't some useless tragedy," I say, "this is real life."

We talk until sun peeks gently over the wooded horizon. She asks me if there's anything she can do to help. I nod. I tell her that, if one thing could be changed about my disorder, it's the hallucinations. I tell her, even with my red dot method, I need her to tell me when I'm awake or asleep. And if I am sleeping, I need her to wake me up. Just for a couple days, I say, until I can finish this play. Then I leave her and walk home, still sitting on her windowsill. No kiss, no hug, no nothing.

This isn't a love story.

I reach the school and once again fall into a deep sleep. When I wake up, I check my palm—and see the dot. A wave of relief rushes over me. I check my watch and realize its ten minutes until Marie is supposed to check on me. I silently count down, with my legs dangling off the edge of the stage. Nine. Eight. Seven. Six. Five. Four. Three. Two. One. And still no Marie. I'm losing my grasp on everything. Where is she? I wonder if I'm dreaming. But the dot is here, and pinching myself doesn't work. I am forced to accept that she has forgotten about me. Production goes on as usual. I ask my friend, Jacob, about Marie.

"Who's that?" he asks.

"You know," I say, "Marie, The actress. She's the star of our play!"

"Never heard of her."

I ask around. Nobody seems to have ever known her. Her auburn hair, green eyes. Apparently they never existed. At this point, I'm certain I am dreaming. Nothing makes sense anymore. And I'm so, so tired. But it doesn't matter, I tell myself, the only thing that really matters is finishing this play. I've begun to settle into the process of directing my last scene when it hits me—the journal! The answer's got to be in there. I excuse myself from the stage and return to my room. I check the closet, grab the book, and flip through the pages wildly. Tomorrow reads:

March 5th, 1965

I don't know what's going on. When I woke up today, my dot was gone. I looked for Marie, but I couldn't find her anywhere. No one else seems to be able to help. I can't tell if I'm dreaming or not. And—

I don't wait around to read the rest. I've come to a decision about that book. Whatever it says or predicts: it can't control my fate. I live my life based off my choices, not some sleep-induced hallucination. So instead of probing through the rest of today's secrets, I continue forwards, blindly. The day starts in the usual fashion. I skip class until theater. I do my best to stay awake.

This is my life. And it is ending, one second at a time.[1]

When production begins, I see Marie, standing in the shadows of the dimly-lit stage. I go up to her and say something like, "Where were you?" She tells me she's sorry she forgot about her promise. She says that her dad kept her home from school because she was sick. None of her explanation satisfies me. It doesn't explain why my dot has mysteriously disappeared, or why pinching myself to wake up doesn't work, even though I'm certain I am dreaming.

¹ *Line from Fight Club by Chuck Palahniuk*

It doesn't explain why everyone thought she never existed.

But for now, it's good enough.

Tonight is the premier of my play, or so Marie tells me. It's going to be a hit. In fact, a professor from Harvard will be in attendance. Perhaps it will get noticed. Perhaps it will become a Broadway spectacle. I could care less. After another tiring day, I allow myself to fall asleep within the confines of my classrooms. The only place I feel safe. The last thing I see is Marie's face, telling me that she's real, real as can be.

When I wake up, I'm sitting in a chair backstage. I turn to Jacob, who's walking past me.

"Where's Marie," I ask.

He doesn't seem to know.

Everything in my life has boiled down to this moment.

I can hear my heart thud against my skin. A single bead of sweat finds its way down my face. I've reached a fork in the road.

I have been presented with two versions of reality, one dream, one not. Whichever I choose now will decide whether I go down in the history books as the greatest and most troubled playwright ever, greater than Shakespeare, or if my fate is to be laid out on a stretcher and locked in a room. I would never last long in an asylum. Some kid tells me that it's time for me to give my pre-show speech.

Everything in my life has boiled down to this moment.

And as I step out from the curtains and up to the blinding light of the podium, I'm not nervous. I can trust myself to give a simple speech.

I am told it was great.

I remember none of it.

It doesn't matter, though. All that matters to me now is finishing this play. And it is finished. Second by second, it drains away. In a half an hour, I will finally be free from this wretched nightmare. Well, I think, might as well go see what I've created.

I walk to my seat from the darkness of backstage and into the light. Quickly, I take my velvet-lined seat and watch. The play is more beautiful than I ever imagined. Its stunning prose, captivating fight scenes, it enraptures the audience and myself.

Yet, there's something I can't put my finger on.

Something is off about this play.

Its words are too dynamic, too descriptive. It isn't my method of writing at all. I think as hard as I can, about the day I created it. About my inspiration for it. And yet the only image I can conjure up is that of the horrible leather journal. The one that shouldn't exist.

Doesn't exist.

And while I try and recall what happened, curiosity gets the better of me. Time to find out. I leave the auditorium to my private room. I dig around in my closet, the last place I read it. When I find it, I open its crackled, yellow pages and search for an entry concerning my play. I find one. It reads: "...*I only hope they never look in the closet in room 513.*" I get up. There's an old hallway that connects my side of the theater to the underground, abandoned attic of classrooms. I go there now, and as my play is performed right above me, I tear apart an enormous closet I never bothered to open.

At least, I don't remember doing it.

I search through the closet and find eight boxes full of journals and writings. With each box I discover new writings. The last box I find is made of metal and locked. I need a key. I consult my journal. Nothing. I look through my pants pockets. I look through my shirt pocket. In it lies the key, thought I have absolutely no memory of putting it there. As my dread grows, I unlock the box. Inside are about fifty manuscripts from different student authors, each new plays. Each a play I've done. Each a play I stole.

Everything in my life has boiled down to this moment of indecision. Because now, in this dimly lit classroom, the truth has been revealed to me. I'm a no better writer then the failures that hid their work in this room.

Now everything is in the light. Nothing has been left out.

With shaking hands, I tear the manuscripts to shreds. For the journal, I take a match that doesn't exist and strike it on the wall. It lights, casting eerie shadows across the boxes and desks. I light the journal aflame, and toss it one last time back into the jumble of paper from whence it came.

Please, let me forget about today until tomorrow.

The room slowly succumbs to the flames. Smoke works its way through the cracks in the stage and startles the performers.

Within minutes the entire auditorium will blaze to life. I can feel my last minutes ticking away as I walk out into gently falling snow. It is midnight, and I don't have much longer. I walk only for a few minutes when I reach a darkened suburban road near the school.

Please.

All that matters now is finishing that play. And as I walk onto Parker Avenue for the last time, I realize I have no regrets. Why should I? Plagiarism isn't nearly the worst crime ever committed. What about arson? Murder or rape? In the long term, what I've done doesn't amount to much.

But it is still enough to break me.

I check my watch. It reads twelve o'clock. Time to die.

Everything is falling apart. Everything.

With my last few breaths, I fall to the ground and inch myself across the road until I've reached the middle. I contort my body into a sitting position and wait in the inky blackness for a light. And then I see it, it's coming up from the hill, they haven't spotted me yet, and yes, they're hurling towards me, and the last thing I see is the blackness being rent apart by the headlights of some ignorant failure, some unaware junkie who has, to my overwhelming happiness, decided to race across the suburban wasteland at twelve o'clock at night, at no less then ninety miles an hour. At this speed, I'll break my neck before sailing across the neighborhood, perhaps in time to scare some off the dull-witted suburbanites.

This isn't a tragedy.

This is real life.

Maybe I'll be reincarnated as a comet. Here, right now, as an icy wind whips across the asphalt, there's nothing I think of that would be more inexpressibly beautiful than to plummet to my death into something as solid and infinite as the moon. I am in the mood for destruction. And, just my luck, my chariot of death approaches. In my last seconds, I am wondering what they will do with my body. Will I be cremated? Used for science? Or maybe nothing. Perhaps I'll rot in the frozen road on Parker Avenue forever.

Kids will play hopscotch with my fibula. A family will suspend my skull from the mantelpiece.

The car gets nearer. So close, I can smell the dank breath of the jock and his single-use girlfriend, currently unaware I'm about to change their lives for the better.

I smile.

Oblivion.

by Christopher Clements, age 16
2014 Silver Key
Thunderbird High School, Phoenix

Gifts, Ghosts, and God

The boy's father taught him how to pray. To pray without kneeling, to pray without altars, to pray without priests. How to pray with ink and balloons.

The people in the churches were wasting their time, his father told him. All their voices just collided with each other's, a deafening roar of wishes, wants, demands. A sound so loud nothing was heard. So a wise man, instead of trying to shout his prayers louder than the rest of them, leaves a note. He sends it up to heaven with his own delivery system. That is how God hears him.

"How's he get it up there?"

"Where?"

The boy looked up.

"How do you think?"

"He ties it to a bird."

"They don't fly high enough."

The boy crossed his arms. "He throws it, and it lands on a cloud. Then it drifts over to God."

"Clouds don't drift high enough."

"What's he do then?"

"I'll show you." He tore a piece of paper from the back of a book no one read, folded the jagged edge so it was smooth, and plucked a marker from his pocket. A magician. Only he had no wand. His cape was missing, too. "Write a prayer."

The boy wrote as neatly as he could: A Prayer

"Now write the rest, and then fold it, so the birds don't see it. They'll try to pop the balloon if they see writing inside of it. They can't read, so they hate letters."

The boy thought and asked God to protect his future prayers from the birds.

They put the note in a red balloon, so God couldn't miss it, pumped it up with helium, and tied a piece of his mother's old ribbon to the end. Then they went outside and let it go. The wind always blew west, so the boy always thought that's where God was. West.

The boy sent up a balloon each Sunday. When his father wasn't around to help, the boy took Webb outside with him, and they filled the balloon with helium, tied the string, and let it go by themselves.

Webb was a parting gift; the boy's mother, the giver.

She was just an idea to him, like pirate ships, or dragons, but Webb was very real, though he lacked most of what a real marten would have. Because Webb felt. When the boy watched the stuffed marten's eyes, he could see joy and pain and all the other emotions of real things. He saw them ten times magnified. And thus, Webb was ten times more real to him than the frogs that lined the sidewalk or the dog that his father allowed to sleep in front of the fireplace.

That dog roamed the street from time to time. She was thin and had fleas. The boy's father would open the door and bid her welcome when the nights got cold. The boy would sit on the counter, his feet tucked safely under his knees, watching as his father went through the trashcan and picked out old fruit cores, ribs, and half eaten sandwiches for her to eat. She snored loudly and would prick up her ears and narrow her eyes when the boy walked past. She never growled, but the boy knew it was because if she did, his father wouldn't let her in anymore. And she didn't have enough fur to keep her warm until winter had passed.

Once, when his father was outside and she was inside, the stray dog snapped at Webb's dangling tail. The frightened boy, who had moments before been searching for faces on the ceiling, gave a startled yank. The dog's nails scratched the wood floor as she lurched forward, but she held with her yellow teeth, pulling. The boy braced his feet against the arm of the couch, pushing. Something split. His head hit the other side of the couch. He was left with his mutilated stuffed marten while the dog scuttled away with the other half of its tail.

The boy cried that night, his mouth stuffed with sheets, so his father wouldn't hear him. He was in a black mood after driving the dog out, for he liked the dog, talked to it, and when she was gone, he cursed. The boy wiped away his tears with his palms, but eventually his palms were as wet as his eyes, and it stung to wipe them. So he stopped trying and kept crying, crying for Webb because he couldn't cry for himself. The marten lay at the end of the bed, shuddering and wheezing and whimpering. But glass eyes couldn't cry tears.

The next morning, as his father slept, the boy went out in the cold with Webb tucked away in the hood of his coat.

The early sunlight was cold, and instead of warming, it bit. He buried his numb fingers in his palms.

They went out into the garage where the helium was. On the hood of his father's truck, he hastily scribbled a note missing so many letters he had to cross it all out and rewrite it. The boy stuffed it into the balloon. It was hard to tie. His fingers were stiff and shaking.

He and Webb went outside, and the boy took the marten from his hood. They held the string of the balloon together, the boy with his hand and Webb with his paw. Then they released and watched it sail away over the tall, jagged trees. When the boy glanced at the lawn, he saw the remnants of Webb's tail. He blanched. Looked to the sky. That was the first real prayer the boy ever sent up.

The second one came with the summer storms. When the thunder and lightning began, the boy began to see ghosts.

They were hideous. Long dried hair. Eyes as hard as bone, dead as skeletons. Ball gowns and dusty suit jackets. They opened his door at night as he and Webb stared at them, bug-eyed. Sometimes, they glanced in and laughed, their breath filling the room like fog. Other times they would come in. They didn't have feet, just stumps. And they would whisper to him with cold smiles in a language he didn't understand, their tongues snaking back and forth through their mouths. Each time they blinked, their pupils grew smaller and smaller until they were pinpoints in ice.

One night, as they hissed and chanted, he recognized a sound. His name. It was as if he'd been standing outside, and the wind had called to him. The boy screamed.

His father threw the door open, and in the hallway light, they dissolved.

"What?"

The boy shrunk at the fear in his father's voice. "Ghosts."

"Where?"

"Not where—when?"

"All right, when?"

"*Al*ways." He paused for seeming lack of breath. When he spoke again, his voice was a whisper. "As soon as you close my door they come, and they open it. Sometimes— sometimes they stand in the doorway for the whole night.

Just staring. And I can't ever sleep."

His father stared at the pale boy with his face half hidden in the sheets.

The boy looked back at him. No, looked past him. Then at him. "I don't think they'll ever go away."

"Why's that?"

"Because I think they're a part o—. I don't know."

His father wiped the circles under his eyes. "I know how to make them go away."

"How?"

"Ask."

"Ask wh—?" He blinked. "But what if they see me writing the prayer? What if they pop the balloon before it ever reaches—."

His father tugged at his wiry beard. "If we go quickly and quietly, they won't catch us. Won't know."

"But—."

"Come on. Quickly. Quietly."

The boy got up and followed his father.

"The most dangerous part is the stairs. Ghosts are always sliding down banisters." He checked around the corner. "But it looks like they're somewhere else for the time being. Quickly now." Their feet pitter-pattered on the wood, and the boy shrank at the noise. But the ghosts stayed hidden, or if they did peer out of the shadows, they did it when the boy's back was turned.

The garage door creaked and whined as it opened. The boy stood tense outside of it and made his father stop when it was high enough for them to duck through. He banged his head, but he had forgotten about it by his next step. When they were both inside, the boy shut the garage door, and, after checking for cracks, finally decided he was safe. He gazed in delight as his frozen breath caught and shattered in the moonlight.

Then he squinted at the shadowy shelves, looking for the marker and paper. When he found them both, he began to write. His father fumbled around in the dimly lit garage for the balloons.

"How will he see it?"

"Who?"

"God."

"It's a lot brighter up there. Closer to the stars."

The boy nodded and continued writing. His father continued looking for the balloons.

He found them. Put the prayer in. Helium. String on the bottom. Raised the garage door. They held their breaths as they passed under the door again. No sound of ghosts. They let the balloon go into the night where it was swallowed up.

When they returned to the house, they went on a ghost hunt. They found nothing. The ghosts had gone.

The third real prayer was the last one the boy ever sent up. He wrote it sitting on the driveway with the paper balanced on his knee and Webb perched on his shoulder. The clouds above were the types that held faces and elephants and dragons, and the birds in the trees were calling to each other, but the boy was too focused on his task to notice them.

The boy wrote something and then drew a line through it. He tried again. He kept trying until the clouds and grass grew too dark to see. Scraps of paper lay scattered on the ground beside him—attempts.

His father called him inside. The boy paused in his writing. The clouds had merged with the dark sky and the birds had gone away. So he saw nothing and heard nothing. His father called again. The boy quickly finished the thank-you letter and ran towards the garage, pressing Webb against his shoulder so he wouldn't fall into the mud. He folded the note. Put it in the balloon. Helium. String. Let it go.

The boy went inside, walking carefully, so Webb wouldn't fall off. When they were inside, the boy took the marten by his half-tail and set him on the counter, where he used to sit when the dog would come in.

The boy's father hadn't let her in again. But he felt bad, so he would give her scraps every Sunday. As a result, she lingered, and the boy saw her sniffing around in the yard from time to time. She narrowed her eyes when she heard his footsteps. He narrowed his.

It was autumn, and the leaves were on the ground, colorful and dying. The wind rattled the bare branches. The boy was on the driveway again, with Webb in his hood. They were being watch dogs, watching the dog. Whenever she got too close to the house, the boy would charge at her, his battle cry ringing through the air. It never came to that though. Battle. She would always snarl and back away. The boy would retire to the driveway, and the cycle repeated.

She got too close. He jumped to his feet and ran at her. She glared and darted away. The boy turned triumphantly to face her. They both froze, glanced at the fallen marten on the ground between them, then back at each other.

The boy had read somewhere that dogs could smell fear. He tried not to breathe, for breath came from his chest and his chest was where the fear was. He glared at the dog to tell her she'd better step away. When she didn't, he yelled. He yelled that he was afraid, but it didn't matter because she couldn't understand him. He shouted and glared with a terrifying intensity.

Then, all of a sudden, his voice caught in his throat, and the silence that filled the yard made him shrink.

The dog launched towards Webb. The boy shot after her. He slid onto the ground and reached blindly, hoping. They grabbed the marten at the same time. Only he had fingers, while she had teeth. They ripped the skin on his fingers, scalded him like fire, burned him like ice, and his hand, of its own accord, recoiled, leaving Webb unprotected. The dog rushed towards the woods, her captive dangling between her jaws.

The boy sprang to his feet.

He shouted words his father used when he dropped something. He shouted words he'd heard on television. He shouted words he made up because the words he knew weren't enough. He shouted them all as he ran towards the break in the trees where he had last seen the dog.

He ran blindly, screaming, screaming. He tripped. Blood in his mouth. He spat it out and rose to his feet. Tracks. He stomped on them as he ran. Fell again. This time he tasted fear. He spat again. It landed on his hand. He wiped it as he stood. Slowly now. His head spun as he ran, and the world spun with it.

"Webb," he called. "Webb." The tracks had faded in a spot, and he had kept running. He had no idea where they were or where he was. He slowed. And began to meander through the trees, calling for Webb.

"Weeee-ebb."

"We-ebb."

"Webb."

He found him.

He found him mangled and strangled and tangled in a heap. The white cotton which flecked the ground sagged with spit. One of Webb's eyes stared at him from where it sat, alone in a heap of white. The other one was still attached. Barely. It dangled uselessly from the split head.

The boy knelt and rubbed the damp little ear. He put his hand over the animal's eye because he couldn't stand to have it looking at him like it was. He was going to cry. He lifted his own eyes.

And then he sank.

Dappling and dotting what must have been the tallest tree in the forest were colors, blue and yellow and red. They looked like globs of paint that had dried as they were about to fall. Only they had jagged edges, where the air had knifed its way out. So jagged. Endless rows of colorful teeth. They belonged to dead things. The murdered bodies of prayers.

When the wind passed through, the notes on the ground rattled. The wind shoved them forward and backward on the forest floor, and so the paper was smeared with mud. The remnants of dried rain dotted the pages, and the ink dripped.

The boy's eyes did the same.

All the prayers he had ever written to God lying in Hell. His strength left him. He sat staring.

Then he stood. He went over to the prayers and read them, collecting them in his opposite hand. They stained his fingers. The mud. The ink. He finally reached the last one. The ugliest one of all. It cracked when he picked it up, that last prayer. He knew what it said.

I want to thank you. For helping Webb. For chasing away the ghosts. For answering my prayers. For making my dad a wise man. And everything else. The whole world, really. It's so pretty I could cry.

The papers crackled in his hands, as if they were burning. He kicked a piece of bark from a rotting stump. The black bugs scurried away in the light. He picked it up. He picked the dead marten up. Opened the belly. Stuffed the marten with old prayers. He placed the body on the sheet of bark. Then started to walk. He knew where he was now.

The river wasn't much of a river, but it would do. It was ten feet across and at its deepest point was four feet. But it would do.

He picked at the scab that had grown over the dog bite. He did it 'til it bled. On the back of a prayer he wrote his last real prayer. The one he never sent up.

Thanks be to God.

He winced. Picked at his finger again so he could sign his name.

Then he sucked it until it stopped bleeding.

He waded into the water, and when it had reached his waist, he placed the bark on the oily surface. It dipped but didn't sink. He took his last look at the corpse. The place where the marten's eye had been was just a pale patch of dried glue. He placed the paper over it.

Ghosts lined the river banks, their hands overstretched as if in blessing. They stood beside each other as far as he could see, with eyes that knew all and faces that betrayed nothing. They emitted a pale glow that frosted the grass of the riverbank.

He wasn't afraid to look away. He knew they would do him no harm. Because he was no longer afraid of seeing ghosts. He was afraid of teeth, and he was afraid of lies, but not of ghosts. He saw them and it was all right. So he looked at the wood with its poor passenger, floating on the water's surface.

And then, like he had with so many balloons, he let go.

They watched solemnly as the current carried the craft farther and farther downstream. Like Moses. Only the water was rough. The basket tipped, and the baby drowned.

by Nicole Dominiak, age 15
2014 Gold Key, American Voices Medal
BASIS Scottsdale, Scottsdale

JOURNALISM

Editor Introduction by Alyssa Tilley

"Journalism is dying," they say. "Why would you write for a newspaper?"

With the popularity of smart phones and tablets, information is at the tip of everyone's fingers. Everywhere you look, peoples' faces are bent downward staring at some sort of screen where they are finding the latest news, whether from an online news site, a meme on Facebook, or a tweet. Journalism is far from dying. Journalism is expanding rapidly and evolving constantly.

Joining the evolution are four young authors. Within this section, you will find a range of topics. Justin Zhu profiles an extraordinary individual who survived the infamous World War II. Tori Cejka interviews individuals who have allowed other peoples' children from all over the world to stay in their homes and become a part of their families. BrieAnna Frank reflects on the tragic Columbine Massacre and how the town and community are doing today. Finally, Navya Dasari joins the discussion of race and identity that is at the center of Arizona politics most days.

Each young author has joined the journalism evolution. Information is being dispersed at faster speeds than ever in today's society. People used to receive news once daily through a newspaper, and now we have the power of the Internet. The Internet is astounding in its ability to spread information, and someone has to find that information, research it, and share it with the world. We are journalists. No matter what the medium, we are sharing information— it is our job to get it out there to the public. Journalism is not dying at all. It is transforming, and young authors all over the world are helping it do so. We are journalists, and we are not going anywhere.

All sources and interviews are valid, as far as YAA editorial staff is aware.

The Call for Courage

Moral courage is the action of one taking a risk for the benefit of others who are less fortunate. Often in life, these less fortunate people are the ones who have been insulted, discriminated and prejudiced against for their whole lives. These people are just like any of us, and yet, they must face the cruel whip of inequity unleashed by society. However, every once in a while, one becomes sickened of this wrongdoing and takes a stand against society's illnesses, not because they want the benefits it brings solely to themselves, but rather for the good of the whole, and simply because of the fact that it is the right thing to do.

In the pursuit of my research, I met a Jewish Holocaust survivor, Oskar Knoblauch. Good-natured, joyful and energetic, this individual was unbelievably optimistic, considering the traumatizing experiences he had to endure.

Knoblauch witnessed anti-Semitism firsthand. When Knoblauch was only thirteen, he had to live in a ghetto with many other Jewish people. They would get little to eat, as their daily rations were nothing but a slice of bread. Soon, in desperation, young Knoblauch had to search for food in the trash. A German trash collector noticed the emaciated boy trying to get the basic nutrition he needed and decided to give him a loaf of bread. This simple action was an action full of love, full of comfort and full of life. The German, knowing the consequences, was risking his life to help a Jewish boy.

Soon after, the Nazi officers came to round up the Jewish inhabitants and send them to death camps. The trash collector knew about this and told Knoblauch to jump in his garbage truck. Knoblauch did so obediently, and when it was time to come out, everybody in the ghetto was gone.

Afterwards, a Nazi official found Knoblauch still wandering in the ghetto. Instead of following his orders and sending Knoblauch to the death camps, the Nazi official sheltered this young Jewish boy in a basement. Following your heart, as the Nazi official did, in a heartless society demonstrates true moral courage.

Soon, the Nazi occupancy was over, and Knoblauch began to start his new life in America by marrying a girl from Florida. Her father had owned a grocery store and decided to pass it on to his son-in-law.

However, Knoblauch was appalled at what was then racial discrimination of African Americans in his community. African Americans were constantly treated like secondhand citizens and deprived of equal rights, all instances reminiscent of Knoblauch's past experience.

"This time not of religion, but color of skin," Knoblauch said. "Yet, it was discrimination all the same."

Knoblauch immediately decided to answer the call of moral courage.

In the grand opening of his store, many of his father-in-law's friends came to see this new owner. At the end of the line, there was an African American woman named Mrs. Harris who introduced herself to Knoblauch.

"This is the first time someone has addressed me as Mrs. Harris!" Mrs. Harris replied, after Knoblauch greeted her.

Knoblauch knew how one simple action could mean so much to another. This episode inspired Knoblauch even more, and he became the first man to employ African Americans in his store. Every time Mrs. Harris came to buy groceries, he would drive her home and roll down the windows so everybody in his neighborhood could see him escorting her to her house. Many people scorned Knoblauch, but he did not care because he knew he was doing the right thing.

Knoblauch's experience is one filled with moral courage, with people risking their lives to fight for a just cause.

"Do what is right," Knoblauch said to me as his final remark.

by Justin Zhu, age 14
2014 Silver Key
Hamilton High School, Chandler

A Toast to the Host

Henri Stotzel walks off the plane and heads into the airport, surrounded by people foreign to him. Though not proficient with English yet, he can still make out some parts of sentences here and there from conversations of strangers and passersby. Stotzel steps outside the gate door, and his eyes search swiftly around the waiting area for Mark Hericks, the man Stotzel has traveled over 5,500 miles to live with, but has never met.

After Skyping and emailing for weeks with families they hardly know, kids from different nationalities spend anywhere from a few short weeks to an entire school year as part of foreign exchange programs. What is the perspective of the families who welcome these students whom they meet for the first time at an airport, welcome into their homes and incorporate them as one of their own?

Hericks, a host dad to German exchange student Stotzel, a junior at Chaparral High School (CHS) in Scottsdale, Arizona, is all too familiar with hosting foreign exchange students.

"I told him from the beginning, 'you're coming here as a friend. I picked you.' My thinking is provide him a home and offer him an opportunity to have fun," Hericks said.

Hericks, a retired law enforcement officer, has been hosting students for over 15 years, making Stotzel his tenth student, following previous students that had come from countries such as Germany, the Czech Republic and Brazil.

Being a host family requires an application, interview and screening process. According to the foreign exchange program American Field Service (AFS-USA), a host family must "welcome a student into your home as a family member for one or two semesters, provide a bed and bedroom, provide an appropriate place to study, provide meals (at home and school) and provide necessary transportation."

Hericks had to fulfill all of these requirements and additionally acted as Stotzel's main source for transportation, as the students are not allowed to drive here in the states. For Hericks, being a host dad brings the opportunity to interact with kids of unique cultures and busy lifestyles.

"It's a real exchange for me. It's an exchange of culture," Hericks said. "He brings youth to my home...we hang out together a lot. I try to help him whenever I can, learning phrases and English sayings, and helping him with English class. The main thing we try to do is have fun together. Just cooking a meal can be fun."

Hericks has been hosting long enough to not be too daunted by the prospect of living with another family's son or daughter for a long period of time. He likes to keep the rules at a minimum and enjoys giving the student a chance to earn a sense of independence.

"I don't think you have to have rules, they know what the rules are. I was brought up where if you were a responsible person and you show that you can handle yourself, who are we to tell you what to do? I think that trust is more important than rules and curfews," Hericks said.

Hericks will be hosting Stotzel for the duration of the 2013-2014 school year, yet the experience for families hosting students for a semester or even just a few weeks appears to be an equally positive experience for host families.

Last year, starting in September, Alan Malone, a junior at CHS, and his family hosted a Brazilian student named Anabel Ruiz for a few months through the Scottsdale Sister Cities Association.

"Originally, I was sort of opposed to it because I'm the kind of person who likes things the way they are with order and everything, but when she actually got there, I actually kind of enjoyed the change," Malone said.

Malone would help Ruiz get from class to class, and along with family, take her to the mall and show her around Scottsdale. This helped Ruiz get acclimated to life in the U.S. because the cultural difference as well as the language can make adjusting for students difficult.

"I think one of the funniest memories was on the first night she got here. We had spaghetti and salad. She didn't know whether to put the ranch on the salad or the spaghetti," Malone said.

Despite having initial reservations about hosting, Malone accepted Ruiz as one of his own family members.

They remain in contact even now, a year later, as Malone can use her input for his debate cases.

"I'll talk to her a lot today whenever we have speech and debate topics involving Brazil, because with things like the protests that occurred there earlier in the year that were kind of big, I got her personal opinion on them and what she saw as a person living there," Malone said.

Delaney Smith, a junior at CHS, also got to experience hosting a foreign student through Chaparral's French program. Their student, Guillaume Fournier, came last February of 2013 with a group of French students from the French school Lycée Les Bressis and stayed about two weeks in the U.S. Essentially, the trip was a vacation for Fournier and an opportunity for the Smith family to show him the best attractions of Scottsdale.

"We took him hiking, and he didn't even know what hiking was. It's just so different, and I think it is really cool to learn about the differences between both France and America," Smith said.

For Smith, one of the biggest takeaways from the two-week experience was learning just how much culture can differ over borders and oceans, and how important relationships can form, even in two weeks. It is a time spent interacting with a different culture that can never be forgotten.

"We even ended up making friends with other exchange students because you all hang out together, and I also met a lot of kids at Chaparral that I didn't know," Smith said. "We all become this tight-knit group, and when they leave, it's just so sad, so you have to try and keep in touch."

by Tori Cejka, age 18
2014 Silver Key
Chaparral High School, Scottsdale

Fourteen Years Later:
The Columbine Shooting

"My friend was laughing and then it turned to crying and I thought 'my God, why is this happening to us?'" states a quote from the Columbine Memorial.

April 20, 1999, started out as a regular day at Columbine High School in Littleton, Colorado. That day soon turned into a national tragedy when two students, Eric Harris and Dylan Klebold, went to school with a plan in mind—mass murder.

Amanda Cooke was sitting in her math class at Columbine when the massacre began. Initially, she was unaware of the events unfolding around her.

"The fire alarm rang to get most of the students out of the building. We heard screams but thought it was students messing around in the hallway. We didn't really think much of it," Cooke recalled.

While the shooting continued at Columbine, Julianne Thomas and her young children were less than a mile away at Leawood Elementary School. Thomas was helping out in her son's second grade class when the school suddenly went on lockdown.

"When we got to the classroom there were rumors about a shooting, but we didn't know much, and because the students were so little, we didn't want to turn on the TV," Thomas remembered.

Rumors about a shooting were confirmed when Thomas began to see dozens of Columbine students desperately looking for refuge at nearby Leawood.

"I went to the office with my daughter in my arms to find out what was going on," Thomas said. "Leawood is the evacuation site for Columbine, and streams of frantic kids were pouring in. The lockdown was briefly lifted at Leawood, and my son's teacher urged me to take my two kids and get out of there."

Thomas arrived at her neighborhood to realize that the entire vicinity was put on lockdown while local authorities tried to maintain order in the chaos. They had not realized that by that time, the killers had already committed suicide in the Columbine Library after murdering 13 people and injuring dozens more.

Immediately after the massacre, Thomas frequently substituted for teachers who wished to attend funeral services of the fallen victims. Many of those teachers had taught the victims before they went on to high school.

Thomas witnessed a victim's young sister come to school for the first time since her brother's death.

"I remember the first day that Daniel Mauser's little sister came back to school. She was in seventh grade, and she carried several helium balloons with her from class to class that day. She had a smile and the balloons, but I knew that smile and those balloons were there to keep her from totally breaking down," Thomas recalled. "I have always thought of that moment and the courage it took for the siblings of the victims to come back to school and face the comments and questions, knowing that at any moment they might break down in front of everyone."

In 2007, the Columbine Memorial opened to the public to remember the 13 victims. The memorial is adjacent to the high school, tucked away in the corner of Clement Park in Littleton. Two aspects make the memorial: the Wall of Healing and the Ring of Remembrance. The wall surrounds the ring of plaques for each of the fallen and is engraved with quotes from injured students, parents, Columbine staff, and public officials.

A student was quoted on the wall saying, "A kid my age shouldn't have to go to that many funerals."

Another survivor recalled his mother desperately searching for him that day, saying, "Once my mom found me, she couldn't seem to let me go for the rest of the day."

The Ring of Remembrance, perhaps the most emotional part of the memorial, is made of plaques where each victim is remembered. Each plaque was written by the victim's parent(s), with the exception of one: Dave Sanders.

Dave Sanders was the teacher killed protecting his students. His life was memorialized by his two daughters. His daughters wrote on the plaque, "His final words: 'Tell my girls I love them.' We love you too, Dad."

Each victim's plaque describes their personality, their philosophies and their passions. Visitors can leave gifts underneath each plaque. Commonly seen items are baseballs, stuffed animals and porcelain angels.

A dried-up bouquet of flowers sat atop a happy birthday card underneath Cassie Bernall's plaque. Bernall was one of the ten students murdered in the Columbine Library. She has been labeled as a martyr for her faith, as some survivors reported that Harris asked Bernall if she believed in God before shooting her in the head at close range. According to the story, Bernall said "yes" and was killed for that reason. However, the story is controversial, as some survivors denied hearing the exchange between Bernall and Harris. They say Harris knelt underneath the table where Bernall was hiding and said "Peek-a-boo!" before killing her.

Fourteen years later, Cooke is now an American history and geography teacher at Columbine. She says that she knew the victims as classmates and even recalled seeing the shooters in the hallways prior to their attack. However, that did not stop her from accepting a job at Columbine.

"It feels like a regular high school," Cooke said. "It only affects other people who I tell that I teach at Columbine."

Thomas is now the librarian of the Columbine Memorial Library, which is in a separate location from the original Columbine Library where the majority of the murders occurred. She says that victims are remembered at Columbine and she tries to make sure they are thought about daily.

"I walk past a wall with the names of the victims every day, and I try to see it every day. Sometimes when something is always there, you stop noticing it. I never want to do that with that wall because those lives were important, and each and every one of them deserves to be remembered," Thomas stated.

Columbine High School and the surrounding area of Littleton have been forever changed by the Columbine Massacre, but the town is still beaming with hope towards the future and how people can improve themselves because of the shooting. The resilience is demonstrated in one prevalent quote from a student at the Columbine Memorial, which triumphantly states, "I think that this caused people to strengthen, rather than to shake their faith."

Works Consulted

"Amanda Cooke Interview." E-mail interview. 11 Sept. 2013.

Inscription, Columbine Memorial, Littleton, CO, 31 August 2013.

"Julianne Thomas Interview." E-mail interview. 24 Sept. 2013.

by BrieAnna Frank, age 16
2014 Silver Key
Maryvale High School, Phoenix

Bridging Divides or Banning Discussion?

In 2010, Tucson's controversial Mexican-American Studies (MAS) program was shut down, and several books about Latin-American history were banned from Arizona's schools. In October of 2013, the Arizona Department of Education approved the program's replacement, "culturally relevant" classes, and the Tucson Unified School District (TUSD) reintroduced the books into its classrooms. To some, the fact that the program and books were ever banned at first seems shocking, especially given that Tucson's population is 42 percent Hispanic or Latino, according to the United States Census Bureau.

With books like *Occupied America: A History of Chicanos* and *Critical Race Theory*, classes entered a discussion of race far removed from the mainstream of ethnic studies in public schools, focusing on topics such as white privilege and modern oppression. According to students and teachers who supported it, the program inspired a strong sense of cultural identity and encouraged students to represent their ethnicities positively, motivating them to achieve in school.

MAS program creator Miguel Ortega, in an interview with journalist Jeff Biggers, asserted that "gang violence on our Tucson streets might be better mitigated by celebrating the cultural and historical assets" of Mexican-American culture. But, according to Tom Horne, Arizona's current Attorney General and former Superintendent of Schools who launched opposition to MAS, it was too divisive.

As reported by the Huffington Post, the law passed to ban programs like MAS in Arizona (House Bill 2281) targets such programs as promoting resentment, addressing students of a particular ethnic group, and inappropriately advocating ethnic solidarity.

Justification for banning the books was that "any book can be inappropriate in a classroom if it's inappropriately used," said current Arizona Superintendent of Public Instruction John Huppenthal, when interviewed by *Fox News Latino*. His objection was to the program, not the books, but banning the books was the option chosen.

However, this reasoning did not just include books about Mexican-American history. One banned book was Shakespeare's play *The Tempest*, due to its themes of colonialism. Such vague reasons for a book ban automatically span a wide variety of books, none of which are inappropriately subversive.

Unfortunately, the situation seems to point to continued resentment and distrust between Arizona's politicians and its Mexican-American population, fostered by miscommunication and a lack of understanding.

According to some, "the race you are born into isn't relevant," but to many Americans, especially the ones involved in ethnic studies programs, their cultural history is an important aspect of their identity.

Reconciling ethnic and national labels may be complex, but need not be negative; it's about celebrating the different parts of identity and how they make us unique.

A new cultural studies program has been returned to schools, and the banned books are back in some classrooms, so it seems that the clashing sides have begun to find middle ground. Both perspectives are understandable.

On one hand, it is important that Mexican-American students in Arizona are encouraged to succeed, feel pride in their cultural identity, feel safe to explore their history, and discuss topics like racism and oppression. On the other hand, it is important they feel confident in their American identity as well, and that racial divisions are not fostered between students. There is a careful balance that needs to be struck, and hopefully, the new ethnic studies program becomes one step closer to it.

Works Consulted

Biggers, Jeff. "Defying Arizona's Ethnic Studies Ban: Tucson Freedom Summer Draws on Mexican American Studies History." *Huffington Post*. The Huffington Post, 27 July 2012. Web. 3 November 2013.

Liu, Eric. "The Whitewashing of Arizona." *Time*. Time Magazine, 1 May 2012. Web. 3 November 2013.

Planas, Roque. "Arizona's Law Banning Mexican-American Studies Curriculum is Unconstitutional, Judge Rules."*HuffPost*. The Huffington Post, 14 March 2013. Web. 3 November 2013.

Planas, Roque. "Neither Banned Nor Allowed: Mexican American Studies in Limbo in Arizona." *Fox News Latino*. Fox News, 19 Apr. 2012. Web. 3 Nov. 2013.

"Tucson (city) QuickFacts from the US Census Bureau." *Tucson (city) QuickFacts from the U.S. Census Bureau*. U.S. Census Bureau, n.d. Web. 3 Nov. 2013.

by Navya Dasari, age 16
2014 Silver Key
BASIS Scottsdale, Scottsdale

PERSUASIVE

Editor Introduction by Billy Gerchick

Rhetoric, according to Aristotle, is the "art of persuasion," and authors may use "available means" to achieve purpose. The persuasive section's purpose is *not* to give SAT and AP models—you have those already; it's *not* to persuade you to change your mind—enough of that going around. You *are* encouraged to read these compositions and then use available means to discuss, research, and develop your own thoughts on five important issues.

"Balance," by Justin Garner, emphasizes a need to re-evaluate personal priorities. Stirling McDaniel prompts humanity to appreciate the importance of imagination, reminding us that the okapi really exists. Rather than society simply blaming media and celebrities, Max Bartlett prompts Americans to consider if and how "mental wellness and social conditions" impact gun violence incidents in America. Last, and an American Voices nominee this year, Kathleen Wu frames the illegal immigration debate, something that's divided Arizonans for years, in the form of a Socratic dialogue between an advocate of the controversial SB 1070 law and an opponent of it. The conversation itself never took place, but Wu uses research and dialogue from non-fiction sources to frame a complex issue as a civil conversation. Regardless of your politics, Wu's characters model a civil tone that all Arizonans can aspire to.

So enjoy these compositions, and at least consider "when to speak your mind and when to shut up," "that beautiful mixture, half-lion, half-eagle," "the mental wellness and social conditions of the assailants," and how "reasonable suspicion" could potentially apply. Above all, use available means to develop your thoughts.

Balance

When a tightrope walker takes his first steps away from terra firma onto a wire, what does he think about? How about not falling? Body position, muscle tension, rope tightness, and weight distribution must be constantly evaluated as he maneuvers across the rope. There's just one central goal in mind: balance.

Physically, the task of tightrope walking must be an ordeal. Every muscle constantly contracting and relaxing, every ounce of focus on staying on that wire, immense coordination, strength, and a perfectly balanced inner ear are all essential for success.

But there's another type of balance that a tightrope walker needs: mental balance. He must decide how to position his arms, which muscles to flex, which muscles to relax, and when and where to shift his weight. Because if any one of these actions is given too much or too little attention, then the walker is certain to fall to his death.

So, it's a trick. These two types of balance allow the tightrope walker to stay perched on his wire and eventually reach his goal.

But surely, balance in itself is a contradiction. It denotes stability but constantly changes. When we are little, balance is simply the ability to walk or to stand on a skateboard. But then, we learn that balance can mean everything from creating a budget to managing a business, or even maintaining a healthy marriage. Balance is knowing when to speak your mind and when to shut up. Balance is knowing when to get homework done and when to catch up on sleep.

Balance makes us who we are because it forces us to make decisions. Consider a teenage girl struggling with anorexia. She must use balance when she decides to eat. Consider a steroid-dependent muscle head. He must use balance when he decides to take time off from working out. And consider an obsessed video-gamer. He must use balance when he turns off his game console and goes for a walk outside. We may not realize it, but balance affects all of our lives simply because we exist.

Balance exists in everything. Without balance, the world as it is today would not be. It applies to all things, and it affects all things, and the second we stop using balance in life, we will, like the tightrope walker, fall.

by Justin Garner, age 17
2014 Silver Key
Mountain View High School, Mesa

A Message to Humanity

Why did you do this? Did you feel *obligated* to ruin the world?

You went around and questioned everything. Everything! *Why is the sky blue? Why is the sky black? What are those sparkling dots? Why is the Sun up there? Where does it go? Why does the Moon change?*

Would it really have been so terrible to have a sense of wonder, of mystery, in this world? I used to love you humans. Really, I did. Once.

Back when you saw witches fly across the face of the moon, when you saw one-eyed giants in fossils, when you wrote "Here Be Dragons" on maps. I loved to walk amongst you and listen to your tales, your stories, explaining the inexplicable. I loved to fear the gods you saw. I loved to hunt the magical stags with you. I loved to cower in fear on the Winter Solstice, the longest night of the year. I loved to celebrate the Harvest Season, to give thanks to your many gods for a good crop. I loved to paint pictures of unicorns and dragons and griffins in your stories, on your walls.

Especially griffins. That beautiful mixture, half-lion half-eagle. Now, what do you have? The okapi? So many stories and tales and myths to account to that creature!

But no. You humans, you despicable humans, you *dissected* it, you found the *truth*.

Unicorns? "Fake!" you proudly proclaim. "Narwhal horns were used to fake unicorn horns."

Mermaids? "Lonely sailors thinking manatees were women."

Dragons? "Silly old people living a thousand years ago mistook dinosaur and whale bones for dragons. Oh, and the idiots thought crocodiles might have been dragons, too."

Those are my friends! I silently seethe, listening in on your conversations. Those are my friends you're talking about!

You humans take the mystery out of everything! *Why is the sky blue?* "Well, Deary, molecules in the atmosphere scatter light a certain way." *Where does the Sun go?* "It doesn't go anywhere, darling. The Earth is rotating so that we don't see it half the time. People on the other side of the Earth see it when we don't."

No! You ruin everything! Why must you be so scientific? So calculated and precise? Why can't you just lie on the grass and wonder? Wonder why the sky is blue and not purple, and not go look it up on the Internet or ask your chemistry teacher? Why can't you just accept it, think about it? Make up some stories, some myths, some legends? *What are eclipses?* "A dragon has eaten the sun! Bang some pots, frighten it away!" *What is lightning?* "The gods are angry; they are warring up in the clouds."

But listen. Just listen, don't ask questions. Listen to the birdsong, the whisper, the howling of the wind. Listen to the trees as they creak and talk to one another. Listen to the fire crackling, dancing.

Listen to me.

Listen to what I am going to say.

I am everything you reject. I represent the things you see in the corner of your eye, the things you hear in the dead of night murmuring to each other. I walk among you, but who am I? Don't analyze what I'm telling you. I'm not your hopes and fears personified. I'm not history talking. I'm not humanity's childish tendencies brought to life to exemplify how much science has destroyed the part of childhood that everyone misses—the wonder.

No. No, of course not.

I am me. But the simple, undeniable fact of my existence defies your science: you can't detect me with your instruments. You can't pin me down and dissect me. You can't tape wires to my head and monitor my brain waves. You can't decode my DNA.

You see me, and all of a sudden – dragons might exist. Witches might fly at night. Unicorns might still be here, hidden in deep recesses of the forests. Who's to say that giants don't lurk in caves on high mountaintops? Trolls? Are they under the bridge? What about all the gods in the old texts, on the cave walls?

And griffins. Do they exist?

The okapi exists. I exist. And I am old, far too old—but not infinitely old. Things came before me.

Now it's up to you, Human, to decide what. Make it something brilliant.

by Stirling McDaniel, age 14
2014 Gold Key
BASIS Scottsdale, Scottsdale

Pointing Fingers

"When will it happen next?" Millions of Americans constantly ask themselves this exact question about violent firearm attacks. Every day on the news, it seems that more and more stories are reported about gun control, causes of violent crime, and methods of stopping future attacks. Contrary to popular belief, violence in the media does not significantly contribute to acts of violence in youth, and other factors such as a lack of mental healthcare influence such events to a much greater degree.

Since the inception of the video game industry, many adversaries of such media have claimed that content within computer games causes young people to commit violent acts. Over time, people have taken this position with little factual evidence. For example, violent juvenile crime in the United States has declined as violent video game popularity has increased. According to fbi.gov, the arrest rate for juvenile murders has fallen 71.9% between 1995 and 2008, and the arrest rate for all juvenile violent crimes has declined 49.3%. In this same period, video game sales have more than quadrupled (*Essential Facts about the Computer and Video Game Industry*). Games do not cause real-world attacks. In fact, video games may actually help in preventing violence.

In a recent study published in the *Journal of Youth and Adolescence,* researchers found that violent video games such as *Mortal Kombat, Halo,* and *Grand Theft Auto* did not cause high-risk teens to become aggressive bullies or delinquents, and can, in fact, have a calming effect and reduce aggressive behavior. Another study done by the *Journal of Adolescent Health* found that 45 percent of boys played video games because "it helps me get my anger out" and 62 percent played because it "helps me relax." For many young people, video games have provided a safe haven where they are able to take out emotions in a virtual setting. However, video games are not the only form of media to be targeted.

After the shooting at Columbine High School in Littleton, Colorado, on April 20, 1999, that left 13 dead and 21 injured, many citizens and public figures pointed fingers at video games, movies, and music as causes of the shooting. Marilyn Manson, a rock star who many blamed for the attacks, was interviewed after the events. When asked what he would say to the Columbine killers had they still been alive, Manson stated, "I wouldn't say a word to them, I would listen to what they had to say, and that's what no one did" (Moore, *Bowling for Columbine*). Could improved mental healthcare impact the rate of shootings?

On the widely used Debate.org, over 80 percent of people said that a lack of mental health causes a vast majority of gun violence. One anonymous respondent said, "Mental health care is very much ignored in the United States, and as a consequence, many dangerously ill individuals go untreated." In addition, significant mental healthcare experts have correlated mental illness to mass shootings. Dr. Jeffery Lieberman, head of the American Psychiatric Association, stated, "in the wake of these series of mass violent episodes, there has been a greater attention, a greater debate and more legislative action to try and address the root cause of the problem, which is the inadequacy and lack of quality comprehensive mental health care services." By means of bringing attention to the lack of mental health support in the U.S., perhaps many lives could be saved.

What is the answer? Although many are quick to blame entertainment media for aggressive action in the real world, the genuine cause may lie much deeper than most want to dig. Because statistics show that games, movies, books, and television shows are not the root for most attacks, it is vital to examine the mental wellness and social conditions of the assailants in order to gain insight into how the next Columbine, Aurora, or Sandy Hook can be prevented. If a strong focus on mental health begins to occur in this country, we won't need to ask, "When will it happen next?"

Works Consulted

Bowling for Columbine. Dir. Michael Moore. United Artists, 2002. Film.

"Crime in the United States, 2008." *Crime in the United States 2008*. FBI, n.d. Web.

"Essential Facts about the Computer and Video Game Industry." Entertainment Software Association. May 2009. Print.

Ferguson, J. Christopher, and Cheryl K. Olson. "Video game violence among 'vulnerable' populations: the impact of violent games on delinquency and bullying among children with clinically elevated depression or attention deficit symptoms." *Journal of Youth and Adolescence.* 2013. Print.

Almeriqi, B. Jason, Lee Baer, Eugene V. Beresin, Lawrence A. Kutner, Armand M. Nicholi, Cheryl K. Olson, and Dorothy E. Warner. "Factors Correlated with Violent Video Game Use by Adolescent Boys and Girls." *Journal of Adolescent Health*. July 2007. Print.

"Can the U.S. Find Consensus in Better Mental Health Access to Curb Gun Violence?" *PBS*. PBS, 16 Dec. 2013. Web.

by Max Bartlett, age 15
2014 Silver Key
Chaparral High School, Scottsdale

Two Years Later:
Illegal Immigration in Arizona
A Socratic Dialogue between a Critic (**CR**) and an Advocate (**AD**) of SB 1070

November, 2012

CR: So, you live in Phoenix, Arizona?

AD: I do. And you're here to ask me about...?

CR: SB 1070. Have its stringent enforcement policies and controversial efforts yielded benefits?

AD: I believe so. According to the Phoenix Law Enforcement Association, several major Arizona cities have "experienced a 30-year low crime rate" since SB 1070 was enacted (qtd. in Pearce). Drug cartel killings and kidnappings have dramatically decreased, and the "state prison population is declining for the first time" (Pearce). The well-being of legal Arizonans must be protected, and just one of the merits of SB 1070 is a safer, stronger state.

CR: Interesting. But perhaps SB 1070 itself is not responsible for the substantial drop in crime rates. Perhaps the increased vigilance of police forces in the state has cautioned criminals into lying low. Once the controversy surrounding the law fades and the zealous enforcement subsides, however, might we expect a resurgence in misdemeanors? Shouldn't Arizona emphasize stricter enforcement of drug cartel and kidnapping laws instead of devoting its energies to upholding an immigration law?

AD: Illegal immigration is inextricably tied to criminal activity. An estimated 80 to 95 percent of illegal immigrants who cross the U.S.-Mexico border are brought over by "coyotes," human smugglers that require fees from their customers in return for passage to the States (McNeill et al.). If clients fail to pay, kidnapping, human trafficking, injury, or even murder may ensue. Tightening border control and discouraging immigration has reduced violence against illegal immigrants by diminishing dangerous crossings and stemming the smuggling business.

CR: What of those still determined to come? The new laws make it even more difficult for them to enter America. Smugglers who are out of business will require even higher fees from desperate migrants; illegal immigrants will be forced to take more dangerous routes hidden from law enforcers (McNeill et al.). Why should Americans allow fellow humans to jeopardize their lives to fulfill dreams or escape persecution? Doesn't that contradict the very premise of American freedom?

AD: Those immigrants can "fulfill dreams" legally. They can "escape persecution" legally. Millions wait to legally enter the U.S. every year. An increasing illegal population forces those who apply for green cards and visas to wait longer. Illegal immigrants delay other immigrants' aspirations.

CR: But most illegal immigrants don't have a chance of entering the U.S. by legal means. There is "virtually no process for unskilled immigrants without relations in the U.S. to apply for permanent legal residence" (Flynn and Dalmia). Employers are banned by both federal law and SB 1070 from hiring illegal immigrants, even though work is often the only pathway to documentation. Many who desire better lives and greater economic opportunities are barred by the government from achieving legal status in America.

AD: That may be true, but granting amnesty to illegal immigrants feeds that vicious cycle. Permitting illegal immigration leads to less legal immigration, which in turn leads to more illegal immigration. It may seem paradoxical, but to grant greater equality and better chances to illegal immigrants, we must first level the playing field for those seeking to enter legally.

CR: Touché. But even if instituting harsh policies now will allow more people to enter in the long run, won't short-term "attrition" of illegal immigration hurt the already weak Arizona economy? Though illegal immigrants may not pay taxes, they still contributed about "8 percent of the state's economic output" in 2004 and held around 280,000 full-time jobs in 2008, before SB 1070 was signed into law (University of Arizona study, qtd. in "Illegal").

AD: On the contrary, an exodus of illegal immigrants would provide legal residents job opportunities and boost Arizona's economy. As Gallup economist Dennis Jacobe observed, allowing companies to hire cheaper illegal labor mirrors corporate outsourcing to countries like China and India. Reducing the number of undocumented employees opens up economic opportunities for tax-paying, legal workers, raising wages and invigorating the economy.

CR: Many legal residents would be unwilling to take those vacant "economic opportunities," however. Princeton sociologist Doug Massey predicts that few will accept work at the same pay illegal immigrants did: "The wages you would have to pay to get somebody to go out in the desert and harvest watermelons would make watermelons uncompetitive in markets" (qtd. in Kurtzleben).

AD: I see your point. But diminishing illegal employment in Arizona "boosts pay and conditions for other workers" and encourages transparency in state businesses (Kurtzleben). The low wages given to illegal workers create unwanted competition at deplorable recompense; SB 1070 helps curb that sort of competition and provides a fairer workplace for citizens, residents, and legal immigrants. Furthermore, SB 1070 reduces the burden illegal immigrants place on legal taxpayers. Illegal immigrants send their children to public schools, borrow from city libraries, occupy state prisons, and use other public services without contributing taxes themselves. Reducing illegal immigration will not only open up higher paying jobs for legal workers, it will lessen the tax money spent on people who do not pay to access public services and facilities.

CR: Okay, so maybe Arizona's law does benefit legal immigrants and citizens, economically and socially. But you still haven't convinced me of its consideration for illegal immigrants. Not only are they still barred from legal job opportunities in the U.S., they are constantly on the run from smugglers demanding payment and Arizona police pushing deportation. In addition, SB 1070 has received national attention for the unprecedented power it gives to local law enforcers. Any officer who harbors "reasonable suspicion" that someone is "an alien" can make a "reasonable attempt [...] to determine the immigration status" of that person ("Senate Bill" 1). This clause has been brought before the U.S. Supreme Court with charges of racial profiling. Many believe that the phrases "reasonable attempts" and "suspicions" invite subjective discrimination.

AD: That is perhaps one of the most misunderstood and disputed portions of the Arizona law. Governor Jan Brewer states that SB 1070 is a "secondary enforcement" law – an official must have a "reasonable suspicion that [someone] is breaking some *other* law before [he] can ask a person about their [*sic*] legal status" (1). Inquiries about immigration status, therefore, cannot stem from racial discrimination; searches must be based on normal suspicions of criminal activity.

CR: If that's true, most of the country, including prominent politicians such as the 2012 presidential candidates, misconstrue a critical provision of SB 1070. Most still perceive the law as an extreme means to ignoble ends. In the second presidential debate, President Obama claimed that "part of the Arizona law said that law enforcement officers could stop folks because they suspected maybe they looked like they might be undocumented workers and check their papers," an unfounded claim, according to Governor Brewer's statement ("Presidential"). In response to an accusation for backing the "reasonable suspicion" clause, Romney declared that he "did not say that Arizona law was a model for the nation in that aspect" ("Presidential"). To satisfy moderate voters and distance themselves from accusations of ethnic profiling, both Obama and Romney denied support for the Arizona law. How can the security and economic benefits of SB 1070 be reaped honorably if many nationwide still do not understand its basic intent?

AD: Law enforcers and advocates of the bill must abide by and publicize the "secondary enforcement" nature of SB 1070 (Brewer 1). They must emphasize that discrimination cannot play a role in detentions or arrests. They must also state that SB 1070 is not a catch-all solution to state and federal immigration problems; it is only a statute meant to help mitigate crime-related and economic issues caused by the growing illegal population.

CR: I see. SB 1070 should not be the only type of response to our broken immigration system. So, along with enacting stricter illegal immigration measures like Arizona's law, would you support reforming the legal process to give greater opportunities to impoverished and persecuted foreigners?

AD: Absolutely. A clearer legal immigration system must be coupled with uncompromising illegal immigration laws to ensure safer and better futures for citizens, legal residents, and applicants for legal immigration.

CR: That is indubitable—I wholeheartedly agree.

As of June 2012, the United States Supreme Court has upheld the "reasonable suspicion" clause of SB 1070, but has struck down the provision prohibiting illegal immigrants from seeking work in Arizona, the provision requiring illegal immigrants to carry their alien registration documents, and the provision authorizing officers to arrest immigrants with "probable cause." The decision will hopefully serve as a catalyst for further action on the immigration problem.

Works Consulted

Arizona Forty-Ninth Legislature. "Senate Bill 1070." *State of Arizona*. AZLeg.gov, 2010. PDF file.

Brewer, Janice K. "Common Myths and Facts Regarding Senate Bill 1070."*Office of the Arizona Governor Janice K.*

Brewer. AZGovernor.gov, 2012. PDF file.

CBS News. "Illegal Immigrants Leaving Arizona over New Law." *CBS News*. CBS Interactive Inc., 29 Apr. 2010. Web. 28 Oct. 2012.

Dalmia, Shikha, Mike Flynn, and Terry Colon. "What Part of Legal Immigration Don't You Understand?" *Reason* Oct. 2008: 33. Web. 28 Oct. 2012.

Gallup Business Journal. "The Real Impact of Illegal Immigration." *Gallup Business Journal*. Gallup, Inc., 14 Sept. 2006. Web. 28 Oct. 2012.

Kurtzleben, Danielle. "Arizona Businesses Hope to Put SB 1070 Behind Them." *U.S. News*. U.S. News & World Report, 25 June 2012. Web. 28 Oct. 2012.

McNeill, Jena Baker, Ray Walser, and Jessica Zuckerman. "The Human Tragedy of Illegal Immigration: Greater Efforts

Needed to Combat Smuggling and Violence." *The Heritage Foundation*. The Heritage Foundation, 22 June 2012. Web. 28 Oct. 2012.

Pearce, Russell. "Arizona's Immigration Law is Consitutional—and Already Working." *U.S. News*. U.S. News & World Report, 23 Apr. 2012. Web. 28 Oct. 2012.

Politico. "Presidential Debate Transcript, Questions." *Politico*. Politico, 16 Oct. 2012. Web. 28 Oct. 2012.

Wall Street Journal. "Court Splits on Arizona Law." Wall Street Journal. Wall Street Journal, 25 June 2012. Web. 22 December 2012.

by Kathleen Wu, age 14
2014 Gold Key, American Voices Nominee
BASIS Scottsdale, Scottsdale

HUMOR

Editor Introduction by Julie Cain

Okay, okay: what do you get when you cross a teenager's perspective on the world with the foibles of modern society? Anyone? No?

Truthfully—I'm not quite sure, either, but however it turns out, it had better have a bloody good sense of humor, or we're all doomed.

Most folks don't realize just how difficult it is to write humorously. Can they toss out an opportune one-liner amongst friends? No problem. Mimic a stand-up comic? Certainly. Make a pun that causes others to roll their terrible eyes and lose their terrible lunches? Psh, hey, why not? But when it comes to the subtle quirkiness that makes for good humor, authors have got to dig deeper, to find the tidbits of life that everyone else takes so seriously, so they can poke their fingers in its sides and remind us that we're not doomed to misery... as long as we keep our senses of humor.

Fortunately for this section, teenagers have a natural talent for finding these tender tidbits and mocking them mercilessly. The writers selected to represent this year's humor category have navigated our human idiosyncrasies in brilliantly well-crafted voices. Alejandra Katz mocks the self-aggrandizing nature of bureaucracies and contrasts them with the innocence of youth. Anthony Mirabito tells a tale of growing up, challenging authority, and standing stark naked in the face of our fears. Bailey Vidler illustrates the fickle impulses of the youthful heart—what could possibly go wrong?

Their stories take us on a trip through Hell and back, streaking all the way.

A Hellish Problem

Although many people like to picture Hell as an eternally screaming pit of anguished, corrupted souls, the reality is much worse: it is a bureaucracy.

It was once said that Hell had been an orderly, even efficient place. However, with the introduction of Order DCLXVI, longer work days and several new procedures plagued the demons and applying occupants, resulting in the gradual accumulation of beings outside the Gates of Hell. No longer was there even a semblance of a line on the dry, rocky plains surrounding the Gates of Hell; instead, there was a mass of Earth's finest citizens, shoving and elbowing each other to get a chance to submit their paperwork to the lone secretary of the Gates, Bulobtepziel, affectionately known to the demon officials as "Betty."

A riot—gruesome even by the Underworld's standards—had erupted earlier that week over one of the many monthly waves of new policies. This time, it was the new pens-only policy. In an effort to cut down on the budget, the High Committee of the Diabolically Inclined had declared pencil sharpeners and the subsequent pencils superfluous, instating pens as the official writing utensils of the Underworld.

At this point, pens were even projected to replace the previously preferred medium, blood. Much to the chagrin of the zealots who loved the dramatics, blood was now starting to look too expensive, despite the fact that it was only used by high-ranking officials.

These soulless policies left the applicants in an infuriating conundrum.

Not only did they, the applicants, have to wait in this line—no, mob—of people to acquire Form Y—a behemoth of a form, ranging from 666,666,666 to 666,666,666,666 pages, depending on the individual and the severity of the sin— but they now also had to go to rejoin the end of the "line" that stretched for miles and miles to wait for a pen to actually fill out The Form. The Form itself left no room for errors; it had to be filled out immaculately, without a single comma or semicolon out of place (lest they have to start the process over again), whilst simultaneously looking out for the lava geysers that erupted spontaneously, carrying their flaming victims to the end of the "line," destroying their paperwork and pen in the process.

It was, indeed, a sight to behold, watching the denizens of this wasteland shriek inanely as they rode these notorious waves of injustice, decades and centuries of paperwork lost by simply being in the wrong place at the wrong time.

It was unanimously agreed that if there was one thing more infernal than filling out paperwork, it was filling out paperwork to receive your eternal punishment. And even more infernal than that—having to do it more than once.

However, those who argued that they were already in Hell were referred to Betty, who would always answer sinisterly with a malicious grin and a diabolical snigger that, no, Hell was much worse than that.

On a particularly desolate day, the monotony of exploding lava geysers and hair-pulling misery was punctured by a rare spectacle: a lone demon—most likely a lesser imp—covered in small horns and boils from head to toe, frantically flapping his pathetic wings through the crowds (enraging several beings as they tried to snatch the loose pieces of Form Y caught in the gust out of the air), making his way through the Gates of Hell.

This imp, known as Hekiel, continued until he reached a lava field, approaching a gathering of cubicles that was reserved specifically for his ilk. As soon as he landed, he wasted no time. The urgent business at hand was unlike any other, and he had to inform the important higher-ups of the situation.

He soon entered a cubicle and accosted a fellow lumpy demon, Fahsxaas—equally hideous, with tentacles and eyes protruding from his spherical body—who looked on the edge of brain death as he mindlessly played a computer game amidst the mountains of collapsing paperwork. Hekiel whispered into what he presumed was the ear—at least, what he *hoped* was the ear—of the tentacle beast, causing a flurry of squawks and incredulous looks. They both paused momentarily, looking at each other darkly, and then took off once again into the air.

Perhaps because he was preoccupied with the current matter, or perhaps because he had just received his Flyer's

Permit, the imp nearly collided with another demon in the sky, Qahtekeach, a furry gargoyle with an obscenely large nose. Although Qahtekeach was only one rank above the other two, it didn't stop him from lording over them as if he was the Prince of Darkness—that is, until he heard what was going on. After many indignant whispers, the trio decided to head to Abaddon's lair.

Now, Abaddon was a demon who liked to think he was unlike any other demon. He was Lord Commander of the several demon legions, overseer of one of the Circles of Hell, Tempter of the Bodily Vices in his spare time (not that anyone had much time anymore, these days), and wasn't too shabby looking, either (at least by Hell's standards).

However, despite this plethora of charming qualities, Abaddon had learned that a demon could be Lucifer himself and still not be exempt from the daily workload that, at times, seemed worse than the punishments reserved for the sinners.

Abaddon was in the middle of said torture when a knock on his door interrupted him. *That was peculiar,* he thought, glancing up at the clock. He didn't have tea with Beelzebub until 3.

"Enter!"

In rushed three underlings, faces contorted in varying levels of perturbation.

"Sir, there's a human in Hell!" one of them squeaked.

Abaddon's pen paused on the paper. "Yes, Infidel. As you know, there are *many* humans in Hell."

"No, Oh Terrorizing Shadow of the Night," said the exceedingly tentacley one. "We mean that there's a manspawn on the loose in the Outer Circles!"

"A child is rare, but not unheard of. Now, if that's all –"

"But, Oh Dark Harbinger of Death, He who Bequeaths Sorrow Upon Mortals – "

Abaddon made an exasperated noise.

" – Uh, what I mean to say is, the manspawn is, uh, innocent. Sinless. It shouldn't be in Hell at all."

Abaddon looked up at the trio disbelievingly. "That should be an issue for the Department of Demonic Affairs, not me."

"But Oh, Grand Master of the Depraved, Adramelech is on leave," wailed the ball of tentacles. "He left with his family for the Vatican last week." Abaddon groaned. "All right. Show me where the child is."

Abaddon followed the trio to the Outer Circles of Hell toward a containment cell reserved only for the most violent of demons. Outside was a small gathering of distressed-looking demons who wasted no time in addressing Abaddon. It was worse than expected. The fiend had offed several demons, and Abaddon needed to do something about it before the situation got real attention. Choosing a middle-ranking demon named Buer and the tentacle mass ("Fahsxaas, your Darkness") to serve as his body guards, Abaddon steeled himself and ducked into the small cell, occupied by a wooden table and two chairs, set up in the typical interrogatory fashion.

At the other end of a table sat a small, plump mass of skin, clothes, and hair—Abaddon decided it had to be a female if there was that much hair. Abaddon tried to guess an age, but it had been such a long time since he had last seen a young human that he doubted it would be correct.

As the demons entered, she stood up and curtsied a, "how do you do?" before sitting back down again.

Not for the first time, Abaddon lamented the incompetence of the demons in Hell. Bested by a little girl. How humiliating.

He motioned for Buer to sit in the chair opposite the girl. Abaddon wasn't going to get caught up in her gimmicks, no matter how innocent-looking she was. Better Buer than him.

The girl gazed at them with large doe-eyes. "I'm looking for my father. Have you seen him?"

Buer squinted at her bemusedly. "Little girl, do you know where you are?"

The girl blinked. "Of course I do! I'm in Texas. Daddy always said that, if you looked closely enough, you could see the fire through the cracks of the ground."

In the background, Fahsxaas coughed nervously.

"You must one of the cows that the cowboys herd up," she gushed. "I can't say I've ever seen a talking, flying cow, but it's nice to meet you."

Buer froze, baffled at the little girl's insolence.

"*Cow?*" he spat, frothing at the mouth. "*Cow? You dare challenge the great power of Buer? The All-Powerful Buer?*" Encouraged by her polite, questioning stare, Buer escalated.

"*I am the Lord of Darkness! Harbinger of Pestilence and Roar of the Damned! The Fist of the Infernal and Destroyer of Children! I AM THE NIGHT!*"

Unfurling his wings and slamming his hands on the table in a thunderous, awesome display of might, he rose to full height—and promptly banged his head on the low-hanging ceiling.

The girl immediately stood up, her face the epitome of concern. "Are you all right?" she asked, reaching out to pat Buer consolingly on one of his hands—alarming both Abaddon and Fahsxaas, who flung themselves backward to avoid her while screeching profanities. Upon contact with her hand, Buer exploded in a cacophony of noise and colors, causing Abaddon and Fahsxaas to flee the room as if the demons of Hell itself were on their heels. They reached the outside, veterans of the traumatizing event.

"Infidels," Abaddon breathed to the remaining demons in the group, trying to keep his calm. "I have a task for you. Search the Catalogues of the Damned and find the girl's father. If he's anything like that monstrosity, then he should've gotten through a loophole in the paperwork or something—though he probably isn't as sinless as her, or else we would've heard about another exploding terror by now—"

"Well, I don't know, maybe he *is* innocent," chirped Hekiel. "Did you hear about that guy we got last week?"

The demons exchanged quizzical glances.

"You don't mean that codger who died of a heart attack during confession before the priest could officially absolve him of his sins?" asked Qahtekeach.

"No, that was ages ago," Fahsxaas interjected. "You're talking about the guy who died with one of those new golden communicating thingies—what were they? Myphones? Youphones?"

"– Iphones – "

"– Right, Iphone, in his hand." Fahsxaas' voice dropped down to a conspirator's whisper. "I heard that Old Grimmy mistook that for the worship of an idol and brought him here instead of Heaven."

A hushed silence grew over the group.

"Poor Grimmy," Qahtekeach said solemnly. "He's getting too old for the job."

Hekiel sighed. "Yeah, but he can't retire now, can he? The Internal Bureau of the Infernal keeps on lowering his pension every year."

Fahsxaas shook his tentacley head, mourning the fate of the denizens of Hell. "There truly ain't no rest for the wicked, is there?"

"Duly noted," Abaddon dryly remarked, looking thoroughly irritated. "Now, go find the girl's father. I don't care if he's lived the life of a saint or eats little children for breakfast. Just *find him.*"

Unfortunately for Abaddon, at that precise moment, the skies darkened ominously, parting with a crackle of thunder to reveal the Prince of Hell. Lucifer landed gracefully on the ground, sporting an elegant suit. For hating humans so much, he sure liked to look like them.

Lucifer addressed the demons in a delicate purr.

"Gentlemen. What seems to be the problem? I take that it couldn't have been too hard to locate and contain the child?

No one answered. They were too terrified, as their negligence had caused the death of several demons.

Lucifer gave them The Look and walked toward the cell to retrieve the girl. He exited the cell, the girl by his side. The girl frowned at him. "Are you going to help me find my daddy?"

Lucifer smiled menacingly. "Of course, poppet." He crouched to her eye level and gestured toward the volcano-like landscape. "There is nothing that I can't fix, for I am the Angel of Light, the Adversary, the Roaring Lion –"

Abaddon groaned internally. The demons in Hell had bored each other to death with the recitations of titles so much that having a new audience (even if it was just a little girl) had caused everyone to burst into a flood of self-affirmations.

" – The Serpent of Old, the Tempter, and the Ruler of Demons. I can give you anything you want in this world."

Abaddon shuddered. In many ways, Lucifer was more terrifying with his suave words and trickeries than his wrathful side, Satan. Abaddon almost feared for the girl—after all, she was facing Lucifer—but then he saw the little girl's mouth curl into a smile so innocently wicked that even the Ruler of Demons faltered for a second.

The girl reached forward, intent on hugging the Devil.

"So, let me get this straight," Beelzebub enunciated deliberately, taking a sip from his tea. "You're saying that there was a little girl—a sinless girl, who should've by all accounts been in Heaven, who, by some inconceivable reason, ended up down here."

Abaddon nodded.

"And then, this girl, not even half the size of most demons, went around poking them," Beelzebub drawled, "resulting in the death of most of the Cabinet of the Despoilers."

Abaddon nodded.

"And further yet, this girl *hugged* Lucifer, causing a detonation of the likes that Hell has never seen before, leaving the Underworld without a ruler."

Abaddon stared at Beelzebub with a pained look and slowly bowed his head in confirmation.

Beelzebub sighed, setting down his tea cup. "Abaddon."

"Yes, Beelzebub?"

"You've been drinking Spirit Tea again."

by Alejandra Katz, age 18
2014 Gold Key
Ironwood Ridge High School, Tucson

A Burly Perrywinkle and
Half-Naked Egyptians

"Son, I am going to have to ask you to remove the loincloth and exit the building immediately." A mountain of Samoan brick was tilting his neck in my direction and glaring rather disapprovingly at my choice of dress. His nostrils flared with the aggression of a gorilla, and like a gorilla, he was all muscle; even his cheeks appeared to lift weights. I was trying, without much success, not to gawk at the size of his calloused, criminal-strangling hands. This was not someone you wanted to pick a fight with. But honestly, what better way to show up at The Egyptian Empire Festival, or as my friend and I liked to call it, The Bare Body Bonanza. I considered it stroke of genius. Loincloths are pretty much a necessity at times like this.

The guard flexed his enormous bicep and seemed to consider my pathetically frail legs that showed with perfect clarity below the hem of my loincloth. "Do not make me give you a second warning. Come back when you are fully clothed and slightly more defined." He chuckled to himself at that last comment and resigned to staring at the crowd of incoming people, as if I had already left. I don't know about you, but I definitely wouldn't meet Ramses the Great in a pair of Levis.

Slinking my way back into the throng of the moving crowd, I shifted my way towards the center of the bodies. Being skinny can help with that. Everyone around me was dressed in normal clothes: black shirts with bloody skulls, pink jackets embezzled with rhinestones, and always the blue designer jeans that all the kids seemed to wear these days. I seemed to be the only one in the entire place who had taken the carnival to heart. Well, everyone except my best friend, Hondo, who was entering on the opposite side of the fair in his own white satin loincloth.

We had been looking forward to this event for months, planning and scheming and anticipating this one night of pure awesomeness. Ancient Egyptian culture was one of my, and Hondo's, favorite things to learn about. We lived, breathed, ate, and pooped pellets of their society, and we tried in every way we could to bring it to the modern world. You can imagine our reaction when The Egyptian Empire

Festival announced they were coming to our hometown of Bellingham, Washington.

Our moms bought us ridiculously expensive tickets for the 25th of February. The tickets included everything at the carnival: wheat and barley beer, spear throwing, pyramid construction, one finger on King Tut's kneecap, and a piece of sand from the Valley of the Kings to name a few. We even get to meet the 224th cousin of Khafra, the pharaoh who built the Great Pyramid of Giza. How cool is that?

With the night finally upon us, Hondo and I dressed ourselves in loincloths that were specially tailored to match our bodies. Using black eyeliner, we painted around each other's eyes in the distinct markings of an ancient pharaoh. We donned pristinely folded headdresses and taped false beards to our chins. After removing our shirts, the makeup was complete.

If you think a three hundred pound security guard is going to stop an eleven-year-old boy from pursuing his obsession, then think again.

I rushed through the crowd, gently pushing aside purses and hanging globs of arm fat to reach the front of the line. The massive man I encountered earlier was looking past me, watching the men and women coming in from the parking lot. Our moms had just dropped us off. Taking this opportunity to make a break for it, I burst out of the protection of the taller adults and into the dangerously open ticket line. I guess those security guards get paid for a reason; and the ones as big as Mr. Perrywinkle tend to do the best job. It was as if my loincloth was painted bright red and screamed delinquent. Mr. Perrywinkle spotted me instantly, whipped his head in my direction, and took off, straight for me.

Complete and utter panic seized me. Clenching my ticket for dear life, I jumped through three old ladies to reach the front of the line and threw my ticket on the table, begging the greeter to hurry up. "My my, you must really want to be here, eh, skimpy?" the smiling ticket acceptor man asked me. He was moving way too slowly at the moment.

"Yes, yes, very much so, sir! Now, please let me go through!" I was breathless, glancing over my shoulder and discovering, to my horror, that Mr. Perrywinkle was politely shoving his way up to my position. He was only ten people away, and his leisurely pace suggested he was in no hurry.

"Alright, alright, son, give me one second, let me just tear this here flap off for you." I barely restrained myself from yelling at him, but instead waited the extra eternity of a second for him to hand me the accepted ticket. Without responding to his closing remark of "have a great time," I sprinted into the carnival, searching for some place, any place, to hide for the moment.

Dirt flailed behind me and curious bystanders cast me various looks of confusion, but I continued weaving my way through the clay houses of ancient Egypt, winding up beside an old, rickety well complete with a roof and bucket that lowered into the ground. Being the immature boy that always fantasized about escaping a criminal by jumping into a well, I leaped into the bucket, somehow managing to squeeze my scrawny legs inside, and cranked the lever to lower myself down.

Mr. Perrywinkle came around the corner just as my head disappeared from surface view. He stopped in the middle of the stone plaza, turning in circles while scratching his head in a very unprofessional way. The people watching the entire episode pointed the barrel-chested guard to the other side of the well. He seemed to believe them and nodded his thanks before he jogged through the opening. A strikingly-pretty, younger girl with dark hair and olive skin peered over the lip of the well and whispered I could come out now. Nodding my thanks, I grabbed hold of the rope and hoisted myself back to ground level. I accepted the girl's hand and climbed out, finally able to breathe normally. "Try not to get yourself in trouble again, little guy. Oh, and nice get-up." She smiled genuinely and winked mischievously, then ruffled my hair in that big-sister way before walking off to rejoin her group of friends. Time to find Hondo, I thought.

Wandering the carnival was a dream come true for me. I passed stands that sold all kinds of different things from ancient Egypt: scrolls, pottery, mummified toenails, embalming fluid, and even a sarcophagus. I thought of all the things I could do with them, like smother Hondo in embalming fluid, wrap him up in my mom's medical gauze, and then stuff him into the sarcophagus for the day. If only he didn't need to breathe.

Moving on from the souvenir stands, I delved deeper into the festival, traveling through the catacombs under a 1/20 scale version of a pyramid. There were torches blazing on the stone walls every ten steps, and dozens of rooms branched off from the main tunnel. Each one intrigued me, but I knew that I needed to find Hondo before I did anything else. It wouldn't be fair to do everything without him.

I emerged from the depths of the pyramid and found Hondo across the way, sporting his own loincloth and listening intently to an Egyptian priest who was trying to convert him into believing in Horus, their sky god. And by the look on Hondo's transfixed face, that priest was doing a darn good job.

I hurried across the open clearing towards them, keeping a left eye out for Mr. Perrywinkle as I went, and caught the tail end of their conversation: ". . . The blessings that I have bestowed upon you shall never cease to aid you, as long as your faith in the mighty and exalted Horus is strong. I sense that you, Hondo, with your name meaning 'war' in our language, will always have a firm grasp of what is worth believing in."

"You said my name means war?" he asked in astonishment. Neither of them noticed my approach, as I was standing quietly, waiting for them to finish.

"Yes, my son, you have a very old, but very powerful name. It is the same name Menes, the first pharaoh of Egypt, gave to one of his sons. You were born with this name for a purpose. You must serve Horus dutifully and happily, forever praising him for rewarding you with such an important gift." Now, this may have been a dotty, old man dressed in an Egyptian priest costume, but to two eleven-year-old boys, nothing could be any better than that.

The Egyptian priest man seemed to notice me for the first time. He uncrossed his legs and rose to greet me, grinning a toothless smile. "And who might you be, young fellow?" he asked. When Hondo twisted his neck around, he recognized me and leaped out of his sitting position.

I embraced him and proceeded to answer the priest. "My name is Nazim, and my mom told me my name means 'disciplined' in ancient Egyptian. Please tell me she was right," I begged him hopefully.

"As a matter of fact, she is. Your name is among the most honored names in our language. Nazim was the supreme general of Hatshepsut herself. She marched gloriously into Nubia and enslaved the entire population, expanding Egypt's empire into the largest civilization the world had ever seen." The priest smoothed down his beige cloak and laid a hand on each of our shoulders. "My boys, I take it that you are truly interested in my work. Let me show you something not many others have the privilege to see." A golden tent was nailed to the ground behind where we were standing; the priest led us towards the entrance, which had a stitching of the great falcon, the symbol of Horus, emblazoned into the fabric.

He threw the tent flap open in the exuberant fashion of a circus performer revealing his tiger and told us to "Please, come in." We practically fell into the tent, overjoyed that we were getting a backstage tour. The tent flap shook itself out, straightening in the doorway, sealing the small space in total darkness. I whispered Hondo's name, keeping my hands outstretched so I didn't run into anything. Hondo murmured his soft reply back to me, signaling he was okay. There was no sign of the Egyptian priest, not so much as a breath to give him away.

"Hello? Are you there, Mr. Priest?" I tried calling him pharaoh, pastor, dude, walrus, baldy, none of them worked. He might as well name himself the Vanishing Priest of Egyptian Carnivals, because he disappeared completely, without a trace of beige robes to be found. "I wonder where he could have gone. It can't be that big in here."

"Maybe there is a trap door. Wouldn't that be awesome, Nazim?" Hondo fantasized. With that, a slight rustling in the back of the tent caught our ears' attention. "Is that you, Mr. Priest?" Hondo asked. All of a sudden, the far wall of the tent lifted up, revealing a shuffling, old man, hurriedly making his escape. Both of us shouted for him to come back, but someone else decided to answer our cries. A giant silhouette blocked the opening the priest just left and stepped into the darkness as it fell shut. Before our instincts could kick in, a candle flickered on, illuminating the combat-hardened face of Mr. Perrywinkle.

My loincloth was soaked. Hondo's knees were quaking, and my heart had frozen with terror. Mr. Perrywinkle's eyes shone demonically and his satanic grin swept all the joy from the room as if the happiness itself had been stabbed with a blood-stained sickle. Hondo and I were petrified to the point that our feet were plastered to the ground and refused to move.

"Two of you, are there?" the security guard mused aloud. Hearing his voice must have jolted me out of my stupor, because my legs regained functionality, and I bolted for the barely visible tent flap. I burst through the entrance, feeling the rush of wind as Mr. Perrywinkle's hand grazed my neck, narrowly missing me. "Come back, you blasted kids! Public nudity is never allowed!" He shouted from directly behind me.

I unleashed every ounce of energy as soon as I cleared the tent. Unfortunately for Hondo, all the energy in his slightly pudgier body didn't amount to very much. Mr. Perrywinkle closed the gap between him and my best friend astoundingly quickly and laid an ogre's hand on his shoulders, lifting him clean off his feet.

Hondo's shrieks got the attention of more than a few other people and soon enough, we had become the newest addition to the Egyptian Empire Festival. The enormous security guard simply slung Hondo's flailing form over his back and continued after me, never breaking stride. My breaths were labored now, each one coming in a ragged gasp, as I never was much of an athlete. On the opposing end, Mr. Perrywinkle's breaths were long and easy. I could hear them now, steadily gaining ground on my faltering feet.

In other words, I was doomed from the start. I should have turned myself in and admitted I probably shouldn't have dressed so scantily. At least it would have saved me from what happened next.

The knot that held my entire loincloth firmly on my waist had significantly loosened. Let's be honest with each other here. If you aren't a boy scout, you are certainly not good with knots. And it just so happens that I am not a boy scout. With a stone-faced Mr. Perrywinkle in hot pursuit and a weakening knot structure in the balance, the stars of embarrassment had aligned themselves perfectly.

Mr. Perrywinkle could have stepped on my heels by now. Oh, how I wish he did. But no, he decided to chase me into the plaza and reach his hand down. The burly security guard drastically misjudged the distance between his hand and my neck, and instead grasped the back of my flapping loincloth. To put it simply, he yanked it right off. I honestly didn't feel anything happen; I continued my frantic escape to the other end of the plaza as if nothing had gone wrong. Actually, Mr. Perrywinkle tripping and falling in surprise was the only thing that had not gone wrong.

By then, I had stopped running, exhausted and prepared to give up. When I turned to find Mr. Perrywinkle sprawled out all over the floor, staring at the white loincloth clenched in his fist, I became suddenly aware of a slight breeze drifting its way across a very breeze-sensitive area. No, I thought. This cannot be happening. I refused to accept what had, in fact, just happened and tried to control the tremble in my jaw. I must have stood there for a full five seconds, staring at my nakedness like I had never seen it before. It was one of those out-of-body experiences, where you see yourself from someone nearby and can't help but feeling sorry, despite your laughter.

My worst nightmare had come true. The huts, the sand, the bricks, and even the people were a deep tan, making my blindingly white butt cheeks a beacon for every pair of eyes in that plaza, including the olive-skinned, attractive girl from the well. She was still in the plaza, sitting on a picnic bench, except she was now giggling her head off. My newly revealed Tutankhamen jewels could have been the most treasured artifacts in all of ancient Egypt at that moment, judging by the way everyone was reacting.

Delayed reactions being my specialty, I cupped my hands over my groin, like that would erase the image from their minds. The blood from every part of my body had rushed into my face, like someone had fed me a ghost pepper and told me to let it dissolve onto my tongue. Tears leaked from my eyes and slid down my cheeks. Hondo was openly gaping at me, as if his whole perception of me had just changed. There aren't many things that could have made it worse, except for a certain five words that finally did me in. Mr. Perrywinkle's face displayed the evil soul harbored within him as he spoke.

"Put some meat on, kid." At that, the security guard came to the conclusion I had received enough punishment for the day and burst into maniacal laughter. I turned quickly and let my embarrassment carry me out of the carnival as fast as it could. I ignored the obvious amusement on everyone's faces and ducked under the fence, out of sight. The comforting arms of the night wrapped their cool hands around my shoulders and asked me if I was going to be okay. With stained cheeks and a running nose, the stars of my embarrassment seemed to know my answer. They shifted out of alignment ever so slightly, waving goodbye to their friends and saying to each other, "I'll see you guys next time."

Clothed in nothing but the pale skin on my behind, I sent a message of my own to all those stars up there. "Egyptians don't give up that easily," I said, daring them to try harder. After all, there isn't anything worse than accidental public nudity.

Unfortunately for me, the stars seemed to consider that a challenge.

by Anthony Mirabito, age 15
2014 Silver Key
Gilbert Classical Academy

Hellfire Love

CAST

HEATHER is excitable and dramatic, but intelligence is not one of her strengths. She is desperate for a date—a quality that her roommate finds exasperating.

JADE is **HEATHER**'S college roommate. She is typically down to earth and studious, but sarcastic and rude, especially around **HEATHER**.

THE **DEMON** is professional and dresses like a businessman. He is analytical and logical as he considers all of his options.

JEREMY is clueless about what is going on around him, but he is infatuated with his girlfriend, **LYNN**, for whom he left **JADE**.

LYNN is jealous and overly-protective of **JEREMY**.

SETTING

Scene opens in a college dorm room with two beds on either side. There is a line of duct tape down the middle of the room. One side is neat and with fresh decorations, whereas the other side is cluttered with books and papers lying on every surface, all the way up to the duct tape line. A girl is lying on a bed on the messy side, reading a textbook and bobbing her head to her iPod.

HEATHER: [*wafts into room, closes door, and sighs dreamily*]

JADE: [*turns page*]

HEATHER: I got a guy's number!

JADE: [*disinterested*] Really?

HEATHER: Yes, and he was totally—Jade, are you even listening?

JADE: [*takes out headphones and looks up*] Sure.

HEATHER: Yes, Jade, he's so breathtakingly cute, since you were kind enough to ask.

JADE: But I wasn't.

HEATHER: Jade, I'm telling a story.

JADE: I'm not interrupting.

HEATHER: Yes, you are, Jade! We've been roommates for a year now, and I've had it with your sarcastic comments whenever I take a breath! I'd just like five minutes without you breaking into my thoughts! God! [*audible sigh*]

JADE: You don't have thoughts to break into.

HEATHER: Jade!

JADE: [*raises hands in submission and goes back to book*] You were saying.

HEATHER: Oh, right. So, I met him at the restaurant, and we started talking, and... [*silence as she trails off, deep in thought*]

JADE: Are your five minutes up?

HEATHER: No! Shut up.

JADE: Shutting up process commencing... [*pause*]

HEATHER: Can I continue?

JADE: No matter how I answer that question—

HEATHER: Glad that's cleared up. As I was trying to say, restaurant, talking... right, so then I had to take off. But he wrote down his name and number! [*waves slip of paper*]

JADE: Is that the back of the grocery list?

HEATHER: [*hands on hips, glare*] Jade!

JADE: [*mocking*] Heather?

HEATHER: You're supposed to do the best friend thing!

JADE: [*chuckles*] No, you've got to be kidding... [*face falls in realization*] You're serious.

HEATHER: [*pitiful look in her eyes*]

JADE: [*rubs eyes*] Um... What was... his name?

HEATHER: You're really bad at this, aren't you?

JADE: Well, what do you want me to say?!

HEATHER: You're supposed to ask me what he was like. "What was he wearing? Who was he with? What did he drive? How much money was in his bank account?"

JADE: How can you possibly—No, I don't want to know.

HEATHER: [*looks expectantly*]

JADE: Ugh, fine! What did he look like?

HEATHER: He was sooo hot—and, I mean, tall, dark, and smoldering. Except he was blonde. And kind of short. But smoldering. And he had this old-style bomber jacket, which was really cool, and this weird black eye, which was actually kind of sexy, and—

JADE: Yeah, I get the picture. He was hot. He was cool. He was up and down the whole thermometer. Do you actually know his name?

HEATHER: You keep asking that! What are you trying to do?

JADE: All right, you caught me. I am trying to make you look a lot less shallow than you really are. I am so sorry for forcing you into that image; I know you don't want everyone to have the wrong impression.

HEATHER: [*flatly*] Jeremy. His name was Jeremy.

JADE: [*sits up*] What? Jeremy Price?

HEATHER: Yeah, actually—

JADE: You were hitting on my boyfriend?

HEATHER: Boyfriend? Jade, you were the one who gave him the black eye!

JADE: Well, ex-boyfriend. He was cheating on me.

HEATHER: So, what's your problem?

JADE: Heather, how can you possibly not understand—fine. I'll put it in your terms. The "dating rules" [*motions air quotes with hands*] say that one cannot hit on any past romantic partners of the "best friend."

HEATHER: This is true... [*Jade rolls eyes*] But maybe I don't want to be right, this time!

JADE: [*grumbles*] You're never right; that's the problem...

HEATHER: I'm going to call him. No matter what you say.

JADE: Seriously? Heather, he was a complete—even I don't want to see you go through those problems.

HEATHER: You're jealous! You can't have him, so you don't want me to.

JADE: No, I'm mostly worried that we actually have similar tastes in something. And, who knows what we might've started. Like, I might actually go on the Internet, the land of celebrities, and cats, and celebrities that act like cats. And you might learn how to read, which would most definitely be disastrous.

HEATHER: That's—I—You are—I'm going to call him. [*grabs phone*]

JADE: Now?

HEATHER: No reason not to.

JADE: It's been an hour since you saw this guy. Who you just met. Who's my ex, anyway!

HEATHER: You're saying I don't care?

JADE: I'm saying that your relationships last about as long as a taxicab ride.

HEATHER: Hey. I think Jeremy and I have something. Just because you can't commit yourself—

JADE: [*stands abruptly*] Commit myself? I gave him

everything! He had my blood, sweat, and tears. I practically handed myself over to him and let him do whatever he wished! [*pause*] I wish my relationship was as dirty as that last sentence sounded! But it wasn't, because he was off with that other chick!

HEATHER: You didn't give enough.

JADE: [*rolls her eyes and flops back onto bed*] The only thing that I could've done to show more dedication would have been to lock him in my closet.

HEATHER: You should've have shown him that he was worth your life.

JADE: And you're saying, what, that you would?

HEATHER: I would! As a matter of fact, I would trade my life... my soul for him!

[*Explosive noise, lights flicker and turn off. DEMON appears. HEATHER squeals and tosses phone over her head, and JADE stands up.*]

DEMON: [*to HEATHER*] Would you like to talk prices?

JADE: [*singsong, looking around idly*] This is why Heather isn't allowed to hire the exterminator.

HEATHER: Jade...

JADE: Who the hell are you?

DEMON: Yes, "Hell" is an appropriate term. I am a demon, summoned here by your offer. [*to HEATHER*] Now, you made the statement; did you not?

HEATHER: I didn't summon you.

JADE: Yes, Heather, you did. You said you would trade your damn soul, and look. Now, we have a demon problem *and* a cricket problem.

DEMON: Your soul is already damned? Because I cannot claim that which another demon already has.

HEATHER: No! I am clean. No damning here.

JADE: Huh. I thought you came straight from Hell.

HEATHER: What are you, some kind of lawyer?

JADE: Funny. The last time I called a lawyer a demon, he got offended. [*to DEMON*] Can you sense who made the offer?

DEMON: Not exactly, but my senses are still finely-tuned to those looking for love. For example, you are physically attractive and well-off. [*to HEATHER*] And I'm sure you have a nice personality.

JADE: No, she really doesn't have that, either.

HEATHER: Wait, I can actually trade my soul for Jeremy's love?

JADE: [*rolls eyes*] Heather, you believe him?

HEATHER: I'll do it!

JADE: What?

DEMON: Done.

JADE: Wait, no. You can't just trade your soul like that!

HEATHER: Yes, I can.

JADE: But—it's not right—

HEATHER: Jade, would you trade your soul for his eternal love? (It is eternal, right?)

DEMON: No, that costs an extra fee of one soul.

HEATHER: What?!

DEMON: You do understand the gravity of the word, "eternity," do you not?

HEATHER: Fine, I'll sell her soul.

JADE: Hang on, you really can't do that!

DEMON: You make an appealing offer.

JADE: Stop! Listen! [*waves arms*] Maybe I want to buy his love.

DEMON: Is that so?

JADE: Yes. I... I... I would trade three souls for his love. All right? I forgive him! I still love him, no matter how much pain he caused me!

HEATHER: Too late, honey.

JADE: Too late? I was through with him before you even met him.

HEATHER: Ours is a love at first sight.

JADE: You're ridiculous.

HEATHER: You're stuck up.

DEMON: [*tries to hold in frustration*] You're both grating on my nerves! [*back to calm and professional*] Please, make your offer before I'm further tempted to ship you two off to the Research Department for Torment.

JADE: I'd trade... three souls.

HEATHER: Three souls? Whose?

DEMON: [*nods*]

JADE: I would trade Heather [*HEATHER gawks*] and... the noisy roommates to our right.

DEMON: The value is not the same. The value of souls depends on the sacrifice, not the quantity. You have no concern for your neighbors, so they are practically worthless.

JADE: Not even a lot of practically worthless souls? I could give all of my professors.

HEATHER: I'll give you everyone in my Political Science class.

JADE: You don't take Political Science.

HEATHER: Taking a class and showing up to a class are two very different things.

JADE: Well, I'll give you the souls of everyone in the Falkland Islands.

HEATHER: Where are the Falkland Islands?

JADE: Exactly.

DEMON: Ladies! As tempting as these offers are, they mean nothing! If I offered to destroy your Political Science class, I think you would give me your own head—not that it's worth anything, anyhow. And you, the Falkland Islands have already been sold to another demon. I'm talking sacrifice!

JADE: Seriously? Fine. I would trade my soul and Heather's.

HEATHER: You would?

DEMON: You, Jade, don't particularly care for Heather, either.

HEATHER: [*hurt*] You don't?

DEMON: Therefore, Heather's offer maintains highest value.

JADE: [*blows out cheeks*] I would trade... my family. Four souls, all very dear to me.

HEATHER: [*shocked*] Jade!

DEMON: Highest offer is currently Jade's.

HEATHER: Seriously? I, uh, I'd trade my extended family! That's... [*Begins to count on fingers. DEMON remains emotionless and still throughout process, while JADE becomes bored and starts to show interest in DEMON'S brief case, which is set on the desk. DEMON swats JADE away. HEATHER looks up.*] It's a lot of people!

DEMON: Four-hundred and ninety-seven souls, exactly. You never specified the definition of "extended."

HEATHER: Four-hundred and ninety-seven souls.

DEMON: And you know only eleven of those people, and care for approximately forty-three percent of those eleven. I'm growing impatient. This transaction is going nowhere, and time won't make his value go up.

HEATHER: Him!

DEMON: Pardon me?

HEATHER: I will trade you his soul. *[JADE looks baffled. HEATHER crosses arms in determination.]*

DEMON: I am intrigued. Continue.

HEATHER: Well, he means a lot to me? Like, he means the world to me. More than that, he means everything to me. That's… why I'm trying to buy his love.

JADE: *[rubs temples]*

DEMON: You present a valid argument.

JADE: Can you even hear yourself?! You're trying to use him… to buy him! It's like, trying to buy money!

HEATHER: You can exchange a dollar for four quarters; can you not?

JADE: *[tosses hands into air]* Sure. If you like your men better sliced into four pieces—hey, I won't question your fetishes.

HEATHER: This is love! Why do you mock me?

JADE: *[sits down in resignation]* You want a soulless Jeremy? Fine! I don't care.

DEMON: I shall summon him. *[claps hands]*

[Lights flicker off. When they flicker on again, JEREMY is sitting on the floor, kissing LYNN. They freeze and look

around, dazed.]

JADE, HEATHER, LYNN: Jeremy!?

JEREMY: [*quickly*] I'm sorry. [*pause*] For whatever I did. (I screwed something up here, right?)

DEMON: On the contrary. You have won the heart of this... lovely young woman. And she is trying to win yours in return.

LYNN: Who's this "lovely young woman," Jeremy?

JEREMY: [*to HEATHER*] Uh, I swear, I didn't mean to cheat on you. I didn't mean it.

JADE: Goddamnit, Jeremy! You cheated on me, not her!

JEREMY: Oh. [*pause*] Then, who is she?

HEATHER: You don't remember me? We spoke at the restaurant? You gave me your number? [*waves paper*]

JEREMY: [*takes paper*] I filled out this form to receive coupons. Were you my waitress?

JADE: [*looks pointedly at HEATHER*]

HEATHER: I thought bringing you your dinner was very romantic...

DEMON: [*looks at watch*] I have a meeting with the boss in half an hour, and I really can't be late. So, if we could just hurry this along, I would appreciate that. Heather, is your offer of Jeremy's soul final?

HEATHER: Yes, it is.

JEREMY: It is?

LYNN: Wait, you can't buy Jeremy's love. I already did! [*EVERYONE looks to her*] I traded my obnoxious neighbors' souls, since he would never leave Jade.

JADE: [*soft look*] Is this true, Jeremy?

JEREMY: [*Looks up from stroking LYNN'S hair. Slow,*

blank look.] Whaaat?

LYNN: I got a good lawyer.

DEMON: [*Frustrated, snaps. Lights flicker off. Crash. JEREMY and LYNN disappear. Lights flicker on.*] Enough has been said.

HEATHER: Just like that? His love belongs to someone else?

DEMON: [*short*] Pardon me, ma'am, but tough luck. If you'll excuse me, I have to report this to management; another demon is up by twelve sales. My reputation is virtually dead right now!

JADE: Hold on, just one moment. You said that the value of a soul depends on the sacrifice. But she bought Jeremy's love with her neighbors!

DEMON: I said that?

JADE: You tried to scam us for souls!

DEMON: You can't prove that. Your statement will hold nothing in a lawsuit.

JADE: Demons! [*storms out*] [*awkward silence*]

HEATHER: So... can I get your number?

by Bailey Vidler, age 15
2014 Silver Key
Mountain View High School, Mesa

DRAMATIC SCRIPT

Editor Introduction by Michelle Hill

"Art is an Adhesive." -Marc Robinson

In his book *The American Play,* Marc Robinson writes: "art should not be artifact" (308). Robinson posits that instead of confining art to the walls of museums or the pages of anthologies, we should interact with it, hopefully using it as a means for connection. Luckily, the genre of Dramatic Literature begs to be shared. The text of a playscript clamors to be read aloud on stage, of course, but it is equally evocative when spoken in classrooms and around kitchen tables.

As I read the nominated short plays, the work of Nailah Mathews compelled me to interact. "Little Things" was the script that I wanted to talk about with friends, asking what they thought of the situation and characters she created. Even now, two months after my initial read, I find myself thinking about the script's multiple conflicts. As you read her work, assign yourself a role, and speak the words aloud. Better yet, assemble a cast of five and devote fifteen minutes to a staged reading. When a playwright writes a play, art is created. When a group comes together to perform this art, the act of creation connects them forever.

Selfish Things

CAST

OLIVIA – A young woman who has just attempted suicide
WILL – A receptionist in the waiting room for Paradise; a young man who shows OLIVIA what she has left behind

JACK – OLIVIA's living ex-boyfriend
SUMMER – OLIVIA'S living younger sister
DENISE – OLIVIA and SUMMER'S mother

SETTING

Time frame: modern day/disjointed
Place: a simple receptionist's office center stage to start, three empty chairs and a desk
Stage left: a small, sparsely decorated bedroom with storybooks and short novels littering the floor

> *(Lights rise on OLIVIA, sitting center stage. Lights are bright, blaring, and uncomfortable in the waiting area for an office of some kind.)*

WILL: *(from offstage)* Name?

OLIVIA: Excuse me?

WILL: Your name. Full name, thank you.

OLIVIA: Oh, okay. Uh... Olivia. Olivia Marie Turner.

WILL: Age?

OLIVIA: Seventeen.

WILL: Reason for being present.

OLIVIA: Reason for being present?

WILL: Yes, Ms. Turner, your reason for being here. Right now.

OLIVIA: I don't really know where I am. I was hoping that you might be able to tell me.

WILL: You're in the In-Between. You know, limbo, purgatory? You're in the 'Waiting Room for Paradise' or whatever. I need to know why you're here. Your cause of death.

OLIVIA: *(pleasantly surprised)* I'm dead?

WILL: Repeating the end of other people's sentences isn't very attractive.

OLIVIA: Well sor-ry. I just... I didn't think it worked. I– I killed myself this morning.

WILL: No you didn't, but you did come quite close. Any witnesses?

OLIVIA: What do you mean, no I didn't? Witnesses? No. My dad's out of town on a business trip. He won't be back until next week.

WILL: Method of self-murder?

OLIVIA: What do you mean, no I didn't? I took five extra-strength sleeping pills.

WILL: *(enters with a clipboard in hand)* And that got you? Extra-strength sleeping pills? Back in my day, it was a bullet to the brain. Now you can just off yourself in a kind, peaceful little way, and you don't even have to mess up your hair.

OLIVIA: Back in your day? You don't look any older than I am.

WILL: Don't let the dashing good looks fool you, I've been dead far longer than you have. I'm Will.

OLIVIA: Modest, aren't you? *(extends hand)* Olivia.

WILL: Yes, I'd gathered that. *(scans clipboard)* It says you've left behind your parents, one younger sister, and one ex-boyfriend? Is that correct?

OLIVIA: Yes, it is, but I can't see how any of that is important–

WILL: Yes, yes, well it's important for me. I've got a job to do, and that involves knowing everything there is to know about the bout of self-loathing that had you offing yourself. Should I assume it was the boyfriend?

OLIVIA: Jack had nothing to do with this. He doesn't even know I was planning on it.

WILL: Mhmm, premeditated self-assassination... And the parents? Your file doesn't read like there was much divorce trouble... Little to no drama between them, loved each other for years, separated, but were very, very fond of you and your little sister, though not of each other. They have any hand in this?

OLIVIA: No.

WILL: So, what, you just got bored one afternoon, took a nice stroll, went to your bedroom, thought 'Well, Dad won't be home for another week, it's a lovely day for suicide?'

OLIVIA: You have no idea what you're talking about.

WILL: Then please, enlighten me. It'll make my job that much easier.

OLIVIA: And what is your job, exactly?

WILL: Ms. Turner, it's my job to find out exactly why you've done this to yourself, and you won't be going up above or down below until I have the answers I need. After I find out, it is my obligation to either help you cling to life or ease you into the last leg of the race to death.

OLIVIA: My reasons are my business.

WILL: So are everyone else's, and they all end up giving them to me, so you'd might as well just spit it out now. People come in and out of the In-Between every day, either ready to die or to turn around and have that second chance at life. I've got all eternity to wait on you, but it seems as though your body can only have those pills in it for so long until it shuts down for good.

OLIVIA: But– But I thought you said I was dead.

WILL: I never said you were dead. The place we're in is called the 'In-Between' for a reason. In-between life and death. You're not the brightest crayon in the pack, are you?

OLIVIA: Stop talking!

WILL: Well, then, you'd better start!

OLIVIA: Fine! Fine... I just... I can show you better than I can tell you.

WILL: Then get up. I've got a ticket to the world of the living with your name right on it, and we simply cannot be late. *(offers OLIVIA his arm)*

(Scene change; OLIVIA and WILL enter through the house. Stage right is an attractive young man; he is JACK, the boyfriend OLIVIA has left behind. Stage left is SUMMER, OLIVIA's younger sister. OLIVIA and WILL come to take center stage, but stand in the shadows.)

OLIVIA: Oh, Summer, you'll never make friends sitting inside all day.

WILL: She can't hear you.

OLIVIA: What do you mean, she can't hear me? Why not?

WILL: Time passes differently here than it does in the In-Between and in the World of the Living, for all you know we could be seeing the past. And, you aren't tangible to people who are alive right now, Olivia. Please keep in mind that you did try to sleep your way to death this morning.

OLIVIA: I didn't want it to hurt.

WILL: Yes, yes, and of course you weren't thinking of the consequences of your actions. You weren't thinking at all of how things could have been different if you had just decided to sit tight and weather the storm.

OLIVIA: You don't know anything about me, so don't start assuming that I just got out of bed one day and decided it'd be a great idea to off myself. That isn't what happened.

WILL: You're doing a poor job at convincing me otherwise.

OLIVIA: Shove it.

WILL: *(rolls his eyes, turns to face JACK)* I'll assume that's the boyfriend?

OLIVIA: Ex-boyfriend.

WILL: Why'd the two of you call it quits?

OLIVIA: He cheated on me. Three times. In the same month. I found out the night before my birthday. I ended it that next day.

JACK: *(on the phone)* Yeah, I know I screwed up... I know she cared about me; really I do, but... Well, we're just kids. We're in high school. We're supposed to have fun, supposed to experiment. I wasn't expecting her to get so touchy about it... Well, yeah, she had the right to... I didn't mean it that way; that came out wrong, look I just... No, just listen. Plenty of people warned her about what kind of person I was–

OLIVIA: They did.

JACK: –and she had plenty of chances to end it before it got to what happened last month. She could've taken any of them–

WILL: You didn't.

JACK: –And ended it. Yeah, she was a great kid... Yeah, she did have a nice smile... And she always did this cute little nose-wiggle whenever she was mad–

OLIVIA: I do not wiggle my nose when I'm mad!

WILL: You're doing it right now.

JACK: Look, the point is, that was then, and this is now. We don't *have* a relationship anymore. I don't even know where she is right now, she hasn't texted me since she called it off.

WILL: Nice willpower you've got there.

OLIVIA: I pride myself on it, thanks.

JACK: She doesn't want anything to do with me anymore... Well, maybe I was wrong to do what I did, but it's not like she's gone and done something stupid because of it.

WILL: You haven't, have you?

OLIVIA: It may have been a contributing factor.

WILL: You can't be serious.

OLIVIA: Of course I'm not serious. He's gorgeous, but not worth my life. Why? Back in your day cheating wasn't a serious offense?

WILL: Of course it was, but we usually just called them witches and burned them alive or sewed a red 'A' on the front of them and called it a day.

OLIVIA: How old *are* you?

WILL: A lady never tells.

OLIVIA: But–

WILL: Shall we visit your little sister?

OLIVIA: No! *(a beat)* I mean, not yet. I don't want to see her.

WILL: You seemed awfully excited to see her only a few moments ago.

OLIVIA: Well, now it seems like an invasion of privacy. Besides, now that I've heard what Jack had to say about me...? It's great to know that I was just another notch in someone's bedpost.

WILL: There's a picture of you in his wallet that says otherwise.

OLIVIA: And how would you know-

WILL: *(walks up to JACK, nicks his wallet before rifling through it and procuring a picture)*

OLIVIA: I thought you said that the living couldn't touch us.

WILL: He didn't touch us, now did he?

OLIVIA: Huh... Well, go give it back.

WILL: You plan on keeping that picture?

OLIVIA: He wouldn't miss it either way. *(returns photograph)*

WILL: If you insist... He really did care about you, you know.

OLIVIA: Of course he did. He really cared about Lauren and Claudine and Farrah, too.

WILL: He had a whole lot of love to give, I suppose.

OLIVIA: Mhm, and plenty of B.S. to go around too. Can we go now?

WILL: Not quite yet.

(OLIVIA'S mother DENISE enters into SUMMER's room and sits down to play with her, until her phone rings. She gets up to take the call.)

WILL: And there goes the mother.

OLIVIA: Unfortunately.

WILL: Mommy issues?

OLIVIA: You could say that.

WILL: Your file says that your parents—as a whole—loved you very much.

OLIVIA: Does it also mention that her child support payments are behind?

WILL: It would seem that way.

OLIVIA: Didn't know as much as you thought you did, did you?

WILL: I've never claimed to know anything. All I know are the basics and what you're telling me.

OLIVIA: *(waits a few moments before taking a deep breath and speaking)* The divorce was fine. I was eleven, Summer was five. Mom wasn't the best person at the time. Dad cited 'irreconcilable differences.' What he meant to say was that Mom found friends in the bottom of a bottle of Jack and that the most she kept around in the house for me and Summer to eat was a box of stale mac-and-cheese. Not exactly the best living environment for two growing girls.

WILL: She seems to be doing quite well for herself now.

OLIVIA: Only because she has full custody over Summer and only partial over me. When Dad sued for negligence, she counter-sued for abandonment when she was pregnant with Summer... Such a load of–! You know, it's crap when a court says that children need their mother. My dad, Summer, and I? The three of us would've been just fine without her. The only reason she isn't in some crappy studio apartment is because she skims from the top of the cash Dad sends for the bills.

WILL: Medical bills?

OLIVIA: Yeah. Summer has this– *(cuts herself off)* It's nothing.

WILL: Well, obviously it's something, and something very important. We're running out of time, Olivia. There's only so long before your body starts shutting down.

OLIVIA: It's my choice. It's what I want.

WILL: To leave your little sister behind with that woman?

OLIVIA: Me dying will do more good to Summer than me living ever could.

WILL: You're not too terribly persuasive, are you? Did you have to convince yourself to take the pills, or did you just down them all in one go?

OLIVIA: Will you just let that go?

WILL: No. I need to know why you would choose to leave such a fragile little thing along with your mother for any extended period of time.

OLIVIA: Summer is much, much stronger than she looks. And our mother... She's bad, but she isn't that bad.

WILL: I sincerely doubt that. You and I both know that she isn't exactly the type of woman to uphold visitation rights.

OLIVIA: She's petty as anything.

WILL: I figured.

DENISE: How's your chest feeling, sweetheart?

SUMMER: Funny.

DENISE: Funny bad?

SUMMER: No, funny strange. I don't feel sick or anything, but I feel strange-funny.

WILL: What's wrong with her chest?

OLIVIA: Nothing you need to worry about.

DENISE: Are you sure, baby? The last time you felt strange-funny, we had to go to the Emergency and we had to stay there all night.

SUMMER: But I got better. 'Livia and Daddy came, and they stayed the whole night, even when the nurses said that visiting hours were over, they–

DENISE: Yes, I know, Summer. I was there. You seem to forget that.

SUMMER: I didn't forget... You were outside smoking. And you kept drinking out of that flask when you thought nobody was looking.

DENISE: *(tone deadly)* Are you accusing me of something, young lady?

SUMMER: *(withers)* N-no.

DENISE: That's what I thought. You need to learn to watch yourself, young lady. One day that smart mouth will get you in trouble.

SUMMER: *(mumbles)*

DENISE: What was that?

SUMMER: Nothing. It was nothing.

DENISE: Don't you dare lie to me. What did you say?

SUMMER: I said that Daddy says that a smart mouth means a smart mind, but talk too much, and you'll be on your behind.

DENISE: *(chuckles)* Well for once that man was right. Clean up this room. You won't have dinner until this floor's been picked up. *(exits)*

> *(SUMMER, looking dejected, begins cleaning up
> the mess in her room.)*

OLIVIA: She hardly eats, anyway.

WILL: Does your mother starve her?

OLIVIA: Why do you need to know?

WILL: Does she beat Summer?

OLIVIA: It's none of your business.

WILL: You know it's part of my job, Olivia.

SUMMER: *(picks a phone from out of her pocket and dials quickly)* C'mon, Livie, c'mon, pick up... Please, please, pick up.... *(hangs up in a fit)* I hate voicemail.

OLIVIA: Summer–!

WILL: She can't hear you.

OLIVIA: Yeah, you said that already.

WILL: Now's not the time, Olivia. We have things to do.

OLIVIA: No, you have things to do. All I have to do is wait until those pills do their job, and then I'm done.

WILL: Stop talking like that, there's still time to save your life.

OLIVIA: I don't want my life to be saved!

WILL: This isn't about you.

OLIVIA: But it was my choice.

WILL: What about Summer–

OLIVIA: Leave her out of this.

WILL: There are other people to consider when you attempt suicide–

OLIVIA: I haven't attempted anything. This morning, I killed myself. This afternoon, I woke in an office with you asking for my name. Now, I'm watching things I really don't want to see while you keep asking me questions. In all honesty, it's putting me in a pretty crap mood.

WILL: Olivia, we do not have– Listen to me, Olivia, time passes differently in the In-Between, and every individual person takes a different amount of time to die. You see, the same way ice melts–

OLIVIA: You have all of 'eternity', isn't that what you said earlier? And soon I will, too. And maybe, once I do, Summer will have a fighting chance.

WILL: Olivia–

OLIVIA: You really wanna know that bad? You really need to know that bad, for your stupid little clipboard? Fine. Fine, I'll tell you. Summer was born with a congenital heart disease. When mommy dearest over there was pregnant, she had a little taste for a shot or two, maybe once or twice. She thought it was all okay. Hasn't stopped since. My dad never knew. He was too excited about being a father again. But one day, when we went in for the ultrasound, we heard something. A weird little noise. A murmur. A freaking murmur! *(a beat)* Do you have any idea how it feels to watch a baby no bigger than your forearm get swept away from the maternity ward to get stuck full of needles because her heart doesn't beat right? At six years old? She was so small, and, and I had never felt so helpless in my life. She needed a new heart... They'd been cutting her open for months and months, year by year, and no change. Other people needed hearts, and they took priority over Summer when she was six, and when she was nine, and when she was eleven. But one day, one day I convinced my dad to take me in, have me tested. Blood type, physicals, the works. We found out that Summer and I were close in more than one way. *(looks to SUMMER)* She needs a new heart. And I'll be the one to give it to her.

WILL: Olivia, that is a bad idea. That is a very, very bad idea, and we both know it.

OLIVIA: Do you know how long the waiting list for donors is? Names, and names, and names of men and women old and young, kids as young as Summer and younger who are waiting for someone to die so they can have the one thing that'll keep them alive? I'm a near identical match to Summer. I can do this, Will. I can save her life.

WILL: Olivia, near identical is not enough.

OLIVIA: The last person who was a perfect match had a heart that went to a man in Nevada. Summer's little defect wasn't high enough of a priority. We were this close, this close to saving her, to making a difference. Someone has to help her. I can.

WILL: You said yourself that the waiting lists are long. For all you know, your heart could go to someone else, to someone in Colorado. And then where will you be?

OLIVIA: Not if I have anything to say about it. Got anything on your little clipboard about a note I wrote?

WILL: *(astounded, flips through his clipboard until he finds the note and begins to read aloud)* 'I, Olivia Marie Turner, on this the day of my death, would like it to be known that all of my worldly possessions should be donated as part of my last will and testament. My body and all of its innards shall be donated to science, save for my heart, which'–

WILL, OLIVIA: –'shall be given, via transplant, to Summer Jane Turner'–

OLIVIA: –'My only younger sister.' What judge is going to deny a girl her dying wish?

WILL: Olivia, you can't do this.

OLIVIA: Who are you to tell me what I can or cannot do?

WILL: Olivia, Summer needs you more now than she ever has before. If she is dying, if she really is dying, then she's going to need you to make her days special. She's going to need you to stand by her and stand with her at every doctor's appointment, even when she's scared the most. You can't just leave her behind like this. You cannot commit to doing such an unbelievably selfish thing!

OLIVIA: Who gives you the right to determine what I should or shouldn't do with my life? It's my life, it's my choice, and it has absolutely nothing to do with you. You're calling me selfish? I've just given my life to the person I love in this world the most, and you're calling me selfish?!

WILL: No, Olivia. I'm calling you selfish because you're insisting on taking from your sister the one person *she* loves most in the world. How do you think she'll feel knowing that you gave up your heart for her? To know that she was the cause for you killing herself?

OLIVIA: I–

WILL: You're her best friend, Olivia. You're her lifeline. She's alive because she wants to be alive with you. You can't take that away from her. You don't have that right.

OLIVIA: But–

WILL: What did she say, that night? I know you remember, that night she ended up in the Emergency room because her chest felt strange-funny?

SUMMER: 'Livia, what if something's really wrong this time? What if they find a hole, or one of my valves is crushed, what if–

WILL: What did you say?

OLIVIA: *(focused on SUMMER)* I told her that nothing was going to be wrong.

SUMMER: How do you know?

WILL: And?

OLIVIA: And I said to her– I said because she was a fighter. I told her that she had been fighting since she was little to make it out alive, and I told her that she could keep fighting.

SUMMER: But I get so tired, Olivia. I don't wanna fight anymore.

WILL: And you said…?

OLIVIA: I said… I said if you don't want to fight for yourself anymore, then fight for me.

WILL: What else did you say, Olivia. You had to convince her!

OLIVIA: I know that you're tired. I know that you want to rest and sleep. But I know you want to go out and play with your friends, and you can't do that if you're gone, and, and I won't lose you. Even if it's just for my sake, for my peace of mind, Summer, keep fighting. Fight for me.

SUMMER: Okay. Okay, I will.

OLIVIA: Promise me, Summer. Promise me.

SUMMER: I promise, 'Livia. I mean it.

WILL: She's only fighting because you told her to. The only reason she hasn't given up yet is because she thinks you'll be disappointed in her if she does. She's only alive because you are. If you kill yourself tonight, you're only sentencing her to die tomorrow.

OLIVIA: I– I didn't–

WILL: Of course you didn't. No one who attempts suicide ever really does. Now come on, before we're too late.

(Lights dim as WILL takes OLIVIA's hand, and they dart into the house. They re-enter to where a single chair is resting center stage.)

WILL: Sit down in that chair, go on, go! You're running out of time.

OLIVIA: *(sits)* Now what do I do? How do I go back, Will? How do I get back to her?

WILL: You have to close your eyes and see what you want. See your body, see yourself waking up and vomiting the pills. Watch it happen, watch yourself come out alive.

OLIVIA: It isn't working, Will. It's not happening.

WILL: Imagine your father! Imagine him storming into your room and calling 9-11! See it, happen, Olivia. You have to believe it. You have to want it.

OLIVIA: He isn't even in this state, Will, he's not coming! Oh, God, oh God, Summer, how do I get back to her, Will?

WILL: *(rushing to his desk)* You have to want it, Olivia. It isn't enough to want to go back to her. You have to want it for yourself. See your body, see yourself breathing.

OLIVIA: It isn't working, Will. It isn't working! I can't do it! I can see my body, but nothing's happening, nothing's changing.

WILL: Oh no.

OLIVIA: *(slowly opens her eyes as WILL, stricken, hands her a pamphlet)*

WILL: Olivia, I'm so sorry. I tried. I told you, Olivia. I told you that time passes differently here. I tried to tell you that things were different, but you wouldn't listen to me. Olivia, oh, I'm so sorry. I tried. You know we both tried.

OLIVIA: *(she reads aloud)* In loving memory of Olivia Marie Turner.

(OLIVIA looks out into the house, overcome with despair, crumbles. Blackout.)

END OF SHOW

by Nailah Mathews, age 16
2014 Gold Key
Ironwood High School, Glendale

SCIENCE FICTION/FANTASY

Editor Introduction by Melissa Williamson

In a world where we are obsessed with reading books with the premise "In a world where...something awful happens," we lose ourselves, although I certainly would not want to live in a world where my community has to send kids off to die in a sadistic game. We wonder what it would be like to love an angel or a sparkling vampire. My best friend could be a Shadow hunter. My town could have a huge Caster library underneath it. This is what I love about sci-fi and fantasy. I enjoy losing myself in worlds that are not like our own (or, the stories might say something about what our world could be, if we continue on a destructive path). It is a way for us to dive into our imaginations and think, "What if?"

What if I had to live my life with a bracelet around my wrist that shows me how many hours, minutes, and seconds I have left before I die, like in Sue Kim's "Numbers?" What if I could not see color and I could be persecuted for all the books I have in my house because of the way society works in "Renegade" by Nailah Mathews? Maybe I could slip into a coma and not wake up. I could be stuck on "The Bridge" with the narrator of the poem by Natali Chausovskaya. While I would love to spend eternity in the embrace of my husband, I would not know how the world continued without us, because we can mess with time in Nichole Kypriano's "The Peculiar Time of Russellville." I would not want to live in those worlds, but I do love reading about them. I hope you will enjoy them, too.

Numbers

Adam was out the door as soon as the bell rang. He always was. Never mind the homework; he had people to avoid.

Phoenix High was a dreary, run-down school, adorned with graffiti and gum and crumbling walls where fights had once taken place. It was the place everyone avoided, the place where poor parents stuck their troublesome children.

Adam Hawke often asked himself that question: Am I troublesome? There was a time when he would have answered no, but now?

Well.

He evaded sneering jocks, dim-witted musclemen with practiced ease. Heads down, eyes on the ground, he told himself. Use the road if I have to. There were no cars. There never were. No one here could afford a decent education, let alone an SUV.

He reached a fork in the road. To the left was home, his father's house, and to the right, where gangs prowled, was suicide, plain suicide.

He went right.

One could almost tell where gang turf began. Trees snaked low to the ground, then suddenly shot up like they had been bent in half by giant hands. Leaves grew in strange, twisted shapes, if at all. Little rivulets of murky water ran in the cracks in the road, occasionally spitting in a miniature geyser-like show.

Scowling, Adam gritted his teeth and punched a nearby tree. His wrist caught the sunlight, pale and unbroken. No matter where he went, resentment followed him, resentment and hate and fear. Because his wrist was plain. No counter, no falling numbers that gleamed ashen from underneath a thin layer of skin. They were a countdown, years days hours minutes seconds, and with them came the inevitable sense of doom that hung over those whose numbers approached zero. It drove people mad, knowing when they would die, but not how, not where, not why.

And Adam didn't have one.

It seemed more a curse than a blessing. He covered his wrist like everyone else, but the fact that he was different was hard to hide, considering that "What's your time" was a more common greeting than "What's your name."

The path opened up into a park, once a popular kids'

attraction but now overcome by years of vandalism. To any other kid, the underworldly atmosphere might have been intimidating, but to Adam, this was home. This was all he had.

Unless, of course, someone else decided to come along.

He sat down on a decrepit bench, mindful of a split in the wood. A blanket of clouds covered the sky; a sudden gust of wind made him shiver. *I should've brought a jacket*, he sighed inwardly, rubbing his hands together and breathing into them.

"You should've brought a jacket, stupid," said a voice beside his ear. Adam started and flew off the bench, whipping out his blade instinctively.

"Settle down, pup," laughed Russell Angelo. "S'only me."

Russell Angelo. Sly, lawless, wild. A regular flirt and kleptomaniac, he took pride in his extensive criminal record. He stayed away from the other gangs, and they mostly stayed away from him. A loner. And also Adam's only friend.

Adam straightened from his defensive crouch and tucked his blade into his front pocket. "Your head's gonna end up on the ground one of these days," he snapped.

Russell flashed a taunting grin. "Little cub like you couldn't hurt a fly," he said, dropping down onto the bench with the loose limbs of one who has had too much to drink. He stretched his legs across the seat. "How's the old man?"

Adam shoved Russell's feet off and sat beside him. "Are you drunk?" As far as Adam knew, Russell had never had more than a single bottle of alcohol at a time before.

Russell seemed not to have heard. More likely, he was ignoring him. "He still obsessed with his girlfriend? Pansy or whatever her name is?"

"Daisy." An illusion of sickeningly sweet perfume and flaking makeup filled his head.

"Pansy, Lily, whatever. Either way, she's hot."

Adam was utterly revolted now and didn't hesitate in telling him so.

Russell's amused smile displayed an array of yellowing teeth. "I know. Got a cig?"

Adam sighed but couldn't help grinning at Russell's shameless antics. He dug a pack of cigarettes and a lighter out of his pocket and tossed them over. "I hope you smoke yourself to death."

"Feisty." Russell lit one, and they sat there in companionable silence, a trail of smoke snaking upward into the darkening sky.

But it wasn't all companionable. Something was on Russell's mind; something was nagging at him. The pause before the grin, the overly hearty laugh, the drinking– Adam hadn't missed any of it. He'd known Russell for too long. "What's wrong?"

Russell continued to stare into the distance. Adam prodded him again. "Russ."

Russell jumped, looked at Adam as if he had just noticed him. "Yeah."

"What's wrong?"

There it was again, the slight pause. "What do you mean, what's wrong? I got the lamest pal in the world, not to mention an abusive dad and a mom who died ten years ago."

"Cut the shit. I can practically taste the alcohol on your breath, Russ."

Russell sighed and looked him in the eye. "Well, if you must know." He pulled up his sleeve to reveal his counter, unprotected and clear.

0000001256.

12 minutes, 56 seconds.

Adam gaped at it, dumbfounded. "You never showed me."

"I never saw why I should."

Suddenly, anger and denial shot through him. "You bastard. You only have twelve minutes left, and *now* you tell me?"

A bitter smile. "What would you have done?"

What *would* he have done? Hug him? Cry? Try to kill him himself? Or perhaps just forget about it?

They were jerked out of their reverie when two meaty hands closed around Adam's throat and lifted him into the air. Adam 's eyes bulged his breath was cut off. He twisted, kicked, tried to get free, but the hands were too strong. He was getting faint.

"Melcrona!" Russell leapt over the back of the chair and lunged at another burly, sallow-faced boy who caught Russell by the wrist. Two similarly-built thugs slunk up behind him.

"Well, well, look who it is," Melcrona sneered. "The loner and the freak. Let him go." This last part was directed at one of his goons, who had been straining to hold the twisting, purple-faced Adam. The goon let go, and Adam fell onto the ground with a squeak. He scrambled to his feet.

"You looking for trouble?" Russell snarled, procuring a knife from his pocket. "We can give that to you."

"It ain't personal, Angelo," Melcrona drawled in a nasally voice, his sneer stretching his thin lips and revealing a gaping hole where his front teeth should be. "We just lookin' for a bit of fun, ain't we, Jace?"

The boy who had choked Adam—Jace—grunted what Adam assumed could pass as an affirmative.

"We're gonna leave you screaming for mommy," Russell spat.

Melcrona raised his eyebrows appraisingly, as if to say, You? "Surround them," he ordered, and his cronies, grinning and snarling like a pack of hungry coyotes, began to slink into place—a ring, a moving, snickering ring. Adam backed up against Russell, and neither of them said anything—there wasn't much to be said.

For a moment, Adam made eye contact with Melcrona, and when the other boy grinned maniacally, Adam saw in his eyes a wild, reckless need for thrill—and behind it, a deep-seated fear, the anguish of a soul that has already given up. This was a desperate man's fight. Adam's gaze never wavered, never showed emotion, but in that moment, he was filled with an inexplicable pity for a boy whose only consolation came in making others suffer.

But then the moment was over, if it had ever even happened. Melcrona smiled nastily, and then everything happened at once. The three goons pounced and Melcrona leapt forward and fists flew and there was a gunshot and a crash and someone shouted and the ground rushed up and met Adam with a crunch. They had him pinned. Had him stretched out and held to the ground like a piece of prey about to be skinned, but the knives were punches, kicks to the groin that he could not deflect. And then, suddenly, they were gone.

It was silent.

Too silent. Where was Russell? Melcrona? Adam craned his head back and looked at the upside-down world. A dust cloud was settling back over the pile of broken wood that was the bench. Melcrona stared, transfixed, as if in a daze. His bloody palms made fists, opened up again. Trembled. His three minions were gone, as suddenly as they had appeared. His bravado had gone with them. And Adam knew why Melcrona was afraid, why he was staring at the bloody, broken bench and the bloody, broken arm that jutted from inside it; why Adam suddenly felt empty and defenseless in the wind, like his whole right side had been torn off.

"Melcrona!" Adam roared, scrambling to his feet. Melcrona jumped, looked at Adam as if for the first time, and the look he turned upon him was that of a cornered rabbit. Adam fought to suppress the rage that boiled in the pit of his stomach, but the blood pounded in his head and he even tasted a bit of it in his mouth. But that was okay because Russell, too, must have tasted it as the bench collapsed upon him; he, too, must have felt this rage, this insatiable urge to kill, to ravish, to avenge...

A furtive movement, and Melcrona was gone, his back vanishing into the trees. "You coward," Adam bellowed, "Come back and look at what you did! YOU COWARD! LOOK—WHAT—you..." He suddenly broke off, gasping for breath, trying to see through the tears that shattered his vision, trying to speak through the sobs that racked his lean frame. He heaved with the effort of drawing breath. His knees trembled and gave out completely, hitting the ground with a thud. Inch by painful inch, he half crawled, half dragged himself back to the crime scene. The death bed.

Russell's arm lay limp, reaching, grasping from the rubble. His counter stared accusingly up at Adam: 0000000000. Zero. Gone. Lifeless. And Adam knew there was nothing he could do to bring him back.

So he sat there, dirt streaking his face, holding the cold, hard hand of the boy who had been so alone yet so happy, a black sheep among bleak violence. He had valued life, Adam knew, even though he hadn't acted like it. He had never gotten drunk, never gone suicidal or given up trying. Russell had cared. He had cared about things when no one else had.

And now he's gone, said a voice in Adam's head. And then—No. He's just playing a joke. He'll wake up and give me hell for crying and holding his hand, and secretly I'll enjoy it. He'll laugh his hyena laugh that makes me cringe and then laugh along.

So why am I still crying? Why is revenge the only thing I can think of? And why, why am I seeing red?

People were beginning to notice the peculiar scene: the freak crying over a broken bench. Groups of gangly, tattooed teenagers jeered and catcalled from the shadows, but none of it registered in Adam's mind. There was nothing in the world but him and Melcrona, and death; nothing else mattered to him now.

His legs carried him up, past the broken body, past the circles of wondering innocents, back onto the splitting roads and splitting sidewalks, until he had broken into a run. He ran blindly, trusting his body to take him to his prey. He ran down sleazy alleyways and forsaken apartments, channeling his anguish through meaningless strings of curses and prayers. He ran until the sun began to fall, and his legs ached from exertion.

He ran until he found Melcrona.

He slowed to a heaving walk at the gas station, hoping to catch his breath. He knew it was a popular gang hangout, but he didn't care; he thirsted for danger and the oblivion it brought. Then he heard the sniffling and retching. It was faint, distant, as if coming from behind the building. In spite of himself, his curiosity was engaged, and he crept over to the back to investigate.

It was Melcrona. Crouched with his head between his knees in a thriving growth of weeds in the rotting parking lot, his back was to Adam, and he didn't notice him approach. An unpleasant feeling rumbled in Adam's stomach, hungry and vile, and before he knew what he was doing, he had called out, "Miss me?"

Melcrona didn't so much as turn, and that was when Adam knew something was wrong. He took a hesitant step, then two, barely feeling his shoes sink into mud. It was as he approached the crouched figure that Melcrona turned and looked at him and yelled "What do you want!" and Adam realized his tormenter was crying. Smears of snot and tears streaked his chin and cheeks, and his eyes were red and bloodshot—from crying or drinking, he didn't know. Possibly both: shards of shattered glass and muddied amber liquid littered the ground around him.

And as he gazed at this pitiful figure, the monster inside him withered and died.

"Well," Melcrona demanded, "are you going to kill me or not?" He threw his arms out in a challenging gesture, and that was when Adam saw the numbers.

0000000614.

So that was what this was about. Melcrona was a dying man, and he simply couldn't handle the fact. He tried to forget about it by doing what he did best; but in the way his eyes danced wildly, in the way his voice quavered, Adam knew he felt the looming imminence of death. Melcrona had watched as the light in Russell's eyes gave in to resignation and then left him completely, and he knew that was what Adam would see in him as the minutes counted down. Adam's voice was hard when he spoke. "I don't kill for no reason. Unlike some."

It was as if Melcrona had been coiled, waiting to explode. "Do you think I have a choice?" he yelled, slamming his hand down into the shards of glass, and Adam had the feeling he wasn't just talking about Russell. "Do you think I fucking enjoy living like this, not knowing who or where I am every time I wake up? Not a single damn person cares!" He was screaming now, driving broken glass into his palm, tears streaming down his bloated face. He looked up at Adam with wide, red-rimmed eyes swimming with pain and hurt, and a clear, desperate cry for help. "Do you think I chose to live like–"

Abruptly, he coughed, violently hacking up clots of blood and saliva. Adam knew what was coming before it happened—he scrambled back just as a stream of concentrated bile splattered into Melcrona's lap.

He watched helplessly as Melcrona dished out another helping; the latter groped blindly on the ground behind him, grabbing a torn paper bag and shoving his face into it as his stomach convulsed again. He crouched there, his face slick with sweat and tears, his hands painted with the product of his sorrow. This boy, this sorry image, was what hid behind every hoodlum, every alcoholic, every confident teen. Every wealthy government puppet. And there was no one to help them. No one who wanted to.

Hesitantly, Adam edged closer, and, as much as his conscience screamed at him not to, put his hand on Melcrona's back, holding in a grimace as he made contact with his damp shirt. Melcrona's breathing evened out under Adam's steady hand; his shaking receded to a tremble.

There was a silent, somber moment in which Adam prayed for Russell to understand.

"You know," Melcrona said slowly, "I can't remember the last time someone's touched me without leaving a bruise."

It was a confession. A token of trust. The realization hit him hard—they were very much alike, Russell and Melcrona. The abuse. The unstable support and the lack of love. The falling numbers.

"But he didn't give in," Adam mused aloud, withdrawing his hand. Melcrona, his mouth still stained with bile, shot him a quizzical look.

"Yes," Adam said, firmly now, "you do have a choice. Or, you did. But you gave it up."

Melcrona seemed not to understand. He took a deep, trembling breath, and said, "Look, just kill me already, okay? Make it quick and easy."

The numbers flashed on his wrist—0000000103.

"I don't have to," said Adam. He stood and walked away.

Melcrona said no more, just gazed at him with uncomprehending eyes, clutching his bag of vomit like it was the only thing he knew. Adam had come to kill Russell's murderer, to avenge his death, but as he left, he realized that Melcrona would bring about his own demise. He had lived his life with an eye on his counter, had put too much stock in it, and in doing so had created this future for himself. It was a self-fulfilling prophecy. He knew he was going to die, and he couldn't change that, so he had given up entirely.

But Russell had understood, Adam realized. It wasn't about when you died—everyone would eventually die someday. But if you have some life left in you, why not enjoy it while you can?

Behind him, the numbers on Melcrona's wrist reached zero.

by Sue Kim, age 14
2014 Silver Key
Hamilton High School, Chandler

Renegade.

His brightest memory of his mother is of the day she dies. He is used to watching his family grow smaller and smaller around him. The nostalgia is overwhelming. It feels like yesterday when he came home from school to find his father's body in the kitchen. Wrists wide open, grey blood flowing in neat little lines, following the patterns in the grey and white linoleum tiles, and the two of them hunched over his twitching body. His mother didn't tell him stories for a while after that, but she did tell him to stop taking the pills.

She whispered to him that there was more to life than fear and pain. That somewhere out there, there were cities, Free Cities where pills weren't rules and nothing was grey. In those cities, there was noise and color. Where living wasn't just being alive—it was exciting and breathtaking and real. Places where living meant something.

She whispered that there was something more, something better there. Something beyond the State walls that kept them in and the rest of the world out. That something was why she kissed his father's weeping wrists and smiled as his body shuddered and bled. It was why she whispered, 'He's free' when he finally died. Why they didn't take their pills the day his father's body was buried in the grave he had been assigned on the day of his birth.

It's why he's standing here right now in his very best clothes. His shirt is white and pressed, all sharp lines and cutting corners. His trousers are dark grey and his shoes are black. His mother is in a pretty white dress. His father had loved his mother in that dress. With straps that wrapped around her neck and a heart shaped neckline; it was made of soft, cottony material that fell to her calves. She always wore her hair up when she wore that dress. Today, her hair is down.

It jumps over her shoulders as the wind picks up, dark brown curls tousling for a spot on her shoulder. She's smiling softly as they read to her, her crimes. He doesn't hear them. He only sees his mother, smiling.

Her lips are not grey.

Refusal to take medication. Refusal to administer medication to a minor.

It nearly floors him, and his mother grins wide and bright and dangerous. It's a secret: the dark color on her mouth isn't the grey his brain tells him it's supposed to be. Instead it's a vibrant, sharp color. It ensnares him with each delicate curve over his mother's cupid's bow and full dark line over her lower lip. She mouths one word to him.

'Red.'

Willing distribution of hazardous materials. Accessory to distribution of hazardous materials. Distribution of hazardous materials to minors. Theft.

They shave her dark brown hair while they read her crimes. Public humiliation always preludes public execution. That's the way things are done. But his mother holds her head high. She wears her secret smile as her thick dark hair falls to the ground in near perfect ringlets about her feet. She looks like she's trying not to laugh. Their eyes are still locked.

Red.

He's been off his medication ever since the day his father died and his mother kissed his wrists bleeding sluggish grey blood, but teachers administer it at school. He does his best to hide the pills around his gums and on the roof of his mouth like his mother taught him, but sometimes he doesn't have any other choice but to swallow them. If he's lucky, he can get away and hurl them back up in the bathroom before they dissolve in his stomach and take away the sight that he had been born with. The sight that had been stolen from him, from all of them with their first pill. The sight that nearly none of them knew had been taken.

Treason against the State. Refusal of cooperation in corpse removal in the case of your late husband. Slander.

It's the same sight that had driven his father mad. He'd promised himself that he wouldn't be the same way. He had to stay strong for his mother. He had to keep her safe.

Red.

He's been off his medication ever since the day his father died, and this is the first, brightest color he's ever seen.

He's hoarded the soft, dull greens and browns that can't be changed no matter how hard science tries. The dark brown of his mother's hair, and the honest black that was his own and his father's. He clings desperately to the shade of blue he had never known the sky was. The first time he found out what yellow was, he stared at the sun until his vision was full of dark black spots and static for two hours afterward. His mother had held him and told him how proud of him she was.

That doesn't compare to this.

This– This *red* is a revelation. It's the last thing his mother will ever give him, he knows, and he takes the gift greedily. He does his best to paint a picture in his mind of how she looks. How the men in their pristine white clothes and thick grey boots look as they hold his mother upright. He does his best to remember the color of her skin, olive with a smattering of dark brown moles criss-crossing her arms. His father used to tell him that they were star maps written onto her skin.

He drinks in the color of her amber eyes, and the way the red makes them seem even brighter. His mother looks deadly like this, smiling her secret smile like she's waiting for the right chance to let everyone in on the joke. Others will only see it as a particularly dark shade of grey on her lips. But he knows the truth. He knows this truth.

Their eyes are still locked as the stool is kicked out from under her. He doesn't flinch when he hears her neck snap. He doesn't blink. She wouldn't have wanted him to.

His eyes flit away from her and land on a girl who looks his age. Her eyes are the same dark brown as his mother's shorn hair. She's doe-eyed and frightened. And that's when he knows that his mother's secret smile wasn't just for him. It was for this girl. It was for Doe-Eyes, too.

He doesn't smile at her. He barely even nods. She seems to understand the gesture. He looks away, but he feels her eyes on him as the square begins to empty and as his mother's body is taken down.

Red.

He finds the lipstick later, hidden amongst other precious little things in a hollowed-out old book beneath her bed. The book alone is enough to get him arrested, much less the treasures hidden inside. He smears one thick line over a piece of paper before folding it up and stuffing it into his pocket. His family's apartment is his now and his alone. It's a heavy burden for an eleven-year-old. He's stuck living where his father took his own life and where his mother was dragged out by the back of her neck for trying to give him something the rest of the State had forgotten.

Red.

He sneaks out after curfew and leaves the paper in a small crack on the stool his mother stood on, not even eight hours ago. He watches from his window as Doe-Eyes scuttles out from the darkness and snatches up the paper. She steals away into the night in her pure white clothes and her dirty brown eyes.

That same night, he takes a knife from the drawer and draws it across his forearm in three deep gashes. Father, Mother, Son. Everything, everything, grey. They well up in wide, bright, dangerous color. They well up red. And when he sleeps that night, he dreams.

When he wakes up, he's twenty-one, and the world is just as ugly as it was *(just as grey, grey, grey, as it was)* when he was a child. The only differences now are his job, the quality of the furniture in his childhood apartment, the regulation beer in his refrigerator, and how much fight is left in him. He has to get out. He's going to get out. He just needs to figure out when.

He arches and cracks his back, rolling his shoulders as he pulls himself out of bed and into the bathroom. He grabs a cloth to wash his face but catches sight of himself in the mirror. He has his mother's eyes. They're grey, but not in the way that everything used to be. No, his eyes are grey but are flecked with green. Damn near vermilion in the right kind of light. He's got his father's hair and cheekbones. His skin is only a few shades darker than his mother's was. He doesn't have star maps written onto his skin, and he's glad for it. He thinks that if he did, he'd end up cutting all of them off.

He cleans his face, shaves, then dresses himself for work at the factory. He has a small breakfast of regulation canned Good Meal: patented and sure to be filled with all the vitamins and nutrients a man of his age and stature needs to keep functioning properly. It smells like motor oil, and it doesn't go down easy. He wonders how long it's been since agriculture quivered in the face of processing. He wonders how long it's been since fruit still grew. He barely remembers what strawberries taste like, or if they even had a taste at all.

He cracks his neck and dumps his dishes in the sink. He resolves to wash them later because he always does. When does he ever not? He's a good citizen. He knows routine. He knows what he's supposed to do when he's supposed to do it and when. He understands what is expected of him. He's a good man, a strong man, perfect for work in the factories. He is a credit to his society, especially after how terrible both his parents turned out.

He picks up the cup containing his medication and pops out his dosage for the day. He can feel the cameras in his kitchen trained on him as he puts them into his mouth. It is a gaze that could turn dry hands clammy. He grabs a bottle of apple juice from the fridge and takes a long pull off of it to wash the taste away.

By the time he grabs his jacket and leaves the apartment, the pills have dissolved with countless others in the juice, and his vermillion eyes are glinting in the warm summer sunlight. The when is now.

by Nailah Mathews, age 16
2014 Gold Key, Silver Medal
Ironwood High School, Glendale

The Bridge

1.
The last thing I remember is a cold needle in my arm.
Through my flesh, into my veins.
There it stayed.
In pulsing blood and skin the color of winter.

After that,
everything is a blur.
I blacked out.
Bits and pieces of that night are faint.

A flash of light here,
a splash of color there.
A mix of words and thoughts.

And the rest is wishy-washy.

I clearly remember,
I didn't pull the needle out,
I didn't have to this time,
as I had numerous times before.

It fell on its own,
out of my hand,
down my arm,
onto the ground.

2.
I need to remember.
I need to remember now.

No, now I need to get up.
I have to get up and find someone.
Anyone.

I slowly open my eyes to see a white room.
Too white. Too clean.
Except for the flowers and butterflies painted on the walls.
Pastel shades of pink and purple.
This place looks too familiar.

This is definitely a hospital.
Fuck.
My parents.
Fuck.

I can't be here.
I gotta go home.

I quickly get up
and throw my legs over the bed.
My head aches.
My limbs feel as if they are coming undone.

I cannot stand straight,
but I manage to hold myself up
and I stumble into the bathroom.

My hand fumbles to find a light switch.
The lights flicker on.
I stare at the reflection in the mirror.
At a sickly looking girl.
Sick and faint.

Eyes a gloomy empty gray.
Hair a brown greasy mess.
Lips a thin bloody cracked line.

I stare hard at this girl.
At me,
But is this even me?
I hardly look anything like myself.

3.

I turn on the faucet
And cup my hands under it.

I expect to feel the cold, refreshing liquid.
But I don't.

The water just seems to go through my hands.
As though they weren't even there.

I keep my fingers there
Still hoping to feel the water.

But I don't.
I don't feel anything.

I look back in the mirror.
I realize something is wrong.

Terribly wrong.

4.

I take a deep breath

I stagger out of the bathroom
        Not even bothering to turn the faucet off.
                Or the lights.

I turn around and start to walk back to the bed.
        Before I can reach it,
                I stop in panic.

There on the white bed,
        under the stiff blanket
            Lays a still girl with her eyes closed.

Each step closer to the bed
        I realize that the strange girl asleep in my bed,
                is not a stranger at all.

5.

I am lying in a hospital bed attached to cords.	I am standing above a hospital bed.
My eyes are closed and I am quietly breathing.	my eyes are open but I can't breathe.
There is a crisp white blanket wrapped around my freezing skin.	I am in an old t-shirt and jeans. My pale skin cannot sense whether it is cold or not.
I am sleeping. I have been sleeping for a while. I must be dead.	I am running. I cannot run fast enough. I must be alive.

6.
This is a dream.
I tell myself.
Wake up.

I push my back against the wall outside my door.
Trying to breathe,
trying to gain composure.

I instinctively push my arm towards my hair.
A habit of pulling out my hair
has followed me through my early adolescence
into my late teens.

I reach for a strand,
But before I can touch it
I notice a band of white
wrapped around my left arm.

I finger the bandage.
I slowly start to unwrap it.
Fold by fold.

Underneath the binding elastic,
is an odd discoloration.
A patch of blue and purple.

A bruise along the
red vines leading to
the inside of my elbow.

I realize,
This is the reason why I am here.
This bruise is the cause and answer
to why I ended up in a hospital.

I can no longer think straight.
I pull myself off the wall.

7.
I wander the crowded hospital halls looking for any sign
that I am alive,
that I am real.

I touch nurses that pass by me.
They pay no attention.
They brush past me
as though I am nothing,
as though I am no one.

What the fuck is going on?
Doesn't anyone see me?
I'm here!
I'm right here.
Just look at me.
Talk to me!
Please.
Please, someone talk to me.

I grab a nurse by her shoulders and shake her hard.
I scream in her face.
She walks right through me.

This isn't happening. This isn't real.
This is just a bad dream.
A nightmare.
I'm going to wake up,
right now.

Angry tears stream down my face as I run through
corridor after corridor.
I run into people
who pass right through me.

I run until I no longer can
and collapse on the tile
in a fit of sobs and rage.

As I sit in a ball on the floor
I realize that I am alone.

8.
After I am able to control my crying,
I take a deep breath.
I close my eyes and open them again,
hoping to wake up from this nightmare
that has gone on far too long.

I immediately feel as though I am no longer by myself.
I lift my head up to see a man
sitting beside me against the wall.
I didn't even hear him sit down.

His dark brown hair,
looks as if it hasn't been brushed in days.

He looks straight ahead
and smiles softly.
He has kind eyes,
and looks as lost as I feel.

He must not realize I'm here.

Are you okay?

He can see me!
I'm not crazy!
I'm not alone.
I wipe away the streams of tears
along my cheeks.

I guess you've realized it then? That you're de–

He stops mid-sentence and looks at me.
Really looks at me.
I quickly look away
Because I realize his eyes
can see through my skin
and I feel an odd electricity
flash inside myself.
A flash that quickly turns into sparks.

I just...I don't know what happened

I manage to say as
I try to ignore the feeling of a burning fire inside me.
A blazing rapid flame.
Whose embers have erupted in body
and I have forgotten all my thoughts.

*Why am I here? I'm not dead, am I? I really
can't be dead. It's not–*

He chuckles.

This really isn't funny.

**I know. I'm sorry. I don't mean to laugh. You
just sound too worried about something you
can't control.**

*So I'm dead then? You see dead people? Is
that what this is? Did God send you down
here to give me my wings?*

**No, I'm in the same place you are. Not here or
there.**

*I don't understand. What does that mean?
Where are we?*

**To be honest, I'm not sure. I know that we
aren't quite living, but we're not dead yet.**

*So when can we leave? I mean...I can't stay like this forever.
It's like I don't exist.*

**I know what you mean. I've been here for a few days.
People call it The Bridge.
I'm glad I found you.**

9.

So how'd you end up here?

We start walking side by side.
Passing patients and nurses
Who pay no attention to us.

**I mean I'm sure you're having tons of fun
being dead and all, but–**

I turned toward him
and give a stern look.

Too soon?

Do you wanna see?

See what?

Come with me.

10.
He followed close behind me as
I made my way past the rooms.
Until we reached my room.

We slowly entered the room.
where my body lies,
but my soul no longer does.

I look at my lifeless figure.
This is the exact place
where my soul left my body.

He looks at the bed,
But quickly turns away.

Did you try to kill yourself?

No, it was an accident. I overdosed,
I guess.

You guess?

I don't really remember much.

I show him my arm where the bruise is.
He gently places his hands on my wrist,
where the hospital bracelet sits.

I realize he is touching me.
This is human contact.
Well, no not exactly human,
But that doesn't matter.
I am no longer invisible.

He reads my name, and age.

You're too young and pretty to die.

What's your name?

Drew.

11.
Drew was in a motorcycle accident the same night I
        overdosed.
It's funny how two separate lives can connect
in the oddest of places
for the oddest of reasons.

An accidental fate,
where two lives are changed forever.

It also funny how fast things happen in The Bridge.
How quickly friendship forms,
how fast love grows.

Things that matter in the real world don't matter here.
Age is but just a number
and ignorance is bliss.

Drew is 25 and full of reason.
I am 17 and full of curiosity.

In the limbo state where Drew and I found each other
where we shared hugs and laughs
and took romantic walks hand-in-hand
through the illuminated hospital.

In the limbo state where our lips first met.

In the limbo state where Drew and I fell in love.

12.
The comatose state of my human body has been lying
     untouched for 3 weeks.
Occasionally I see my parents visit.
but not too often,
because it makes my mom cry
and it makes my dad angry.

I have overheard the nurses talking
and it's safe to say
I should have a full recovery
sooner or later.

Drew on the other hand
is on life support
and has too much brain damage
to ever fully recover.

I wouldn't mind being in The Bridge
with Drew forever
but nothing lasts forever
not even a state of non-existence.

13.
Love is the gap between thinking and feeling
When I am with Drew,
I don't need to do either.
I just am.

There was something breathtaking in the way my name
flowed out of his mouth,
like he had been saying it for years.

I had never experienced
such a strong connection
with someone.

I don't care if we aren't even alive anymore.
Human love is bullshit.
Love in The Bridge is the real deal.

14.
Drew and I sat side by side,
in the patient waiting center.

We spent a lot of time there,
watching, and listening to families
crying over losses,
smiling over births.

It was a place of comfort,
of hope,
of loss.

Drew took my hand in his.

> They have to take me off life support.
> My mom can't do this anymore.
> She comes in everyday,
> and sits and cries.

So what happens then? Where do we go?

> Well, since I can't stay here
> and I can't go home,
> I guess I'm going to die.

We can't just die like that!

> No, I'm going to die.
> You're going home.
> You've heard the doctors.
> They all say you're going to be fine.

What do you mean I'm going to be fine?
I'm not going if you're not coming with me.

> You know I can't. It's not my choice.

Then I'll die, too.

> Don't say that.
> You have a family to go home to.
> They miss you.

Drew, you can't let me go alone.
I won't do it.

> I don't have a choice.
> And neither do you.

15.
The last day I spent with Drew
was the last day I spent
in The Bridge.

Drew and I sat in his hospital room together
and watched his mom cry
and the nurses hold their clipboards.

I held Drew's hand so tight,
I thought maybe someone would decide
it would be best if he and I stayed together.

But slowly and surely
Drew's fingers were no longer
In-between mine,
and I felt his spirit leave me.

Every nerve inside of me,
every bone and every muscle
had also left me.

The empty shell of my ghostly body
walked back to my hospital room
in hopes of finding a way to die.
Or a way to live.
Anything to get me out of here.

16.

Mind	Soul	Spirit	Body
brain	energy	ghost	physique
intelligence	being	apparition	carcass
reason	essence	phantom	figure
sense	conscious	eidolon	flesh

What will you leave behind when your time comes?

17.
I look at my figure on the white bed.
The mattress has patches of yellow discoloration now
and has formed to the shape of the lifeless body occupying
    it.

I've been here long enough.
It's time to go home.

I slowly prop myself onto the bed.
An array of various cords surrounds me.

I lay above my body
desperately hoping to reconnect.

I push myself through the skin and bones of my body.
and I slow my breathing to match.

Knowing that if I can fight through this,
I will make it out.
Alive.

I take a last look at the strange place I have been.
And as I close my eyes,
I feel myself slowly drifting away from The Bridge.

    by Natali Chausovskaya, age 17
    2014 Gold Key
    Sahuaro High School, Tucson

The Peculiar Time of Russellville

When passing through the small town of Russellville, an intriguing sight is seen. Two lovers, embracing each other near a park bench, stay in the same positions for hours, still as statues. Financial workers, blurs to the human eye, move at an exhilarating speed to prevent being late to work. A child, eyes widening at the sight, stands mesmerized by the beauty of a doll at the local department store and seems to remain completely motionless for days on end. Everything appears to move at its own pace, at its own time.

Just now, a student at a local high school is taking an important examination. If he does not pass the exam, he will not be accepted to a college. If he is not accepted into a college, he will not acquire an adequate education. If he does not have an adequate education, he will not be able to hold a job with a sufficient salary to provide for himself. Halfway done with his exam, the student looks up at the clock to find that he only has ten minutes left, not nearly enough time to finish. Instead of panicking, the student merely picks up his pencil and continues the examination at his own pace. After he checks his work twice and is confident with his answers, he turns in the examination with ten minutes to spare.

On the other side of town, an old man is fishing in a little boat at Lake Dardanelle and is said to have been there for hundreds of years. Memories of his youth dart past him like bullets just missing a target—attending his first formal dance, studying at the university, meeting his future wife at the business corporation, holding his firstborn child in his arms, watching his children grow up, smiling at his grandchildren. The old man, his eyes glazed over as he recounts his memories one by one, can be seen from the shoreline and is a monument visited by tourists who venture to this particular town.

In this world the passage of time is controlled by people. Time can be frozen, sped up, or slowed down all in accordance with the wills of the people. This is a world where time is compliant and can be plucked from space just as an apple can be plucked from a tree. However, just as an apple cannot be placed back on the tree from which it was taken from, a decision to interfere with time is irreversible. Ignoring the consequences, people are able to do what they wish with time and take their precious lives for granted.

Although many outside observers look upon this town with jealousy, thinking that these people have been bestowed a great gift; the great tragedy of this world is that everyone eventually finds themselves in solitude. The two lovers sitting near the park bench will realize that in the hours spent embracing each other they have missed repeated calls from bosses, friends, families, colleagues, and have made many enemies. The little girl, staring intently at the doll, will be rudely awakened from her days of dreaming with the news that her parents have been killed in a car accident trying to find her. Sooner or later, the old man of Lake Dardanelle will wake from his stupor and realize that his wife, children, grandchildren, friends are all long gone.

Some who live in the outskirts of this town have completely ceased to meddle with time. They have seen what has happened to people who interfere with time and are fully aware of the consequences. These people are the ones who teach their children about the effects of time in this world of theirs. They are the ones who, even in old age, are able to greet you with a smile and make a sound conversation. They are the ones who walk with the confidence of people who are at ease with one another. They are the ones who live life to the fullest, accept all mistakes made, and truly enjoy life as it is.

by Nichole Kyprianou, age 14
2014 Gold Key
BASIS Scottsdale, Scottsdale

CONCLUDING SECTION
About the Authors

Jacob Abukhader
Jacob is from Mesa. His Indie, Pop Punk, and Alternative musical influences are reflected in his poem "The Start," which explores the wonder of space travel and the mortality of man through the eyes of an astronaut on a rocket launch gone wrong.

Oscar Aguirre
Oscar was born in Phoenix. His poem "Sí Se Puede" considers how society has stigmatized Hispanics, how Hispanics are branded, and how many allow themselves to be stereotyped by their actions. He feels Hispanics should stop their actions that degrade the culture.

Dylan Angle
Dylan, a soccer player, reader, and nature-lover, was born in Maryland and raised in Arizona. He uses the books he reads as inspiration for his writing, but the work "Missing in Action" is dedicated to his uncle, a great man who serves in the Special Forces.

Katie Barnhart
Katie lives in Scottsdale and attends 7th grade at Desert Canyon Middle School. She enjoys putting her thoughts and ideas on paper in any format, although her favorite art is poetry for its beauty and rhythm. Katie also participates in Martial Arts, softball, Science Olympiad, and band (percussion). She loves old music, school, reading, and chocolate.

Max Bartlett
Max was born and raised in Scottsdale, and "Pointing Fingers" is an essay on gun control in America. Max also received a Silver Key for a poetry collection and earned Honorable Mentions for essays "Behind the Door," "The Virtual Gridiron," and the poem, "I'll Make You Read."

Hannah Bernier
Hannah goes to Desert Canyon Middle School and enjoys playing music and soccer. Her poem "Would You Believe Me?" reflects on her religious identity. She likes ukuleles and reading.

Adwoa Buadu
Though born in Fukoka, Japan, Adwoa currently lives in Tucson. She wrote "It's a Lovely Day for Fighting, Isn't It?" for her school literary magazine a few weeks after a Zumba dance session. The essay chronicles a glimpse of Adwoa's struggles to accept herself and love her body.

Raina Burchett
Raina, child of the Sun, was born and raised in sunny Scottsdale. She was inspired by the time she spent with her grandmother "Ruthie" and memories of being a young child. Raina finds writing a form of art in and of itself, as well as a way to verbally express her visual art.

Tori Cejka

Inspired by her newspaper teacher at Chaparral, Victoria Cejka aspires to be a journalist and always maintain her passion for writing.

Natali Chausovskaya

Natali is originally from Kiev, Ukraine, but currently resides in Tucson. Her interest in dark romanticism and love of free-verse poetry is what inspired her to write "The Bridge." She would like to thank her English teachers and family for encouraging her writing.

Hyeji (Julie) Cho

A first-generation Korean immigrant, Hyeji (Julie) Cho is from Scottsdale. She is a proud violinist of the Phoenix Youth Symphony and attends BASIS Scottsdale. Her poems "Farewell to the South" and "Unholy Trinity" portray the struggles in the everyday lives of North Koreans to promote awareness of the oppressed conditions in the country. This is her first attempt at poetry, inspired by her close friend, Haley Lee.

Christopher Clements

Chris Clements is a Sophomore at Thunderbird High School in Phoenix, Arizona. He has a tasteless sense of humor and a cultured sense of pessimism that you smell a mile away. He's been writing ever since he was told that being a writer was the worst occupation to make a living. He's known for his apathy and his sarcasm, especially against "The Man."

Alex Cohen

A debater, participant in academic quiz tournaments, and volunteer teacher's assistant, Alex lives in Scottsdale. As a Jew, he often composes poetry that considers past struggles of the Jewish people; these, coupled with the adversity that children face on the playground, inspired "Schoolyard." Reflecting on general themes of loss and desperation that many face at tournaments he attends, he was inspired to write "Metal."

Navya Dasari

A lover of storytelling in all forms, from nonfiction essays to abstract painting, Navya is from Scottsdale. Her fascination with music and language inspired "Crescendo," while her Indian heritage drew her to a story of race in America, "Bridging Divides or Banning Discussion?" The poems "Passion" and "Trust" both reflect her view of the world and her interest in the relationship between chaos and identity. Her work has also been printed in publications like the *Dartmouth Undergraduate Journal of Science* and *Sharodargho*, the Arizona Bengali magazine.

Vy Doan

Vy spent the first five years of her life in Vietnam and drew inspiration from her childhood home in "Rain." For her, writing is a visualization of her jumbled thoughts and a way to bypass sleepless nights. She plans to study biomedical engineering and always be writing.

Nicole Dominiak

Nicole Dominiak, author of "Gifts, Ghosts, and God" is a human being who enjoys the company of non-human beings—books, silence, and Nutella—more than is probably good for her. She alternates between wanting to clap herself on the back and wanting to slap herself in the face.

Megan Dressler

Megan, preferably Meg, was born and raised in Bullhead City. In a small town with little to do, Meg developed an interest in not only writing, but also in music. When she isn't writing, she can be found practicing ukulele or guitar. Her pieces "King of Gods" and "Ones and Sixes" focus on the struggle with feelings of inadequacy, and on how the two different narrators cope with these feelings—one by painting, the other by embellishing tales about her life. "One Thousand and One Pieces" explores a young woman's heritage and interest in her cultures of origin. Finally, Meg's poem "The Hipster Manifesto" tells the daily routine of the social niche that everybody loves to hate.

Tal Eitan

Tal was born in Israel and has always had a love for music and science. Playing music at the Barton House for the last four years, he's inspired to continue to do so and perhaps to explore the science behind Alzheimer's disease.

Alex Elbert

Alex was born and raised in Arizona. She wrote "Chewing Bubble Gum in the Rain" as a nostalgic reflection on the simplicities of childhood and her disparate desire for more rain in Phoenix. In addition to writing, she spends her time with sculpting and technical theater.

Audrey Ennis

Audrey, the author of "The Preference of Darkness," is from Fountain Hills. She is deeply interested in exploring the nature of humanity, analyzing in her writing both the faults and virtues of man that never seem to be lost through time.

Devin Farr

Devin was born and raised in Mesa, Arizona, and is still living there today. He got his inspiration about writing poetry from a woman named Sarah Kay, who, through her writing, inspired him to dive into the realm of spoken-word poetry. Devin wrote the poems "Sour Milk" and "Diamonds," which send strong, powerful messages that all people would be able to relate to in their everyday lives.

Antonio Flores

Antonio Flores is a junior at Mountain View High School in Mesa. His poem, "To the Young Men," can be characterized as "an ode to Jimmy Santiago Baca, the new godfather of poetry."

BrieAnna Frank

BrieAnna is a junior at Maryvale High School in Phoenix. She's been deeply inspired by stories of survivors of school shootings in America. A trip to Colorado led to "Fourteen Years Later: The Columbine Massacre." She thanks her family, friends, and mentors.

Angelica Garcia

Angelica is a 16 year-old thespian, singer, and aspiring writer. She wrote "Suspension of Disbelief" and "Last Smile" on a whim. She began writing poetry after her eighth grade teacher simply told her she was "good at it" after a poetry lesson. Most importantly, she'd like to thank her parents and little brother for always believing in her!

Justin Garner

Justin is a senior at Mountain View High School in Mesa who participates in competitive swimming when not in class. "Balance" is an essay that addresses the societal shift from being balanced and even, and how we as humans can get back to that balance.

Tiffany Gong

Inspired by conflicting duality of self, Tiffany Gong's poems "The Monster" and "Mother Was Wrong" both reflect the urge to give in to one's own demons and demonstrate the struggle to contain them. Tiffany Gong is currently a high school senior who will attend ASU in the fall.

Callie Gregory

Callie is from Mesa. "A Mother's Love," prompted by the sudden death of Callie's beloved mother, Lynette, is about the days and memories of her mother. She'd like to thank her dad for being so loving and supportive, her brothers, and all her loving, smart, and awesome friends.

Heather Griffin

Heather Griffin was born and raised in Mesa, Arizona. She wrote "The Juggler" during the end of her first semester of her senior year in high school while undergoing the stress presented by the pressing forces in a typical teenager's life.

Anvita Gupta

Anvita was born and grew up in Phoenix. She wrote "A Chipped Peacock" based on her experiences as a second-generation Indian immigrant and her reflections on her home and heritage.

Taylor Hammond

Taylor Hammond plays the bassoon and clarinet in the Mountain View Marching Band and has marched in the Macy's Thanksgiving Day Parade in New York City. She has a Chinchilla named Paisley that she takes for long walks in the desert. She finds inspiration in the life around her. She doesn't know what the future will bring, but she is optimistic and looks forward to all the amazing things she will accomplish.

Anna Hawkins

Anna hails from Mesa. When not studying for Academic Decathlon, she enjoys practicing harp or reading Russian literature. Her poem, "Lament—An Elegy for the Fairy Tale," compares childhood expectations to reality.

Samantha Hayes

Samantha is an 8th grader at Tesseract. Along with writing, she enjoys participating in her school musical every year and playing different types of sports. The arts are her passion; she plans to have a career in that area. She considers herself a "whole package."

Madi Hinze

Born and raised in Arizona, Madi has dreamed of leaving her home state from the time she was little. This desire to explore new places led her to instead travel within her own mind, and writing has been her passion ever since. "Blasphemy" draws from her personal experiences with homophobia while "What Is Good Enough?" is based on the struggles of being a high school senior.

Hannah Jarvis

Hannah is an Oreo enthusiast and recovering Nutella addict who uses writing to make sense of the outside world. When she isn't feverishly scribbling in a notebook, Hannah is busy playing her ukulele, climbing trees, and painting murals. In the future, she dreams of pulverizing the gender binary, becoming a world-renowned muralist-poet, and being able to afford Starbucks every. single. morning.

Hyunjeong Jun

Hyun, author of "Eastbound" and "Teddy," currently lives in Tucson. She has a fondness for learning new languages, her primary linguistic domains being Korean and English. She loves writing because she's fascinated by the artistic expression of language and the influence of language on ideas and culture.

Alejandra Katz

Alejandra enjoys painting, saving puppies, curing cancer, and writing bloated author's biographies. Inspired partially by Dante Alighieri, her short story "A Hellish Problem" deals with the problems one might find in Hell. Alejandra lives with her family in Tucson.

Lina Khan

Lina resides in Scottsdale but is originally from Kentucky; she experienced a culture shock when she moved. Lina wrote "Woebegone" in response to the different types of people she encountered in Arizona. The story deals with a girl whose lack of appreciation of a blessed life drives her to wish ill upon herself.

Sue Kim

Sue has lived in Arizona for most of her life, after moving from Korea at the tender age of three. She writes short stories such as "Numbers" to explore the potential of humankind while staying true to her roots as a lover of fantasy and science fiction.

Nichole Kyprianou

Nichole, a sister, swimmer, and pianist, is from Scottsdale. She wrote "The Peculiar Time of Russellville" after reflecting on Einstein's theory of relativity and pondering the idea of time being tangible so as to have the potential to be controlled by people.

Haley Lee

A triplet, fencer and musician, Haley is from Scottsdale. She wrote "They Are the Patriots" after reflecting, in the post-9/11 era, on her family history during WWII—her mother's Polish and Austrian family in German concentration camps and her paternal family's displacement after the Japanese invasion of China.

Adrian Lamas

Adrian is a fine arts student at Mountain View High School in Mesa. He designed this book's cover art, which will also become YAA's logo.

Kimaya Lecamwasam

Kimaya Lecamwasam is the daughter of immigrants from Sri Lanka, and is a 9th grader at BASIS Scottsdale. She is a budding singer-songwriter and a third-degree black belt. She enjoys travelling and spending time with her family and friends.

Chase Lortie

Chase is 16 and a Junior at Red Mountain High School in Mesa. He enjoys inventing, drawing, designing, writing, and engineering. He thanks his many teachers for inspiring him.

Katherine Lu

Knowing she won't define herself in a short autobiography, Katherine is just a student too preoccupied with metaphysical reflection for her own good. Her poem "a blind (science)" discusses the perpetuation of ignorant folly, oppression, and bigotry belied by scientific and religious tradition.

Lauren Ludwig

Lauren enjoys dancing and trips to California. She loves visiting her grandparents' ranch and going horseback riding and loves to laugh and smile 'til her face hurts. Any chance she gets to eat at Gecko Grill, she accepts. Not a day goes by without an exciting moment in her life.

Christina Luu

Christina is an Arizona native who likes singing while playing piano, reading fantasy, and listening to melodic death metal. She wrote "Impasto" to give a voice to those entangled in an abusive relationship, intends to keep writing, and thanks her family for their support.

Brigitta Mannino

Brigitta's romantic short story "I Should Have Taken the Stairs" was inspired by Disney's California Adventure Hollywood Tower of Terror, and her favorite creative writing book! Brigitta also blogs about all things books on her blog, *Escape Inside the Pages*. Brigitta thanks her friends and family for supporting her writing endeavors.

Gloria Martinez

Gloria lives in Oro Valley and loves vivid imagery and diction. She labels herself a "nefelibata," someone who lives in the clouds of their own imagination and dreams, and who disobeys the conventions of society, literature, or art. This love of imagination and vivid imagery impacted her two poems, "The Mahogany Dealer" and "Sleeping Boy," as well as her flash fiction piece "Abandoned Memories."

Nailah Mathews

"Zoni" award-winning actor Nailah is a native of Detroit, Michigan, who migrated to Arizona at the age of eight. After devouring every book she could get her hands on, she decided it was high time she started writing her own. Combining her love of theater and prose, Mathews penned "Selfish Things": a dramatic script and brief study of human emotion and motivation. Her science fiction/fantasy piece "Renegade." was inspired by Orwellian dystopia, and personal narrative "Chasing Infinity" was born of teenage existentialism. She would like to thank Meridith, Brian, and Kit for helping her find her voice. Much love.

Stirling McDaniel

A martial artist, fencer, and full-time nerd, Stirling hails from Fountain Hills. Her story, "A Message to Humanity," was written when her pent-up frustration at reality exploded. Naturally, she would like to thank her parents and teachers, and, unnaturally, her cat.

Anthony Mirabito

Anthony believes that the written word commands a deep-rooted, conscious respect of its power. In every word, there is meaning; each word carries its own individual message. Alone, they are strong, but together, massed as an army born from the mind, they become lethal: weapons for destruction, tools to serve a purpose, or extensions to share imagination. Anthony writes with the hope that all his work, his proudest being "The Devil's Bane," can demonstrate that power.

Jordyn Ochser

Jordyn was born and raised in Newport Beach, California, and currently lives in Scottsdale. Her fascination with Greek mythology is exhibited in her two poems, "Birth of Courage" and "Birth of Grief." She has a thirst for knowledge that drives her to write about what she doesn't know in order to gain understanding of life yet unexplored.

Sydney Portigal

Sydney Portigal is from Paradise Valley, Arizona. The inspiration for her piece, "Too Rockstar for Starbucks," came from one of her favorite activities—people watching. The piece comments on various themes in our modern day society, such as the importance of outward appearances. She would like to thank her parents for always supporting her.

Mandri Randeniya

Mandri was born in Sri Lanka and moved to the USA in 2007. The personal essay "Waves" recounts her own experience of the Indian Ocean tsunami in 2004. She would like to thank her family for helping her be her best and her friends for putting up with her.

Kolbe Riney

Kolbe lives in Tucson, Arizona, and rides horses and debates in her free time. Mostly, she just really likes puzzles.

Emma Rymarcsuk

Emma, originally born in Virginia, moved to Scottsdale at the age of eleven. Besides writing poetry, she enjoys swimming, playing the violin, and riding her horse, Mickey.

Archanna Smith

Archanna plays the harp and rides English saddle. She hopes to study literature in the United Kingdom. Her poetry is inspired by music that draws her into the emotion of her writing. Archanna's poem "Patchwork" arose from mourning the death of a loved one.

Lydia Spire

Lydia lives in Phoenix. Her works, "Ordinary Courage of a Father" and "Ordinary Courage of a Normal Teenager," deal with the unappreciated everyday courage of normal people. She enjoys seeing other people smile.

Bailey Vidler

Bailey, hailing from Mesa, divides her spare time between writing, drawing, and playing saxophone. She has an obsession to various degrees of unhealthiness for the supernatural and a general empathy for snark and sass. "Hellfire Love" combines these elements.

Kathleen Wu

Kathleen Wu is from Scottsdale, Arizona. She wrote her work, "Two Years Later," for an AP Language and Composition class, and finds the topic of illegal immigration urgent and inextricably complex. In her spare time, she enjoys playing the flute and watching her cat.

Alice Zhao

Alice is from Paradise Valley. After a conversation with her grandfather over the summer, she wrote "In the End, You and I" as a meditation on youth and life, age and the end. She'd like to thank her grandfather for teaching her the power of a story.

Justin Zhu

An enthusiastic volunteer, soccer player, pianist, and club president, Justin Zhu has always been inspired by moral courage. His composition "The Call for Courage" depicts the heartwarming triumph of one Holocaust survivor. Justin would like to thank his parents and mentors for their extraordinary support and dedication over the years:

> *"As a result [of Oskar Knoblauch's call to do what is right], I have joined many religious and social organizations in helping those who are less fortunate. I have learned moral courage comes not from others, but from within. Though my actions are nothing compared to the actions mentioned above, I know that soon in the future I will have to answer the true call for moral courage. Righteousness may be a hard thing to see in many different cases, but only those who can see it, fight for it and risk their lives for it are the ones who demonstrate true moral courage."*

Cassidy Zinke

Cassidy is an enthusiastic writer that never wants the reader to be bored. She dreams of being a novelist and strives for her goal by reading and having fun with writing pieces like "The Young Dreamer," a short story about a young girl with an abyss of youthful imagination.

About the Editors

Billy Gerchick, Executive Editor and Persuasive Editor
Billy teaches English at Coronado High School, Paradise Valley Community College, and Scottsdale Community College in the Phoenix area. YAA Co-Founder and President, Billy values the power of language and media arts collaboration and thanks all who made *Bloom* happen.

Julie Cain, Assistant Editor and Humor Editor
Julie graduated from ASU, has taught in Arizona, advises college students, and is VP of Education for Blended Learning Solutions in Phoenix. When not plotting to reform school systems & save the world, she's YAA's Secretary and goes undercover for the grammar police.

Haley Lee, Student Editor
Needs to get credit for her role as student editor.

Jon Jeffery, Design Consultant
Jon teaches digital photography and graphics as Mountain View High School in Mesa and is Vice President of Fountain Hills Artists' Gallery. John has taught college photography, works in the field, and is inspired by Jerry Uelsmann, Henri Cartier-Bresson, & Richard Avedon.

Taryn Gutierrez, Copyright and Legal Consultant
Taryn Gutierrez currently advises college students, but she feels like she attends Clown College, where she hopes to beat the record for most clowns in a car someday. She's also eyebrows-deep working on her master's degree to prepare for the publication industry.

Christine Porter Marsh, Personal Essay/Memoir Editor
Christine Marsh has been teaching for 22 years at the school from which she graduated, Chaparral High School in the Scottsdale Unified School District. She got her undergraduate degree from UCLA in English Literature and is currently working on her master's degree in Teacher Leadership at Grand Canyon University.

Tracy Weaver, Poetry Editor
Tracy has 20 years of experience teaching English and has coached Speech and Debate for 18. She currently teaches at Mountain View High School in Mesa, serves as YAA Vice President, and is a National Writing Fellow. Her Master's degree is in Speech Communications/Secondary Education, and she is involved with the literary art magazine MOSAIC, Poetry OutLoud competitions, Toro Link Leaders, AETA, NCTE, and Heinemann. Her passion, though, is rooted in reading...reading everything.

Heather Nagami, Poetry Co-Editor
Heather teaches English and Creative Writing at BASIS Oro Valley. Her book of poems, *Hostile*, was published by Chax Press. She enjoys reading and writing poetry, swimming, and playing video games and Words with Friends.

Kelly O'Rourke, Poetry Co-Editor

Kelly teaches language arts at Desert Canyon Middle School in Scottsdale. She encourages students to broaden their knowledge of poetry by exposing them to poets from Naomi Shihab Nye to Wallace Stevens, and her own personal favorite: Mary Oliver.

Laura Turchi, Poetry Co-Editor

Laura is a University of Houston assistant professor of curriculum and instruction with a passion for Shakespeare and contemporary poets Heather McHugh, Eleanor Wilner, Ellen Bryant Voigt, Steven Orlens, and Stephen Dobyns.

Jay Tucker Morganstern, Flash Fiction Editor

YAA Co-Founder/ Board Member, Associate Professor, Mary-Lou Fulton College of Education, Arizona State University, Adjunct Professor of English, Chandler-Gilbert Community College, Adjunct Professor, Upper Iowa University. Jay Morganstern cherishingly thanks: his parents, Stanley and Paulette, who taught him how to write and appreciate the written word, his Great-Aunt Frieda, who introduced him to the spoken word, and his 10th Greenberg, for supplying the most important words he ever read, "Invictus," by William Earnest Henley.

Chelle Wotowiec, Short Story Editor

(Mi)Chelle works at ITT Technical Institute Phoenix West Campus and teaches English at Chandler Gilbert Community College. Her writing is influenced by Paula Vogel and Anne Carson and she believes in the power of language. Words will change the world.

Alyssa Tilley, Journalism Editor

Alyssa is a sophomore at Northern Arizona University majoring in secondary English education with a minor in journalism. She has been working for *The Lumberjack* newspaper for two years. Her favorite hobbies include reading and binging on Netflix.

Michelle Hill, Dramatic Script Editor

In May of 2013, Michelle completed coursework in two doctoral programs at Arizona State University: Theatre and Performance of the Americas and Theatre for Youth. She also received a Master's Degree in Theatre Education and Outreach from the University of New Mexico.

Melissa Williamson, Science Fiction/Fantasy Editor

Melissa is a doctoral student in English Education at Arizona State University. She reads about 98% young adult fiction. Most of it is sci/fi and fantasy. When she was young, she picked up a collection of stories by Edgar Allan Poe, leading to her obsession with sci/fi and fantasy.

About the Scholastic Art & Writing Awards

Since 1923, the Scholastic Art & Writing Awards have recognized our nation's exceptional youth, providing an annual opportunity for grade 7-12 students to be noticed for their creative talents.

Past participants include artists like Andy Warhol and Cy Twombly, writers Sylvia Plath, Truman Capote, Ned Vizzini, and Joyce Carol Oates, photographer Richard Avedon, actors Frances Farmer, Robert Redford, Alan Arkin, and John Lithgow, filmmaker Ken Burns, and more. Outside the arts, Awards' alumni become leaders in fields like journalism, medicine, finance, government and civil affairs, law, science, toy design, etc.

Students' submissions are judged by visual and literary arts luminaries, some who've also been past award recipients. Many notable past jurors have participated, including Francine Prose, Paul Giamatti, Langston Hughes, Robert Frost, Judy Blume, Paula Poundstone, Billy Collins, David Sedaris, Roz Chast, and more.

Today, teens in grades 7- 12 (from public, private, or home schools) can apply in 28 categories of art and writing to earn scholarships and have their works exhibited or published. In the last five years, students submitted nearly 900,000 original works of art and writing. During that time over 60 arts institutes and colleges have sponsored the Awards to make $40 million in scholarships and aid available to regional and national Awards winners.

The Alliance for Young Artists & Writers was founded in 1994, as a 501(c)(3) nonprofit, to present the Scholastic Art & Writing Awards and expand upon the Awards' legacy of bringing exceptional artistic and literary talent of teens to a national audience. Today the Alliance works with 100-plus regional affiliate programs nationwide to bring the Awards to local communities and over 60 scholarship partners. 2012-13 marked the 90th Anniversary of the Scholastic Art & Writing Awards.

The Alliance upholds four core values: scholarship ($250,000 in annual scholarships), recognition (including the annual ceremony at Carnegie Hall in New York City), exhibition (various exhibitions like *ART. WRITE. NOW.* and with partners like the U.S. Department of Education), and publication (featuring multiple art and writing "best of" national publications).

About the Young Authors of Arizona

Beginning as Scholastic Writing Awards affiliate
Since 2012, YAA has facilitated the Scholastic Writing Awards in the state of Arizona. All entry fees go toward YAA's affiliate fee with the Alliance for Young Artists and Writers, hosting our annual spring awards ceremony, and extending community outreach for future years. Working pro-bono, we encourage young authors.

First three years
Thanks to individuals and sponsorship from the Arizona English Teachers Association (AETA), in 2012, YAA became Arizona's first Scholastic Writing Awards affiliate in Awards' history. Our inaugural year blazed the authorship trail with 200-plus Scholastic Writing Awards entries from grade 7-12 students from Bullhead City to Phoenix to Tucson.

Scottsdale's Coronado High School hosted the spring ceremony, where Valley poets Tomas Stanton and Myrlin Hepworth wowed the crowd. Five Arizona authors earned invites to Carnegie Hall in May, and 14-year old Haley Lee became Arizona's first American Voices Medal winner. Haley's poem, "They Are the Patriots," earned publication in the national *Best Teen Writing of 2012* book.

2013 saw entries increase: the spring ceremony was hosted at Arcadia High School in Phoenix and featured a Skype chat with acclaimed author Jessica Brody. Beyond YAA recognition, six young authors of Arizona earned invites to the national ceremony. Haley Lee repeated as our American Voices Medal winner, and two works earned publication in the national *Best Teen Writing of 2013* book: Lee's poem "Expanding" and 13-year old Gloria Martinez's science fiction/fantasy story "Don't Be Afraid of the Dark."

2014 saw even more entries, necessitating a bigger venue for the spring ceremony: Mountain View High School in Mesa. At the national level, eight Arizona entries earned invitations to Carnegie Hall, and 14-year-old Nicole Dominiak earned the Arizona's American Voices Medal for her short story "Gifts, Ghosts, and God." Some key precedents and organizational growth have truly made 2014 a year of, well, "bloom" for YAA.

YAA emerging as a non-profit

YAA is a State of Arizona nonprofit organized exclusively for educational and charitable purposes, within the meaning of Section 501(c)(3) of the U.S. Internal Revenue Code. Without limiting ourselves, YAA is focused on growing responsibly and is now positioned to:

a. Conceive, develop, implement, sponsor, and maintain progress in all aspects of language and media arts, which will advance the interests of and provide the incentive for the growth and appreciation by the public of language and media arts in Arizona and beyond.

b. Undertake projects that will encourage and assist young authors and young-author advocates by helping them achieve standards of excellence and bringing these projects before the public.

c. Strengthen scholarship, research, creative work, publication, exhibition, and performance in language and media arts throughout Arizona and beyond.

"Bloom!" needs your help from May 2014 – May 2015

YAA plans to grow in 2014-2015. Our state has over 1,400 middle schools and high schools combined, with many more home schools. Starting in May of 2014, YAA's "Bloom!" outreach campaign seeks to involve more Arizonans with the 2015 Scholastic Art & Writing Awards as the scope and centerpiece for our growth. We welcome involvement from:

1. Professional language and media arts leaders—teachers, librarians, sponsors, luminaries—to support and promote this book (see page 300).

2. Educators, parents, and volunteers to be outreach leaders in specific counties, districts, and professional communities.

3. Students to enter the 2015 Scholastic Art & Writing Awards by December 17, 2014 (see pages 301-302).

4. Business and civic leaders, volunteer educators and parents, and other supporters to forge financial partnerships with YAA to create scholarships for Awards participants and to continue growing YAA.

If interested in partnering with YAA, e-mail: youngauthorsofaz@gmail.com.

Bloom: User's Guide and Resources

This *Best Arizona Teen Writing of 2014* anthology is the first of its kind in state history: by young authors, for Arizona, earning publication through the Scholastic Writing Awards. YAA may be the only of Scholastic's 100-plus affiliates with our own "best of" book, but we need you to help it reach its educational potential:

1. Please support a 2015 "best of" book by purchasing *Bloom* individual copies and discounted class sets.
2. Be aware that this book contains some slang and sensitive content; teachers are encouraged to preview and use works in class. While these compositions may not be "classic" models, they have been judged as top works, written by teens, that can connect with grade 7-12 language arts students who may prefer studying peer authors.
3. YAA hopes that educators will identify Scholastic Writing Awards categories that align to *your* first-semester writing projects, then use *Bloom* and the Awards as inspiration for students to embrace all writing process stages—notably revising, editing, and proofreading—incentivizing them to earn positive recognition and even 2015 publication.

Bloom in individual copies, class sets, and e-readers

Bloom is available for sale in individual copies, in discounted class sets, and in e-reader format through Amazon's Kindle platform. All proceeds help YAA support Arizona language and media arts and to produce future YAA "best of" publications. See YAArizona.org, go to Amazon.com, or check your local bookstore for details.

Bloom teaching resources at YAArizona.org

YAA is gradually sharing standards-based lessons and other resources to supplement works in this anthology.

Future YAA publications

YAA looks to our *Best Arizona Teen Writing of 2015* book and publishing our 2015 "best of" art works. If skilled and interested in helping YAA with print and digital publishing, e-mail: youngauthorsofaz@gmail.org.

2015 Scholastic Art & Writing Awards: Call for Entries

Young Authors of Arizona (YAA) invites Arizona's grade 7-12 students to enter your original works in the Scholastic Art & Writing Awards by December 17, 2014 (the 2015 Scholastic Art & Writing Awards entry window).

Art Categories

Each of the Art Awards' categories—Architecture, Ceramics & Glass, Comic Art, Design, Digital Art, Fashion, Film & Animation, Jewelry, Mixed Media, Painting, Photography, Printmaking, Sculpture, Art Portfolio—gives Arizona's grade 7-12 students creative options to meet Common Core standards by sharing their original, technically proficient, and uncensored art.

Writing Categories

Each of the Writing Awards' categories—persuasion, personal narrative/memoir, humor, journalism, poetry, flash fiction, short stories, science fiction/fantasy, scriptwriting, portfolio writing, novel writing—gives Arizona's grade 7-12 students creative options to meet Common Core standards by sharing their original, technically proficient, and uncensored writing.

Benefits of participating

- Earn scholarships for art and writing submissions.
- Earn Honorable Mention, Silver Key, or Gold Key Certificate for the State of Arizona and an invite to YAA's Scholastic Awards Ceremony in April of 2015.
- Select Gold Key and Silver Key-winning compositions offered publication in the *Best Arizona Teen Writing of 2015* book; 2015 "best of" art publication opportunities will also be available.
- Educators can use Awards as a 1st semester tool for enrichment, PLC collaboration, and portfolio-based assessment of Common Core-aligned writing projects.
- Educators earn professional development credit as a YAA volunteer judge from the comfort of home.
- More benefits available; see next page on how to enter.

How to Enter the 2015
Scholastic Art & Writing Awards

Arizona's entry deadline for the 2015 Scholastic Art & Writing Awards is December 17, 2014. To help educators and students, here are five steps to enter:

1. Create your Scholastic Student Account

Students can begin creating 2015 art and writing works as early as desired and make Scholastic accounts, beginning in September of 2014, at artandwriting.org/Registration.

2. Access, read, & share YAA's 2015 Awards entry guide

Arizona middle and high schools will get 2015 entry materials mailed, and anyone can go to YAArizona.org or YAA's Scholastic Art & Writing Awards affiliate page to access, read, and share the 2015 Awards entry guide.

3. Submit your work(s) according to specifications

Because YAA now accepts entries for art and writing in 28 different categories, pay attention to category-specific submission requirements and remember to:

1. Review category descriptions and guidelines.
2. Revise, edit, and proofread your work.

Learn more at artandwriting.org/the-awards/categories.

4. Print and complete each work's entry form

In addition to completing account registration and submitting work, each student must:

1. Print the submission form *for each entry*.
2. Obtain required signatures from a teacher and guardian on each entry form. Guardian signatures are not required if the student is 18 years or older.

5. Mail forms and payment by December 17, 2014

Submission is complete once you mail your signed submission forms and payment (if applicable) and they are received by YAA. Please mail your envelope as soon as possible, but it must be postmarked by December 17th. Individual submission entries are as follows:

- $5 per work (submit as many entries as desired)
- $20 per portfolio submission (12th graders only)
- Federal free- and reduced-lunch students can qualify for a fee waiver (see 2015 Awards entry guide).

Made in the USA
San Bernardino, CA
30 March 2014